Writing:
Craft and Art

WILLIAM L. RIVERS
Stanford University

Prentice-Hall, Inc., Englewood Cliffs, New Jersey

Library of Congress Cataloging in Publication Data

RIVERS, WILLIAM L
   Writing, craft and art.

   Includes index.
   1. Authorship. I. Title.
PN187.R5   808'.02   74-26703
ISBN 0-13-970210-5
ISBN 0-13-970202-4 pbk.

Printed in the United States of America

Prentice-Hall International, Inc., *London*
Prentice-Hall of Australia, Pty. Ltd., *Sydney*
Prentice-Hall of Canada, Ltd., *Toronto*
Prentice-Hall of India Private Limited, *New Delhi*
Prentice-Hall of Japan, Inc., *Tokyo*

Acknowledgments

p. 1. From WRITERS AT WORK: The Paris Review Interviews, Second Series. Copyright © 1963 by The Paris Review, Inc. Reprinted by permission of The Viking Press, Inc.

p. 28. Reprinted with permission of Farrar, Straus & Giroux, Inc., from RADICAL CHIC AND MAU-MAUING THE FLAK CATCHERS by Tom Wolfe. Copyright © 1970 by Tom Wolfe. *Radical Chic* originally appeared in *New York Magazine*.

p. 30. Reprinted by permission of Charles Scribner's Sons from "In Another Country" (copyright 1927 Charles Scribner's Sons) from MEN WITHOUT WOMEN by Ernest Hemingway.

pp. 45, 92. From A SHORT WALK FROM THE STATION by Phyllis McGinley. Copyright 1951 by Phyllis McGinley. Reprinted by permission of The Viking Press, Inc.

p. 54. Dylan Thomas QUITE EARLY ONE MORNING. Copyright 1954 by New Directions Publishing Corporation. Reprinted by permission of New Directions Publishing Corporation and J. M. Dent & Sons, Ltd.

p. 56. From FAME AND OBSCURITY by Gay Talese. Reprinted by permission of Harry N. Abrams, Inc.

p. 69. Reprinted by permission of Charles Scribner's Sons from "The Short Happy Life of Francis Macomber" (copyright 1936 Ernest Hemingway) from THE SHORT STORIES OF ERNEST HEMINGWAY by Ernest Hemingway.

p. 73. Reprinted with permission of Farrar, Straus & Giroux, Inc., from THE PUMP HOUSE GANG by Tom Wolfe. Copyright © 1968 by Tom Wolfe.

pp. 76, 77. Reprinted by permission of Charles Scribner's Sons from DEATH IN THE AFTERNOON by Ernest Hemingway. Copyright 1932 Charles Scribner's Sons.

pp. 79, 80. Reprinted from THE SCIENTIFIC OUTLOOK by Bertrand Russell. By permission of W. W. Norton & Company, Inc., and George Allen & Unwin, Ltd. Copyright 1931 by Bertrand Russell. Copyright renewed 1959 by Bertrand Russell.

p. 83. From TRAVELS WITH CHARLEY by John Steinbeck. Copyright © 1961, 1962 by The Curtis Publishing Co., Inc., Copyright © 1962 by John Steinbeck. Reprinted by permission of The Viking Press, Inc.

pp. 85, 86. From THE YEARS WITH ROSS by James Thurber. Reprinted by permission of Atlantic-Little, Brown and Company.

p. 95. Reprinted with permission of Farrar, Straus & Giroux, Inc., from THE ELECTRIC KOOL-AID ACID TEST by Tom Wolfe. Copyright © 1968 by Tom Wolfe.

p. 96. From LOLITA by Vladimir Nabokov, reprinted by permission of G. P. Putnam's Sons.

p. 133. From SPEAK, MEMORY by Vladimir Nabokov (New York: G. P. Putnam's Sons, 1966), p. 19. Copyright © 1960, 1966 by Vladimir Nabokov. All rights reserved.

For Dr. Samuel Kountz and Dr. Folkert Belzer,
whose skill as transplant surgeons I have good
reason to remember

Contents

Preface

This book expresses my two strongest convictions about writing. First, as the introduction emphasizes, writing can be learned—or the *craft* of writing can be learned. We cannot learn to be literary artists the way we learn to multiply by nine or cook pork chops, but we can learn the techniques of the craftsman. Many who have mastered the techniques produce writing that is either art or so much like it that we cannot tell the difference between art and craft.

My other strong conviction is that the plain style is basic in most good writing. Chapter 2 analyzes plain style, which is at once precise, concise, and informal, and resembles the spoken language but is not a transcription of it.

I bring my convictions together in chapters 3 through 8 by analyzing the techniques of craftsmanship and showing how one can master them to give color and life to plain style.

Because everyone must have something to write about, this book has a companion, *Finding Facts: Interviewing, Observing, Using Reference Sources*. Studied together, *Finding Facts* and *Writing: Craft and Art* should enable writers both to conduct research that will develop their ideas and to express them in pleasing and persuasive sentences.

As always, I needed help, especially from critics of various drafts. Charlene Brown of Indiana University was, as usual, the strongest critic— and thus the most helpful. Peter Sandman of the University of Michigan, Ed Nickerson of the University of Delaware, and Jeffrey Fleece of the University of Hawaii provided sharp critiques that caused me to revise heavily, as did two colleagues at Stanford, Ellen Nold and Alfred Grommon.

Sprinkled through this book are bits of evidence that students teach the teacher, especially when he tries to criticize their writing. Terri Anzur, Kathy Beckett, Katherine Bird, Sri Krishn Chopra, Roberta Farb Colson, David DeRoche, Carol Goodhue, Lynne Hart, Tim Ord, Nancy Read, David Rubin, Pat Thomas, George Tibbits, and Connie Revell taught me much by being excellent students.

Like other writers, I also needed editorial assistance when it came time to put words on paper. Janet Collom, Carolyn Sellers, Elizabeth Jones, Irene Wong, and Gwen Yamashiro provided expert assistance. My daughter Gail was similarly helpful and also prepared the index.

Why Learn to Write?

Reading maketh a full man . . . writing an exact man.
—FRANCIS BACON

INTERVIEWER: *How much rewriting do you do?*

HEMINGWAY: *It depends. I rewrote the ending of* Farewell to Arms *thirty-nine times before I was satisfied.*

INTERVIEWER: *Was there some technical problem there? What was it that had stumped you?*

HEMINGWAY: *Getting the words right.*

—Writers at Work, *1963*

A correspondence school advertisement that once appeared frequently in popular magazines asked in bold type: ARE YOU ONE OF THE LONELY ONES? Under these words appeared the quiet face of a thoughtful young man, then a line of large type: YOU MAY BE A WRITER. The ad went on to explain how the school could make writers of the lonely ones. So many people *are* lonely, or at least quiet and thoughtful, that the ad lured thousands into taking the correspondence course.

It would be easy to argue against everything this advertisement implied: that professional writers are lonely and private people (actually, some are, some aren't), that anyone who is lonely may be a step away from a writing career, and that the correspondence school could teach many lonely ones to become professional writers. Worst of all, though, the advertisement separated writers from everyone else. Because a few people make their living solely from writing, *professional writer* is a useful term; and we tend to think of professional writers in a category by themselves—like lawyers or insurance salesmen or morticians. The trouble is that nearly everyone must write. Placing only professional writers in the "writer" category enables others to justify mistakes with airy explanations such as: "Well, maybe I didn't make that clear, but I'm not a writer."

Everyone benefits from writing well. Although all enterprises require good communication, it is usually their weakest link. Some people have other abilities that enable them to succeed in spite of their bad writing, but the junior executive or the young government bureaucrat who can write a clear, concise memorandum is so unusual that he will probably be marked for promotion. Most college graduates who disliked the many writing assignments they received as students have discovered that they must write much more in the world of work. Many suffer because they write sentences that are imprecise, illogical, and confused.

Those who dislike or fear writing often try to talk instead. But relying only on what comes quickly into our minds and off our tongues causes many explosions of anger and enormous wastes of time, energy, and money. So many mistakes grow out of misunderstanding what someone has said that this little sign appears on the walls of many offices and on the desks of many executives:

> I KNOW YOU BELIEVE YOU UNDERSTAND WHAT I SAID,
> BUT I AM NOT SURE YOU REALIZE THAT WHAT YOU
> HEARD IS NOT WHAT I MEANT.

Perhaps there are people whose minds are so orderly and agile that they can state facts concisely and express ideas clearly and logically without putting them on paper. If they exist, these fortunate few may be able to shape in their minds a speech, a story, an explanation, or an argument, organize it carefully, and deliver it smoothly. Most of us cannot. We may persuade ourselves for a time that we have built our thoughts on expressive language, but if we try later to write them, we discover that the structure was flimsy. Holes appear in the logic. One idea does not follow and build on another. What appeared to be an absolute truth suddenly needs qualifying. Instead of a solid structure, we have fragments of thoughts.

Comparing writing to speaking can teach you so much about good communication that you may begin to doubt that anyone can actually develop a speech, a story, an explanation, or an argument without writing. You may even wonder how anyone can know much without first working it out in writing. All of us, including those with orderly and agile minds, can improve our thought and expression through writing. In writing you must test your thoughts in your mind as you are putting them on paper, then test them again as you read what you have written.

Because all college students and nearly everyone who holds a responsible job must write, you should begin to think of yourself as a writer in addition to whatever else you plan to become. Although I refer occasionally in this book to "professional writers," "novelists," and "journalists," nearly all the references to "the writer" and "a writer" mean you.

CRAFT AND CREATIVITY

Unfortunately, by the time most students reach college, they are likely to think of themselves as belonging in one or two fairly distinct categories: those who write well and those who do not. They may be right. Some students were so captivated by words from the time that they began to talk that they quickly learned to weave facts and ideas into readable writing. And there *are* those whose writing ranges from mediocre to awful, perhaps primarily because their sensitivity to language did not develop as early.

The worst mistake is to think that you cannot learn to write well, or that you cannot improve your writing. You may share the widespread and erroneous belief that no one can be taught to write, that writers are born, not bred; but that belief is based on thinking of writing only as a creative art. Although no one can be taught to be creative in steps 1–2–3–4, writing is craft as well as art, and we should be aware of both aspects.

Craftsmanship is the conscious use of reason in applying rules, training, lore, systems, and standards to choose themes and forms and to organize facts and ideas. Most of this book is devoted to the techniques of the craftsman.

Creativity, on the other hand, seems to be a miraculous kind of mental effort that produces something from nothing. To some extent, it is miraculous, or at least mysterious. The novelist E. M. Forster tried to explain the mystery of creativity with:

> In the creative state a man is taken out of himself. He lets down as it were a bucket into his subconscious, and draws up something which is beyond his reach. He mixes this thing with his normal experiences, and out of the mixture he makes a work of art.

A striking number of creative people, from mathematicians to poets, have worked out individually the same method for letting the bucket down and drawing something up. It is to work hard at a problem of discovery, then to relax the mind. Their discoveries sometimes come at night, sometimes on waking, sometimes when they have returned to their work and have begun to review it.

The novelist Louis Bromfield said that he had trained his subconscious to take over after he had concentrated, then relaxed. "Very often I have awakened in the morning to find a problem of technique, or plot, or character, which had been troubling me, completely solved while I had been sleeping."

In some large measure, then, creativity seems to depend on recovering submerged knowledge and forgotten experiences and combining them in new patterns, then using craftsmanship to present them. Creativity is craftsmanship and more. Here is a creative combination of words:

> Abandoning the world of black, white, and yellow journalism, the City
> of *San Francisco Oracle* has managed to seduce more than 100,000 readers
> in her first year of publication. And it's a beautiful seduction. *The Oracle*
> comes on with all the brutality of a soap bubble—gentle, exquisite, delicate,
> reflecting the tints of its surroundings, the Haight-Ashbury district of
> San Francisco.

The writer's obvious joy in the sounds of words and in the rich colors of the English language probably began soon after she learned to talk. What did she learn from teachers and books about the craft of writing? She was taught at least to spell words correctly and to combine them appropriately to frame sentences and paragraphs. No doubt she was taught much more, and certainly the suggestions of many teachers, and perhaps other students, helped give her a feeling for proportion and a sense of structure. She was assigned to read artistic prose, and that led her to read much more on her own. Much that she was taught shaped her talent—the craftsmanship helping her to develop the creativity—and so did every aspect of her life. It may be that we can analyze the making of this artist no more precisely than: She was born of such parents and lived in such an environment and read such writing and observed such events and reacted to them in such a way that a creative writer was produced.

That guess about the making of an artist suggests that it is impossible to assign a certain amount of credit to learning, intelligence, curiosity, heritage, or experience. It is clear, though, that the techniques of craftsmanship are an essential part of her creativity. Can craftsmanship be mastered to the point that it combines with mysterious personal qualities and becomes artistry? It would seem so, judging by the careers of a great French writer, Honoré de Balzac, a great American writer, Mark Twain, and a great English writer, Winston Churchill. All of them were dismayingly bad writers when they were young, and all became master craftsmen.

Balzac's teachers called him a blockhead. His family tried to starve him into giving up writing. The only critic he knew was a friend who advised him to try anything in the world but writing.

The triteness and commonplace style of Mark Twain's early writing is suggested by this slow-moving passage from "The Dandy Frightening the Squatter":

> A tall, brawny woodsman stood leaning against a tree . . . gazing at some approaching object, which our readers would easily have discovered to be a sailboat. . . . Now among the many passengers on this boat, both male and female, was a spruce young dandy, with a killing moustache, etc., who seemed bent on making an impression. . . . Observing our squatter friend. . . .

Churchill failed so often in school that he had to study the fundamentals of writing over and over again. He wrote of that time: "I gained an immense advantage over the cleverer boys. I got into my bones the essential structure of the English sentence."

Like Balzac and Twain, Churchill became an artist, but the marks of craftsmanship are clear on nearly everything he wrote. Here is a passage from a speech he gave when Nazi Germany threatened to conquer England in 1940:

> Even though large tracts of Europe and many old and famous states have fallen or may fall into the grip of the Gestapo and all the odious apparatus of Nazi rule, we shall not flag or fail. We shall go on to the end. We shall fight in France, we shall fight on the seas and oceans, we shall fight with growing confidence and growing strength in the air, we shall defend our island, whatever the cost may be. We shall fight on the beaches, we shall fight on the landing grounds, we shall fight in the fields and in the streets, we shall fight in the hills.

"We shall fight, we shall fight, we shall fight . . ." shows Churchill's mastery of a tricky technique, repetition, which often produces monotony but which a careful craftsman can use to produce the effect of hammer blows. More important, Churchill did not name the areas of battle at random. He speaks first of fighting in France (where the English were then engaging the Germans), then in the seas and oceans (all areas, of course, at distance from English soil), then in the air, on the beaches, on the landing grounds, in the fields, and in the streets. He concludes with the retreat into the hills, where the English will continue fighting. One might consider the speech a defeatist vision of the Germans sweeping over England, but its strongest effect was to rally the English to fight. Churchill ended with the climactic point, "We shall never surrender."

Those who heard Churchill and those who read the speech later did not analyze his method, of course, but they were strongly affected both by the fervor of his words *and* by the careful way he put the words together.

Like most writing, Churchill's speech is a mixture of craft and creativity. How much of each? No one knows, but we can identify in general the points at which each is usually dominant in the writing process. The following analysis reflects in part some of the ideas of Jeffrey Fleece, who writes both fiction and nonfiction.

Every piece of writing begins with an idea or a fragment of idea— what Fleece calls "the germ." Although having an idea is essentially a creative process, its source is usually identifiable and commonplace: a chance remark, a picture, a person, a novel, an essay, an incident. (A fiction writer, T. Harris Downey, says that "A writer's short story begins when someone he knows falls down a well.") All of us have ideas; the important thing is what we do with them.

When we examine an idea to determine if we can do anything with it—most ideas turn out to be useless—we work as both craftsman and creator. Each writer's examination of an idea depends on his abilities and preferences, and often on his memory of how he or another writer shaped a similar or related idea.

Examination then merges into the next phase, developing the idea, which is mostly craftsmanship. In his mind, on paper, or both, the writer chooses a topic and theme, develops an outline (or, in writing fiction, a plot summary) and decides on a point of view. He may also consider how he will handle transitions, flashbacks, and other devices. Because there is a limit to the number of patterns and techniques that will give the writing unity, tension, and believability, this phase relies on craftsmanship. To make every feature of the work novel is likely to produce confusion—creativity gone wild. Some creative impulse should also be at work, however, because mechanically selecting traditional methods and techniques produces formula writing.

In the act of writing, craft and creativity are so mingled that measuring their proportions is impossible. In every paragraph a writer makes thousands of decisions (most so subtly that he is unaware of making them), some as a craftsman, some as a creative artist. The proportions of craft and creativity vary from writer to writer, from piece to piece, and even from morning to afternoon. Fleece points out:

> The ability to handle this subtle process successfully is probably as narrow a definition as we can find for "talent," and the necessity to maintain lively, affirmative creative activity and accurate, largely negative critical judgment is perhaps the best explanation for the small number of literary geniuses. The individual writer's balance or lack of balance

between the impulsively creative and the systematically plodding may be a major factor in his "style."

In the final phase, editing, the writer works almost entirely as a craftsman unless he discovers a need for major revisions that will cause him to create anew.

Why is it important to know that writing is a mixture of craft and creativity? It is because you can learn the craft, and mastering the principles of craftsmanship may give your writing at least touches of artistry. The rest of this section sketches three principles: using prose conventions, writing for an audience, and learning how and what to revise.

USING CONVENTIONS

There is so much more to learning the craft of writing that it may seem odd that I begin with simple conventions of writing such as grammar, spelling, punctuation, and usage. One who can control them is only literate. He may actually be an incompetent writer, unable to define the boundaries of a subject, unable to organize, extend, and support ideas, unable to explain, narrate, describe, and persuade effectively. The conventions are fundamental in writing, however, just as the ability to saw a plank evenly and drive a nail firmly into place is fundamental in carpentry, which, like writing, requires many additional skills. Consider what happens when readers are confronted with writing that is riddled with errors in spelling and punctuation:

> Any false statment, written or, broadcast, is libelous if it causes anyone to suffer public, hatrid, contimpt, or ridicule; or if it causes one to be shuned or avoided; or if it injures us in busness or occupation.

Many young writers dismiss such errors as "typos." Some say off-handedly, "I never could spell." One asked, "What difference does correct spelling make if you can understand what I'm saying?" He thus argued that readers can guess, and quite easily, that "hatrid" actually means "hatred," that "contimpt" means "contempt," and so on. He should have realized that readers are accustomed to correct spelling. They have read "hatred" and "contempt" and "shunned" and "business" thousands of times. Readers see misspellings as oddities—like a troop of bald Boy Scouts—and must give their attention to them. Distracted by the oddities, readers find it impossible to follow the sense of the writing. Because readers are accustomed to pausing slightly or changing pitch when they see commas, the commas after "or" and "public" are confusing. Finally, the change from "one" to "us" is an attention-compelling oddity, a cause of confusion, or both.

So it is with all the conventions. Readers are so accustomed to them that they cannot fail to see and be distracted by obvious errors. If readers must pause and try to puzzle out what the writer means, their smooth pace is interrupted. They must stop and dig for the meaning rather than read.

Conventions are not ironclad rules. One convention requires that a paragraph develop a thought, another that a sentence be complete; but a writer who has learned those conventions can also learn how and when to use the unconventional. Here a student begins with a two-word paragraph and uses sentence fragments effectively:

> It hurts.
> Stretching, bending, and leaping to music hurts. In your ribs. In your calf muscles. Even your head hurts from thinking so hard. The patterns and tempo become more complex. And that woman. She demands perfection. After an hour you have sympathy for students at the Bolshoi School of Ballet. You feel a sweaty, if not spiritual, affinity with Rudolph Nureyev. And when people see you dance they murmur, "What grace. What style."

Readers begin the first paragraph not knowing what it is that hurts, but, intrigued by the unconventional, they want to know. The first sentence of the next paragraph begins to tell them. Then the short sentence fragments—neatly mixed with complete sentences so that they seem neither self-conscious nor abrupt—help readers sense the pain and make it clear that the writer is describing how it feels to be a student in a dance class. Knowing the conventions, the writer knew how to be effectively unconventional.

In short, you should observe the conventions of spelling, punctuation, grammar, usage, and sentence and paragraph structure, not merely because they exist and are sometimes called "rules" but because communication with readers usually breaks down when you ignore them. When you can use the unconventional to good effect, you should, but infrequently.

WRITING FOR AN AUDIENCE

Because a writer's first obligation is to his readers, knowing how to address an audience is central to craftsmanship. Perhaps a few writers are concerned for a short time with self-expression alone, or self-discovery, and actually write for an audience of one, themselves. Properly analyzed, writing can teach a writer about himself. However, except for the finger exercises played privately in personal journals by those who are practicing to become professional writers and except for the kind of short-hand notes careful housekeepers jot down to remind themselves to carry out the garbage before the truck comes Wednesday, nearly everything is written for an audience that extends beyond the writer.

The writer's sense of audience should pervade his writing. No comma is inserted, no word is chosen, no phrase is fashioned, and no sentence is written except for the audience. Yet, if we were to try consciously to gauge the effect on readers of each of the infinite number of decisions we must make in writing, we would soon become unhinged. One must learn to develop a sense of audience and practice keeping readers in mind without actually concentrating on them.

In trying to organize sentences and time elements so that the writing will run smoothly, a writer may forget that readers do not have all the information the writer has. Writing about the active life of a 33-year-old woman she admired, a student included this passage:

> Books have influenced Linda's life. "I used to read more than be outdoors," she said. "The prospect of a good book on Saturday morning was more than I could bear. I must have read every Nancy Drew mystery ever written, because Nancy Drew *did* something!"

Because the preceding paragraphs were about Linda as a woman, most readers would be startled by the thought of a woman reading children's books. Startled, they might stop and wonder, interrupting their reading. Linda *was* quoted as saying "used to read," but that could have referred to the year before; in any case, the words are not a strong enough signal to readers. The writer knew that Linda was referring to her childhood and unconsciously assumed that readers knew it as well. The writer should have made the time element clear, perhaps with:

> Books have long influenced Linda's life. She said of her childhood, "I used to read more. . . ."

Other problems in writing for an audience are not so easily solved, even by talented writers. One who ordinarily writes persuasively for a clearly defined audience tried in the following paragraphs to address journalists and others who know about journalism. His argument is vigorous, but he failed to think through all the implications of writing for his audience. The comments at the left suggest values in persuasive writing and point to the strengths and the weaknesses of this passage:

<table>
<tr><td>

COMMENTS

The writer makes it clear with strong words at the start that he will argue vigorously. Accuracy is essential in all writing, of course, but it is critically important in vigorous argument. If some readers who are undecided about the issue and are thus open to persuasion find an error, they are likely to think less of the argument and may close their minds to it. Those who have made up their minds before reading and have a strong opposing viewpoint may consider any *error sufficient reason to discount the argument.*

If the writer were addressing readers who know little about journalism, he would have to provide more information.

Situation ethics is known to so few that the writer should have spelled out its principles. He refers to some of the principles later in a way that makes it difficult for readers to understand because situation ethics has not been explained adequately here.

The writer was wise not to explain everything in this long passage on the tactics of the late Senator McCarthy. The writer does not even mention that McCarthy became nationally prominent by alleging in many speeches that many government officials were Communists. The writer assumes that his readers know that. In the second paragraph, the writer does not explain

</td><td>

ARGUMENT

The First Amendment freedom of the press has, over two centuries, become encrusted with the dogmatic and unbending attitudes of American editors on the handling of news. Editors have become a legalistic group who base their approaches to news reporting on tradition and precedent. In 1790 there were no wire services, no public opinion polls, no newspaper chains, no radio or television, no "big lie" techniques. In 1790 Americans needed the protection *of* freedom of the press. Since 1950, we have needed protection *from* freedom of the press.

American journalism has cherished for too long the abstract good of a free press at the expense, quite frequently, of innocent individuals and the welfare of the country. The time has come for the newspaper industry and the electronic media to base decisions concerning who will have access to the media and with what information on a case-by-case basis. "All the news that's fit to print" must be redefined to cope with Twentieth-Century American problems and Twentieth-Century media. A major step in this redefinition is the establishment of a situation ethic for the newspaper business as a substitute for what Harvard theologian Joseph Fletcher calls an ethical system of "prefabricated, pretailored morality" which guides papers today.

The press' legalistic system betrayed both the American people and the spirit of the freedom of the press amendment most clearly in the case of Senator Joseph R. McCarthy of Wisconsin. The McCarthy coverage from 1950–1954 and the damage that resulted are an excellent starting point for consideration of a situation ethic for the American press.

</td></tr>
</table>

COMMENTS

what is meant by the "I-hold-in-my-hand" speech. He assumes that his readers know that as well. It is not only wise but necessary to make these assumptions. Having decided that his argument will be addressed to journalists, the writer must interest them. If he were to explain in primer fashion who McCarthy was and what is meant by the "I-hold-in-my-hand" speech, he would not hold the attention of those who already have the information.

A statement such as the one in the last sentence in this paragraph must be accurate. How does the writer know that neither of the wire services reported that the political scientists had voted McCarthy the worst senator? If the statement is wrong, journalists who are irritated by the strong argument may pounce on the error, say that it is typical of the entire piece, and cite the error to discredit everything.

The writer seems to go out of his way to antagonize with "the editors would whimper." Not only is "whimper" too strong—and degrading—he cannot possibly know whether all editors said that they were bound to report all of McCarthy's charges. There are too many editors (the United States has 1,760 daily newspapers). In fact, editors of some of the smaller papers could not have printed all his charges.

ARGUMENT

Newsman Jack Anderson has called the press a "Dr. Frankenstein" which created the McCarthy monster. It pushed McCarthy to national prominence in 1950 after the famous Wheeling, West Virginia, "I-hold-in-my-hand" speech. It then brought him to immense power by regularly sanctioning his tirades with blazing headlines, and it provided him with the most powerful platform in America for attacking innocent citizens. The daily paper became, against its will, a party to the violation of the civil rights of many Americans, all in the name of a free press.

. . . Editors criticized the Associated Press and United Press International for moving so much news about McCarthy's antics. Yet the wire services, for example, provided a picture of the Senator sweeping the Capitol steps clean of the "Communist influence in government," according to the caption, instead of sweeping away the *alleged* Communist influence. They did not report that a group of distinguished political scientists had voted McCarthy the worst senator in the nation.

To any requests for censorship the editors would whimper that they were bound to report all that McCarthy charged. After all, he was a U.S. Senator, and something he said might have contained a grain of truth. Furthermore, editors felt they were not in the business of passing judgment on the truth of his charges. Their job was simply to print the news. Any comment was reserved for the editorial page. And then, of course, the editors employed what Fletcher calls "the generalization" argument: what would happen if everybody judged the value of news? This ploy blocked a blackout of Mc-

<table>
<tr><td align="center">COMMENTS</td><td align="center">ARGUMENT</td></tr>
</table>

McCarthy made too many charges for that to be possible.	Carthy, or at least some form of more balanced coverage.
Because the writer did not present the principles of situation ethics near the beginning, some readers may not understand what is meant by the "generalization argument." By reading the passage carefully and thinking about the term, readers can puzzle out the meaning, but a writer should not require that his readers work so hard.	With the generalization argument news editors absolved themselves of personal responsibility for stopping Mc-Carthy. Fletcher calls this attitude "a fundamentally antisituational gambit, a form of obstructionism, a delaying action of static morality." In the words of the Washington *Post,* they hoped that "McCarthyism would disappear overnight if Eisenhower were elected." Had they faced the . . .

This long piece ended: "Once editors recognize that freedom of the press requires judgment, responsibility, and positive action, the nation's readers will be better informed." Those words suggest that editors, *all* editors, are thoughtless, irresponsible, and inactive. Even if that were true, in an essay addressed to editors such acidity would repel rather than persuade them. Like the other faults cited in the comments above, this one shows that the writer did not think about persuading his readers.

The passages quoted in this section represent extremes of failing to focus properly on the needs and sensitivities of readers. The first is easier to clear up than the second, but many such problems may be solved by writers who reflect on these questions:

1   For what audience am I writing?
2   What do my readers know; what information do they have?
3   What am I trying to persuade them to do (if anything more than reading my writing), and what tone and attitude will engage them?

LEARNING HOW AND WHAT TO REVISE

The principles of effective writing are so embedded in the thoughts of most professional writers that they can answer such questions without asking them. But few professionals find it easy to write effectively. Frank O'Connor said that he usually rewrites his stories twelve times. The late Dylan Thomas wrote seventy-one versions of one of his poems. Most professional writers tinker with their work, revise it, and rewrite it as though they agree with the late Bernard DeVoto, who said that the best reason for putting anything on paper is so that one may then change it.

The nagging problem for most students is that they do not know how to be intelligently dissatisfied with their writing. Nearly all have had the experience of hopeless dissatisfaction, and thus sympathize with the student who complained, "Everyone tells me that I should rewrite, but I look at what I've written and can't find anything wrong. How can I know what to change?"

Learning principles of effective writing is the first step. They should not be memorized like multiplication tables because trying to remember many principles and use them in the heat of writing is distracting and often frustrating. The mistaken belief that "rules" come first may be the main reason many students dislike writing. You should read principles first so that at least a few will be in the back of your mind. Your theme—what you want to say—should be the focus of your writing. If you care about what you are saying, your own interest is likely to carry readers along even if you fail to observe all the principles.

You can usually improve your writing a bit by reading it carefully immediately after completing it, but only a few small flaws are likely to reveal themselves then: an imprecise word or phrase, a sentence that staggers under the weight of too many words, a rough transition. Even those who have rewritten often and well tend to overlook major flaws at first.

Later, when you can stand off and look at your writing as a whole piece, you can revise more thoughtfully by asking questions that grow out of the principles covered in this book: Have I used all the relevant techniques? Are my words precise and my sentence concise? Have I used visual words and phrases? Have I organized facts and ideas, sentences and paragraphs smoothly and logically? Does the piece hang together and make a statement?

Finally, you can read a piece written by a professional writer on the same or a similar topic. The comparison should show you how much depends on the writer's ideas and his control of the tone he uses to express them. You may discover flaws, or apparent flaws in the professional's writing. This word seems imprecise. That sentence is not concise. This passage is overwritten. Whatever you find, an honest comparison of your own work to that of a professional writer will probably suggest how you can improve yours.

It is tedious to follow the pattern: read about principles, write, read your work immediately after writing, ask yourself questions about principles in a later reading, and finally compare your work to that of a professional. But that is a straight road to craftsmanship, and faster than the most-traveled one. Most young writers take years to learn simple principles, or never learn them because they expect their natural ability and inspiration to make them artists. One who recognizes that writing is a craft he can learn is far ahead of the others.

Learning the craft of writing may not lead you to artistry, but in judging nonfiction (we can be less certain about fiction), we usually find it difficult to distinguish the work of the careful and imaginative craftsman from that of the artist. I refer fairly often to artistry in this book, but I emphasize craftsmanship. Working to become a good craftsman is a worthwhile goal.

How to Begin

Good writing, like a good house, is an orderly arrangement of parts.
—MORTIMER ADLER

1 For most of us, writing the first paragraph, even the first phrase, is agonizing. So much depends on what comes first that perhaps no method will make the task of beginning a light one. But we can reduce the agony by recognizing that writing the first word is almost never a true beginning. Only love and hate letters should be written with no planning—and perhaps neither should be mailed until next week.

In preparing to write a short piece, such as a book review or a news story, a writer usually does no more than make notes while reading the book or watching the event, then keep them at his elbow while writing. The laudable work of placing a book or an event in a larger context that will give it a larger meaning requires more research and planning, which hints at the true beginnings of most writing.

FINDING AND DEVELOPING A TOPIC

Some professional writers confess that they have occasionally finished writing a long piece without knowing what they were trying to say. They regret such writing, which is always a failure that takes more time and sweat than planned writing. Failure results when a writer tries to plod his way through a general subject: love, crime, philosophy, baseball, metaphysics, the environment, the freshman year. He must narrow the scope. The first question is: What is my subject? Its companions are: What shall I say about which aspect of the subject? What is my topic?

Basketball is a general subject. Too general. A student at UCLA may choose to write about its great basketball team. That narrows the scope, but the writer still has a subject, not a topic. Several books have been written about the UCLA team, including chapters and passages on the head coach and his methods, the players and their abilities, the spirit of the fans, and charges of professionalism. One who will write only four or five pages cannot cover everything well; he can only skim. He must further narrow his focus, perhaps to the adroit recruiting methods that lure high-school stars to UCLA. Even that could be treated at book-length, but it is a topic that a writer can treat fairly satisfactorily in a few pages.

A woman student interested in athletics developed a topic out of her interest in a way that illustrates how one moves from subject to topic-and-research and then to writing. Learning that after menopause women who do not exercise are in danger of heart disease, she interviewed an authority who recommended that women begin jogging while young to promote the supply and use of oxygen. Then she read several articles and a book on exercise and heart disease, interviewed other authorities, and began to take a fitness orientation course at the YMCA to obtain a first-hand view. Using all this research, she wrote a twelve-page piece that was not about jogging or heart disease in general but one that combined both subjects into one topic: women should start jogging early to help prevent heart disease after menopause.

Knowing that writing well is a process of selection, she had gathered much more information than she needed. Without a sharply defined topic, she might have gotten lost in all that research. But had she gathered only a minimal amount of information, she would have been forced to use the peripheral as well as the pointed. Her topic guided her to the most useful facts and ideas, then the sharp definition of the topic enabled her to write an excellent piece.

A smart writer changes topics in the midst of research if a better topic comes up. She might have considered that physical exercise is boring or worse than inactivity for many of us. Because she learned much in the process of research about self-discipline, including tricks and gimmicks some people use to make themselves continue jogging, she could have written about the self-discipline methods of others, keeping herself out of the writing entirely, or about her own methods in a personal piece.

Narrowing a general subject to the size and shape of a specific topic is usually a nagging problem for most writers. This focus, however, may help solve the next problem: developing the topic.

Imagine that a class has been assigned to write about the plight of minority groups. Surely only dull reading can result from writing the first thing that comes to mind: a general discussion of the terrible problems that confront minorities. A student who is a member of a minority group can develop a topic from that general subject by relating some of his experiences. Personal experiences are often solid topics, especially those that are dramatic or humorous. If the writer does research on minority groups, he may be able to place his experiences in a larger context that lends them greater significance. But what of the students who are not members of racial or ethnic minorities? They must usually rely on research and should interview and observe minorities as well as use the library.

One student who is not a member of a racial or ethnic minority group thought of his own plight as a member of a peculiar minority, left-handed people. Not wanting to limit his writing to his own experiences, which seemed flimsy, he searched the library. He found little on left-handedness: a book and a few articles in scientific journals. He talked to his roommates about the disadvantage of a left-hander in a right-handed world, which helped him remember incidents. Then he used a bit of his library research and much from his memories to develop this topic, "Life on the Left":

> Ever since I was a baby, kicking and gurgling at the world from my crib, my parents knew I was left-handed. They'd offer me my bottle, or a toy, or just a finger to play with, and I'd snatch it with my powerful left cross. I got more food in my mouth left-handed, I banged more loudly on the left side of my crib, and stuffed animals seldom lasted a week before my left hand unstuffed them.
>
> So it was that I earned my membership in a select group of people who go through life backwards. Members of my organization are not hard to pick out in a crowd—we're the ones who sit at the far end of dinner tables, the ones who write with pen and paper at all sorts of bizarre angles, the ones who tell time by the wrong wrist: we do nothing the "right" way.
>
> The "right" way is what nine out of ten people do, although doctors and psychologists are still puzzled over the reason for such a large right-handed majority. Presently, it is believed that one out of three children is born with a tendency toward left-handedness, but that parents coax their children to adjust to the right-handed world, and so cut down the troops in the left-handed army. Although psychologists once warned parents that suppression of a child's left-handed tendencies may lead to a number of nervous disorders, including stuttering, recent studies have disproven these theories.
>
> Just the same, repeated punishment of the child who regularly uses his left hand may build hostility in the child, and so should be avoided. Perhaps for this reason, parents have become more permissive in allowing their left-handed child to grow up left-handed, which has put the percentage of left-handedness in the United States on a gradual increase. This is certainly a hopeful sign for the cause of "Lefties Lib."

Interestingly enough, the tendency of a society toward predominant right-handedness seems to be universal: the ancient Greeks and Romans, Eskimos, Africans, Indians—all are right-handed. It seems that the language-makers of these and other societies refuse to let left-handers forget they are outnumbered. Our word "right" suggests some inherent correctness in using the right hand, while the left hand is "left out" of most tasks. The French word for right, *droit,* also means just, or honest, and is the root for our word "adroit," while their word for left, *gauche,* means awkward. In German, *link* for left also means awkward, and *recht* for right is like the English "right"—just and true.

Although left-handers can tolerate being called names, the offenses against them by the right-handed world do not stop at that. Each day a left-hander receives a barrage of reminders that the rest of the world is doing things differently, and that he had better learn to adjust—or else.

For a glimpse at the hardships of left-handed living, let's spend an imaginary day in the lives of Sidney and Sally Southpaw, and their son Seymour. The Southpaws are a very normal American family, except for one not-so-subtle difference: they are all, by some ill-fated quirk of Nature, left-handed.

Young Seymour hops on his bicycle and gets an early start off to school, since it is mostly uphill from his house. Oh, it wouldn't be too bad if he could take the hills in low gear, but the gears on his bike are over the right handlebar—last time Seymour tried to shift gears left-handed, he lost control and smashed into Mrs. Dexter's bird bath. Seymour doesn't try to shift gears any more. Seymour has extraordinary leg muscles for an eight-year-old.

At school, Seymour and the rest of his classmates sit in their neat rows of tiny chairs, awaiting their teacher's orders. The school bell sounds, and she asks them to rise for the Salute to the Flag, instructing them to "put your hand on your heart." *Seymour's* hand is his left hand, and he obediently covers his right breast with it. There is no hint of a heartbeat. He gropes about his chest, he holds his breath, he fidgets, but his heart will not respond. Seymour is certain he is dead. As the rest of the class proudly recites the Pledge of Allegiance, he mutters the Lord's Prayer.

About this time, Seymour's dad is backing the family Volkswagen out of the driveway, on the way to work. The entire neighborhood knows Sidney Southpaw is off to work: they can hear him savagely grinding his stick shift with his inept right hand. While he drives (on the right side of the road), he gesticulates wildly with his left hand out the window— Sidney loves hand-signals.

Sidney Southpaw is a shoe salesman. His first customer of the day asks for some 6½ flats, and he takes out of the box the shoe *he* would put on first, the left shoe. He crams it on the lady's extended right foot. It doesn't fit. Before Sidney can ask her if she'd like to try some 7's, the lady limps away. Nothing goes right for Sidney.

Back at home, Sidney's wife Sally faces her morning—she is trying to bake a cake. The past half-hour was spent poking holes in the top of a can of flour—last time she used their right-handed can opener she wound her sleeve into the pork and beans—and now she is using the egg-beater with the crank on the right. The eggs are winning.

Having finished mixing the frosting, Sally notices idly that her engagement and wedding rings are missing. This is nothing new. She begins browsing patiently through the chocolate-chiffon.

Meanwhile, Seymour's morning lesson at school is on handwriting. Seymour reluctantly leaves his pencil hanging in the right-handed pencil sharpener, having broken its lead five times, borrows a pencil, and sits down. The teacher tells the class to turn their papers slightly counterclockwise, and to write the alphabet. As Seymour writes, his letters ignore the lines drawn on the paper, and all converge on the upper-right corner of the page. Each letter is reeling backwards, precariously close to falling over, but before it falls, Seymour's hand passes over it and mercifully smears it into illegibility. Seymour never sees what he writes, but he doubts that it was right, whatever it was. So does the teacher.

Father Sidney rings up the final sale for the morning, but the sound of the bell as he punches the "TOTAL" button is drowned by the thud of the cash register drawer into his left elbow. Sidney notes on the way to lunch that the bruise has turned from navy blue to splotchy magenta. He runs for the elevator, but misses it: the buttons are on the right side.

At the luncheonette downstairs, Sidney and the right-handed stranger on his left are rubbing elbows over soup. Sidney delivers a quick jab to his opponent's ribs, but the fellow counters with a devastating uppercut, splashing Sidney's chicken-noodle all over his best pants. Sidney concedes the bout, moves over a seat, and discovers that to use the cutting edge of his dessert fork, he must hold it backhand. He feels it only proper to order upside-down cake.

Back at home after lunch, Sally Southpaw is just putting the last stitch in some knitting she has been doing. As she holds up the vest she had made, she realizes that the instruction manual she has been following is intended for right-handed knitters. Peculiarly, her opposite-handiwork has left no neck-hole in the odd garment. This upsets her terribly, since she has spent so much time on the vest: now she has lost her head. In her rage, she grabs a pair of scissors to slice up the vest, but she cannot make the right-handed shears cut. So Sally sits sadly, sulking in silence.

School is out, and Seymour goes bowling with some of his friends. But the bowling ball he borrows is for a right-hander, and when he throws it, it hooks stubbornly into the gutter. After 17 rolls without pinfall, Seymour decides to call it a day.

Meanwhile, Sidney is late coming home from work, as usual—his watch stopped. After all, it *is* dreadfully hard to wind, what with the spindle on the far side . . .

At dinner, Sidney, Sally, and son Seymour commiserate about their trying day, over the most fitting dish for the Southpaw household: left-overs.

The harrowing day we spent with the Southpaws was only a brief sample of what left-handers must put up with. I, as a member of the left-handed community, feel that we are being treated with discrimination, and that we cannot allow the right-handers to take the upper hand any longer. Something must be done now, to give lefties the equal rights they deserve. All those in favor, raise your left hand!

Whether a writer cloaks his own experiences in light and imaginative writing like this example or treats his topic seriously, he is likely to write the last word of anything worth reading only after he has extracted a topic from a subject, then has developed the subject through research. As the following section indicates, we can seldom move swiftly along a straight line from locating a subject to writing the last word. If we do no more than concentrate on a subject in the hope that a topic will emerge and perhaps develop itself, we will probably waste time and thought. We can usually work most swiftly and profitably by asking: How can I narrow this subject to a topic that will interest readers? Try to keep that question in mind as you explore the subject by reading, observing, interviewing, and talking casually to friends and acquaintances.

OUTLINING AND ORGANIZING

A student who had become friendly with a teacher said to him one day in a tone that mixed challenge and confession: "You make us hand in a full outline with our papers. What you don't know is that most of us write the paper first, then write the outline from it." What the student didn't know was that the teacher had done the same when *he* was in college, and that the outlines the teacher now makes before beginning his own writing are sketchy, quite unlike the blueprints he requires of his students.

Outlining. Many writers detest the word. It suggests putting together a mere skeleton. Hours of labor go into it, then the entire task of writing remains. In contrast, writing is the pleasure and agony of shaping words into phrases and phrases into sentences that become a full-fleshed figure. When that is done, the writer really *has* something. Except for those who so dread the agony of writing that they like to construct elaborate outlines to put off writing, nearly everyone wants to avoid outlining.

But few experienced writers will avoid it, or something resembling it. Nearly all professional writers and many others who write often have learned that some kind of plan for writing is necessary to save their sanity while writing.

The Case against Formal Outlining

For good reason, a professional writer usually feels an itch to begin writing. When a fragment of an idea shapes itself in his mind, he knows that he must put it on paper to prevent it from escaping. He also knows that pinning one fragment down and developing it in words and phrases will cause another to form. Developing the second will create a third—and writing about *that* idea will probably cause him to go back and revise the first, whereupon the second must be revised before he can rewrite the third. That revision may lead to another idea, another sentence, and perhaps another revision of an earlier sentence. By the time he has written a few paragraphs (which is likely to take hours), he may start again; a comprehensive theme has emerged from thinking and writing.

Because a writer knows that one idea grows out of another, one sentence out of another, and one paragraph out of another, he also knows that any formal outline he constructs will have little resemblance to the finished writing. Preparing a full outline—Roman numerals and Arabic numerals, capital letters and lowercase letters—seems absurd. How can he realistically outline the *last* half of an essay when writing the first few sentences of it may change everything?

Although formal outlines can help students learn about order, organization, and the relationships of facts and ideas, your arguments against it may be almost as persuasive as those of a professional writer. The following explanation may persuade you of the value of informal outlines and their use as a compass.

The Case for Informal Outlining

An author who became a professor of English had written books and articles for two decades and was confident that he could fill the classroom hours spontaneously, class after class. On the first day he talked without preparation. The lecture was a reasonable success, if somewhat rambling, but the professor returned to his office dismayed. He confessed to a friend, "I've told them *everything* I know. What do I do next?"

He had not actually exhausted everything he knew, of course. Because he did not try to order and organize his knowledge, he was not even aware of the many things he knew that were pertinent to the course. He staggered through the semester in a similar manner, half-developing in one lecture a point he had mentioned in the first, adding to it three weeks later, and scattering other pieces of ideas and experiences as they occurred to him.

Writing spontaneously produces similar results. To begin writing without organizing your notes and thoughts invites half-developed fragments of facts and ideas to take over. A spontaneous writer does have an important advantage over a spontaneous teacher. Eventually, the writer can organize and develop his work before exposing it to public view—at high cost in time and sweat. Because writing is hard work, agony will be mixed with pleasure whatever a writer does. But he can decrease the agony and increase the joy by resisting the temptation to start *now*. If he dislikes the sound of "outlining" he can think of the work of preparing his notes and thoughts as "organizing." The longer and more complex the writing project, the more likely it is that organized writing material will resemble an outline. The important matter is not the fine detail of the plan but how the writer uses it.

The Case for Organizing

A psychologist's experiment suggests a reason and a method for organizing. After reading to an audience a list of twenty-one ideas, the psychologist asked that his listeners note those they could remember. Few could recall as many as eight. But when the psychologist classified the ideas under three labels, most listeners could recall over sixteen ideas. In effect, the psychologist suggested that his listeners organize the ideas in a way that would bring them to mind.

Material for writing can be organized in somewhat the same way. If you have, for example, a few notes, two articles, and a book, they should be arranged on the desk or table, not stacked but placed separately on labeled sheets of paper. A step toward outlining a short piece is to write at the top of another page a summary of the topic in a few words that serve as a working title, then to scribble the labels beneath it so that you can see the major divisions of the writing in one place.

When confusion sets in, you should organize the divisions and fill them out in a form that resembles a full outline. This point of confusion will vary with the individual as well as with the length and complexity of the piece. No matter how much material you can hold in your mind, notes, books, and articles eventually crowd your desk, and spill onto the floor; you will then need to resort to another system of organization.

Professional writers develop their own organizing methods for writing at length. One jots on small cards notes that represent his article or book, arranges the cards in an order that seems logical before he begins writing, then shuffles the cards—and discards many—as the act of writing creates new ideas. Another puts *sequences* (a fairly common term for notes about long passages) on sheets of paper, one sheet for each note, then fastens them to the wall above his typewriter. One of the most successful magazine writers describes his method:

> First, I cut up the small pocket notebooks that I use in note taking and paste the pages on sheets of typewriter paper, four pages to a sheet. Then I add to that stack of sheets whatever notes I've made on tablet paper and organize the releases, tear sheets, bulletins, and books, which also go on the stack. My live field notes—most of my best stuff from interviews

and on-the-scene reporting—go on top of the stack. Then I go through all this and number each sheet and item.

By this time, I'm warming up to the task ahead of me and am eager to get to the writing. But I don't start beating any typewriter. Instead, I take a large sheet of paper, about the size of a newspaper page laid sidewise, which is divided into four columns, and which has a space at the top of about three inches deep for random notations like lead sentences or titles that might occur to me. I use so many of these special pages in my work that I have them printed.

Then, reading through my notes and the other material, I jot down sequences in my prospective story in the columns on that big page. I number each sequence to correspond to the page number in the stack of notes. This is for quick reference when I'm writing, so I won't have to thumb through a wilderness of notes for a fact, a figure, an anecdote, or a quotation. After I've outlined all the material, I scan the whole sheet for what seems to be a lead, then mark that sequence with a red pencil, "1." Then I look for the next sequence and mark it "2," then "3," and so on. Soon, my story is organized on that big sheet of paper right down to the last paragraph.—*Frank Taylor*

The difference between such intricate organizing and the elaborate kind of outlining mentioned at the beginning of this chapter may seem to be one of form only. After all, the professional writer merely arranges research material on a huge sheet instead of typing on conventional paper notes marked by number and letter symbols. But there are also basic differences. Anyone who tries both systems will probably agree that the professional's method gives him a feeling of working directly on the writing. In contrast, the formal outline seems to be at arm's length from the writing.

Moreover, the professional's plan is not a formula. As he writes, he changes the order of some sequences and discards others. When he discovers that the information he has gathered for one sequence is too scanty or that writing based on a sequence has suggested another sequence for which he has no information, he does more research. His writing is not restricted by his plan; rather, his plan is reshaped by the writing.

Whatever the form of the plan for writing, reshaping it is usually essential. You can alter guidelines, just as a sensible mountain guide takes his party on an alternate route when the weather changes.

By shaping guidelines that anticipate common problems, you will avoid some changes. One problem is illustrated by the following paragraphs, which appeared in the middle of a newspaper report on the frustrations of drivers and gasoline station dealers in 1974:

Gas-station attendants are taking a lot of verbal abuse, says James V. Cresente, executive director of the Northern Ohio Petroleum Retailers

Association. "Remember Available Jones from Li'l Abner?" Mr. Cresente asks. "For five cents he was available to be kicked in the teeth. We dealers are Available Jones today.

"People want to blow their stacks at somebody," Mr. Cresente says, "and the most convenient person is the gas-station attendant. The public doesn't have a chance to see the chairman of the oil companies or Nixon. They see us, so they take it out on us."

"Threats are a daily situation," says Ron Feldman, who operates a gas station on Chicago's South Side. He tells of one customer who had run out of gas and walked more than two miles before he found Mr. Feldman's station open. He had only $1, and Mr. Feldman required a $4 deposit on a can. "When I refused to give it to him," Mr. Feldman says, "he threatened to throw a rock through the window, but we got five guys at the station and they can generally keep things under control."

The abuse isn't always verbal. Jerry D'Angelo, manager of a gas station on Route 22 in Union, N.J., says a friend of his, an attendant at another station in Union, had three teeth kicked out by a hot-tempered driver who grew angry at the station's $3 purchase limit Wednesday. Mr. D'Angelo says that another friend at a service station in Cranford, N.J., was recently knifed by a customer in a similar situation.

Note that in the first paragraph Crescente speaks of the comic-strip character who was available to be kicked in the teeth and declares that gasoline dealers are Available Jones today. Three paragraphs later, the writer mentions an incident in which a gas station attendant had three teeth kicked out. Although writing can be organized in many different ways, the quoted passage would have flowed more smoothly had the incident been placed immediately after Crescente's comment. Simplicity of organization is usually valuable, but the writer's primary aim should be to help and interest the reader, not merely to make the writer's work easier. It is easiest for the writer to group all quotations by one speaker in one paragraph, and all those by another in another paragraph, but the result is usually disjointed. If a topic might be stated, "Here are some interesting things said by various people," such a plan of organization might work. In most instances, however, interview notes should be arranged so that a point made by one speaker is connected to a related incident and to a similar point made by another speaker.

It should be obvious that a topic is usually organized not only at the stage we call "organizing" but also before and after that stage. In choosing and developing a topic, we must try to imagine what its parts will be. If we fail to gather enough information then, we must gather more while organizing for writing. In the writing we are almost certain to discover that we did not foresee the final shape (indeed, could not have foreseen it), and we may even be forced all the way back to the stage of developing the topic. In the end, then, pre-writing and the act of writing are usually one process. Dividing the process into parts, however, is not just convenient for discussion. One who begins work as if all pre-writing could be completed before sitting down to write imposes order on a process that might otherwise be overwhelming.

THE PHYSICAL ACT OF WRITING

Although teachers differ in what they require, most prescribe much the same format: papers typed double space on one side of the page, with sizable margins (usually more than one inch and less than two). Many students wonder whether the drafts of their papers should be written in longhand or typed, and whether they should write a piece straight through in rough form before polishing or polish each sentence before writing the next. No one can say which is better in either case. Just as individuals vary in the kind of organizing and outlining they find suitable, they work differently in the physical act of writing. Temperament, willpower, habit —all the qualities that make a writer one kind of worker or another— determine the approach.

Ernest Hemingway developed the habit of "thinking on a type-writer" during years of newspaper reporting. When he began to write novels, he retained the habit in writing dialogue, which came into his mind rapidly, but the rest of his writing was in longhand. Robert Benchley, the late humorist, also worked for newspapers for years. He typed everything. Hemingway wrote most of his stories straight through, then wrote draft after draft in revision. Benchley rarely wrote more than one draft, a fairly common habit among those who write short humor pieces, but he spent almost as much time on some of his short humor items as Hemingway spent on his short stories. Benchley wrote most of his sentences the way he wanted them the first time, but he sometimes spent an hour writing a sentence.

In short, you should adopt the method that suits you. You should be aware, however, of the principal advantages and disadvantages of each. For concise writing, longhand is ordinarily better than typing. The very tedium of writing in longhand seems to cause us to make each word count. But the hard work of writing in longhand may cause the impatient to fail to include long passages that may be needed.

Typing is much faster for those who have learned to type even moderately well. Often, though, a writer who types uses too many words, and the speed of the work encourages him to type passages that later prove to be useless. Soon, the typist is likely to find himself inserting pages and yanking them out so often that longhand might have been faster in the long run.

Whether you use longhand or type, it is likely that in the course of writing one passage you will develop an idea or find a fact that will be useful in a passage you plan to write later. Scribble a note to yourself before continuing. Thoughts and facts have a way of disappearing if they are not captured immediately.

This chapter should have made it clear that so much of the work of writing is disorderly that you cannot bring all of it under tight control. Realizing that, you should plan and organize the part of the work that lends itself to planning and organizing, which will leave your mind free to develop the rest imaginatively.

PROJECTS

1   Practice narrowing a subject to a topic by thinking first of a general subject. For example, "History" can be covered adequately only in thousands of volumes. "American history" is also a huge subject. Narrower (but still huge) is "the teaching of American history on this campus." The subject approaches topic size when it is narrowed to a particular course in American history. The topic is a size you can grasp when you reduce it to your attitude toward one course in American history or what the teacher hopes his students will learn in the course.

Choose a broad subject (for example, science, sports, or language) and write a list of at least five topics that gradually narrow the subject to a size that could be covered reasonably in a five-page paper.

2   Examine any ambitious paper that you have written for any course. Write 800 to 900 words *about* that paper, using the sections of this chapter headed "Subject and Topic" and "Outlining and Organizing" to describe how and why you planned and wrote the paper as you did. If, for example, you outlined the paper, then found that you could not follow the outline while writing because new ideas occurred to you, that aspect is worth extended comment. Consider each of the major points in "Outlining and Organizing." If you have developed your own method for organizing long pieces of writing, describe it.

3   Write your next assignment in longhand. Type the assignment after that. In each instance, analyze both the act of writing and the completed piece to determine whether the points about writing in longhand and writing on the typewriter apply to you.

You Can Choose
a Style

Every writer, by the way he uses the language, reveals something of his spirit, his habits, his capacities, his bias.—E. B. WHITE

2 The saying "the style is the person" is only partly true. E. B. White, who is probably the best American essayist, says that from some place deep in our writing we do reveal ourselves; the personal voice comes through. Certainly White's gentleness is revealed in his writing. So is his humor, even when he writes seriously. But if the style and the writer are the same, why do so many executives and bureaucrats write as though they were business machines? No doubt their warmth comes through in letters to friends, and perhaps if we were to read samples from all their writing, not just the part that is the professional pose, we would find that the style fits the person after all. But the pose hints that one can choose a style.

Think of "the style is the person" as *personal style,* which may be different from the *style of choice.* A writer's personal style may limit the choices he can make, may even dictate the one he will make. But writers who seem to be alike in person have chosen different styles, and some who are quite different from one another in person have chosen the same style.

STYLES OF CHOICE

John Fischer, the former editor of *Harper's* magazine, has written that the easiest styles to master are "the Murky Academic, as found in practically any doctoral dissertation, or the Rococo Breathless, typified by

Tom Wolfe (the youth culture kid, not the novelist), and the Long-Winded Profound, a specialty of the *New York Review of Books.*" Fischer's tone betrays his distaste, but the styles he identifies with such names are certainly familiar to us.

Writers of the Murky Academic style use long and abstract words in long sentences like these from *Attitude Change: A Critical Analysis of Theoretical Approaches:*

> The second issue is whether or not the classical conditioning paradigm as opposed to the instrumental conditioning paradigm is indeed the correct one for research procedures such as those of Staats and Lott. The epistemological importance of definitely evaluating the appropriateness of the classical conditioning paradigm for these experiments partly lies in social psychologists' conceptualization of attitudes.

The Rococo Breathless, an ornate style that may produce strong effects but sometimes makes the reader work too hard, is typified by this passage from Tom Wolfe's book *Radical Chic and Mau-Mauing the Flak-Catchers:*

> But she is not alone in her thrill as the Black Panthers come trucking on in, into Lenny's house, Robert Bay, Don Cox the Panthers' Field Marshal from Oakland, Henry Miller the Harlem Panther defense captain, the Panther women—Christ, if the Panthers don't know how to get it all together, as they say, the tight pants, the tight black turtlenecks, the leather coats, Cuban shades, Afros. But real Afros, not the ones that have been shaped and trimmed like a topiary hedge and sprayed until they have a sheen like acrylic wall-to-wall—but like funky, natural, scraggly . . . wild . . .
> *These are no civil-rights* Negroes *wearing gray suits three sizes* too big—
> —no more interminable Urban League banquets in hotel ballrooms where they try to alternate the blacks and whites around the tables as if they were stringing Arapho beads—
> —*these are* real men!

The Long-Winded Profound is represented well by this paragraph from the *New York Review of Books,* part of a review by Jean Staro-binsky of two books on the philosopher Jean-Jacques Rousseau:

> We can also say, more importantly, that when he traces the lines linking Rousseau's thought to the tyrannies of our century, Crocker is extrapolating and giving reality to themes which in Rousseau remain in the realm of imagination or of historical reminiscence. In a passage which carries an important reservation, Crocker concedes that there is

some anachronism in talking of Rousseau's totalitarianism. Plutarch's
Sparta, to which Rousseau so often turns his gaze, is not a modern
totalitarian state. When Rousseau mentions Lycurgus, he is not
prefiguring Stalin or the loyalty oath of the Fifties. In order to see this
in him we have to play the game of analogies, starting from our modern
experience and reducing to a common denominator every system where
the individual is obliged to conform to the will of a "guide" or a
tyrannical majority.

Fischer himself writes the style I prefer, the plain style, which is
much more like the spoken language than other styles but is not simply
written talk. Except for direct quotations, all writing changes speech at
least by ridding it of imprecise words and duplications. Plain style emphasizes precision in using words that are easy to understand and conciseness
in framing sentences readers can comprehend without the spur of thinking that they *must* read this to improve themselves.

Plain style is informal, language in its shirt sleeves. It usually avoids
bookish words such as *hitherto* and *amidst;* stilted expressions such as *He
was graduated from college;* genteel words such as *perspire* and *luncheon*
(*sweat* and *lunch* are fine, even if not together). Plain style also avoids
using euphemisms that misguided gentility has brought into the language,
such as substituting *casket* for *coffin* and *passed away* for *died.* Plain style,
however, is not vulgar: euphemisms are used for expressions such as
pissed off and *bullshit.* Nor is plain style slangy or colloquial. *Boost,* as in,
"The employees got a pay boost"; *fixin's,* as in, "dinner with turkey and
all the fixin's"; and *check into,* as in, "I'll check into that and let you
know"—all are on the other side of a line that plain style does not cross.
Plain style sounds like everyday speech in that *let you know* in the preceding sentence is used instead of *inform you.* It is more formal than
speech in that an everyday expression such as *swap* becomes *trade,* and
help but, as in, "He could not help but see the signal," becomes "He
could not avoid seeing the signal."

Simple as plain style seems, it is difficult to write, largely because
most of us are afraid of it. Wilbur Schramm, one of the few social scientists who is able to bring himself to use it, once advised young social
scientists, "Have the courage to write simply." It takes courage, and not
only for those who lean toward the Murky Academic. We avoid simplicity
partly because we want to sound lofty or otherwise important, partly
because we fear that sending plain sentence marching after plain sentence
will seem simple-minded.

When our thoughts are not worth expressing, the fear is well-
founded. Writing plainly does *not* mean stating the obvious. One way to

avoid simple-mindedness is to obey "Klaver's law," laid down by Peter R. Klaver of the University of Michigan, which holds: "Nothing can effectively be said to be X unless it could reasonably be said to be non-X." That warns against stating a truism such as "Men and women are different" or a platitude such as "It's not what you know, it's who you know" as though it were new and important.

Those who write the plain style well also avoid oversimplifying by using techniques that make it obvious that "plain" is a relative term. The style is plain*er* than other styles. Some of those who choose other styles exaggerate techniques to try to produce strong effects. They are more likely than the plain stylist to use literary devices such as periphrasis, an indirect, roundabout way of stating ideas. The writer of plain style seldom uses more than a touch of any bold technique, much as the writer of background music for a film underscores subtly to avoid drowning out the dialogue.

Ernest Hemingway, who learned to write simply when he was a reporter for the *Kansas City Star,* is an example of the plain stylist at work. Not content with mere simplicity, he worked hard to orchestrate sounds and rhythms, nearly always using short words and short, carefully varied sentences. The first paragraph of his story "In Another Country" illustrates the technique:

> In the fall the war was always there, but we did not go to it any more. It was cold in the fall in Milan and the dark came very early. Then the electric lights came on, and it was pleasant along the streets looking in the windows. There was much game hanging outside the shops, and the snow powdered on the fur of the foxes and the wind blew their tails. The deer hung stiff and heavy and empty, and small birds blew in the wind and the wind turned their feathers. It was a cold fall and the wind came down from the mountains.

In these few rhythmic sentences Hemingway establishes a mood as well as a setting, placing his readers with himself and his friends in the midst of war but out of it. He repeats words, especially *wind,* in a way that is not at all monotonous but helps create a dreamlike feeling. That is the work of a craftsman who made himself an artist.

Few writers will ever match Hemingway, but his work makes it clear that one who uses the plain style is not restricted to bare words in terse sentences. Plain style begins as a neuter; having made no commitment to a technique, plain style leaves it to the writer to choose among the many techniques (described in the next two chapters) that give writing its color and life.

PRECISE WORDS

The word *precise* may suggest formality, which is foreign to plain style. But precision means exactness, and one who writes the style that is first cousin to informal speech must use precise words; he is always in danger of drifting into the imprecisions of speech.

Confucius suggested why we must use words precisely. When asked what he would do first if he were put in charge of a national government, Confucius answered, "It would certainly be to correct language. If language is not correct, then what is said is not what is meant. If what is said is not meant, then what ought to be done remains undone. If this remains undone, then morals and arts deteriorate. If morals and arts deteriorate, justice will go astray. If justice goes astray, the people will stand about in helpless confusion. Hence, there must be no arbitrariness in what is said. This matters above everything."

During the Vietnam War, government spokesmen used euphemisms to make the harshness of bombing sound softer; they described the war as a series of tactical movements rather than bloody action. We were told of "interdicting enemy supply lines," "defensive ordnance drops," "neutralizing a free-fire area," and "protective reaction." General Curtis LeMay used more precise words: "We ought to bomb them back to the Stone Age." One can wince at his brutal goal and at the same time applaud him for using words that said exactly what he meant.

In a famous essay, "Politics and the English Language," George Orwell lamented that "In our time, political speech and writing are largely the defense of the indefensible." But focusing only on the language of politics and war is unfair. All of us are addicted to euphemisms, words that make harsh things soft and little things lofty. We let our language lie for us. Many salesmen certainly do. The proudly promoted "lifetime warranty" sometimes turns out to guarantee a product for *its* life rather than the buyer's. And when a youngster who is headed for a place his parents do not approve answers "Where are you going?" with "Out," his purpose is usually to mislead—like the politician and the salesman.

Although misleading words sometimes serve particular purposes in conversation, writers need precise words. The lofty practices Confucius wanted to protect—morals, arts, and justice—certainly suffer when what is written is not what is meant. Many lesser practices—carrying on the everyday business of living, relating experiences, describing persons or places, expressing emotions and ideas—also suffer because of our failure to use the right words.

Diction: Using the Right Words

Gustave Flaubert, one of the great masters of realism in fiction, told his writer friend Guy de Maupassant, "Whatever the thing you wish to say, there is but one word to express it, but one verb to give it movement, but one adjective to qualify it. You must seek until you find this noun, this verb, this adjective."

Flaubert exaggerated, but not much. J. D. Salinger, author of *Catcher in the Rye* and other stories, sometimes sits for hours making lists, searching for the precise words that will shape the meaning of a sentence. Truman Capote, author of *In Cold Blood,* also writes slowly, largely because he weighs and tests each word. The late Robert Ruark, who was a fast (and slovenly) writer, one evening boasted of his own speed and teased Capote with, "Truman, I'll bet you spent all day writing one word." Capote responded, "Ah, but it was the *right* word, Robert." Only professional writers need be that fussy, but anyone who writes should seek the right words.

A few professionals have worked to build large vocabularies because writing is their business; they learn words the way a financier learns monetary exchange rates. But most good writers work slowly on their vocabulary frontiers. When they hear or read an unfamiliar word, it usually becomes part of a list they have in mind. When they come upon the word again, they learn it.

Few writers, however, show off the words they know. Salinger, Capote, E. B. White, and especially Ernest Hemingway almost never use words that send their readers to a dictionary. Here and there we find them using an unusual word, ordinarily because no other word carries exactly the same shade of meaning, sometimes because they want to produce an unusual effect. A writer should strip language clean, Hemingway said. Most professional writers agree. Not only is clean prose easier to understand, its simplicity is persuasive; the writer does not seem to try to persuade. When we try to overpower readers or force their admiration by dazzling them with unfamiliar words, we impress only the small-minded. The writer Daniel Maue said, "When you don't know what you mean, use big words—that often fools little people."

If you have or develop a large vocabulary, you must resist two strong temptations: trying to make your writing seem important by clothing it richly, and showing off the words you know. Only the small-minded will praise you for yielding to either. The true measure of a writer's vocabulary is not the number of words he can use but the number he can use effectively.

Instead of memorizing six-syllable words, train yourself to think about the meanings of ordinary words. Several simple words now have more than one meaning because many writers use them as though they were elastic; dictionary-makers then list the secondary meanings. You too can stretch these words—the dictionary says you can—but that is seldom wise. You can, for example, use *since* for *because* like this:

> Since it rained Sunday, the ground was too wet for our picnic.

But you should think of *since* as a time-sequence word. The reader begins, "Since it rained Sunday," tunes his inner ear for words that will tell what happened later ("we've had nothing but sunshine"), and is unable to focus properly on a sentence that actually ends, "the ground was too wet for our picnic." The writer meant *"Because* it rained Sunday." The reader may not be conscious that his inner ear becomes confused, but the imprecision bothers him just below the level of consciousness.

Some substitutions of *since* for *because* leave meanings unclear:

> Since the union advanced its deadline for negotiations and set a tentative strike date of May 12, a number of questions have arisen concerning the status of employees and others in event of a strike.

Does that mean "because" the union advanced the deadline? Or is *since* used here as a time-sequence word? The writer probably meant the latter, but we cannot be sure.

To understand how much small imprecisions affect readers, consider what happens when a paragraph carries one sentence in which *since* is substituted for *because,* another in which *as* is substituted for *because* and still another in which *while* is substituted for *although.*

> Since it rained Sunday, the ground was too wet for a picnic. As I was going to take Sally, I was sorry we had to call it off. While I may not be the best conversationalist, I think she likes me.

As the reader starts each sentence, his inner ear signals a time sequence. He cannot read the paragraph at the same pace and with the same instant understanding that would be possible if the writer used words precisely. (*Since* is sometimes useful as a weak form of *because.* When time and cause are joined, *since* and *because* are the same.)

In reviewing *For Pete's Sake,* a movie in which one scene pictures a stampede through a New York City intersection, a movie critic stated: "Surprisingly, the bull and the cows took direction better than the actors and it only took three takes." By using *take* first in the past tense as a substitute for *accepted,* then for *required,* then in the present tense as a movie jargon word, the critic undoubtedly confused some readers and caused others to pause and puzzle out the meaning.

Such examples teach an important lesson: Given a choice between a word that *can* carry the proper meaning and one that *must* carry it, choose the latter.

Some phrases that are almost meaningless are used so widely that we write them without thinking. Surely you have run across "needless to say" hundreds of times. But if something really is needless to say, why say it? "Remains to be seen" is also familiar, but the phrase has no meaning worth the words. Aside from events that have already run their course, *everything* remains to be seen.

Using such phrases thoughtlessly encourages us to gum sentences together with other thoughtless words. We may use the various words that attribute quotations—said, declared, stated, added, claimed, maintained, implied, insisted, suggested, and the many others—as though all have a single meaning. In fact, *said* is the only neutral word in that list. To *declare* is to say emphatically. To *state* is to say formally. To *add* is to say secondarily, without any of the emphasis given primary points. It would be easy to list thirty words that are used to attribute quotations, all with different meanings, some with subtle shades of meaning. That helps to explain why careful writers labor over their choices of words.

To become discriminating in using words, we must think about the words we write. For example, in an article about broadcasting, a student wrote, "The daily news has become one of television's largest productions." If he had thought about *largest,* he would surely not have used it. Size of daily news production in television can be measured in number of employees, dollars spent, or hours of broadcast time. But in none of these measurements is news one of the *largest* productions. Consider television program schedules, which show how much time (and, usually, money and manpower) goes to situation comedies, movies, crime dramas, soap operas, talk shows, and sports broadcasts.

Editors wince when they see thoughtless writers use *well-known* without thinking, as in "Larry Czonka is a well-known athlete." The term does not mean what it tries to say: that Czonka is known well by a great many people. A more precise expression is *widely known*—known to a great many people who do not actually know him well.

Unless you think about the meanings of ordinary words you may drift into using words such as *area* to refer to almost anything. An area is geographic. Like most words, *area* can be used in other ways; but it should not be substituted for a specific word that the writer cannot think of at the moment. "Learning to play a musical instrument is an area that. . . ," one student wrote. Learning to play a musical instrument can be a hated chore, a happy experience, drudgery, or torture. But it is not an area. It *is* an activity, but *activity* is an all-purpose word primarily used in completing thoughtless sentences. Like *situation,* another all-purpose word, it is not often used by writers who care about what they are writing.

One cannot think about the meaning of each word while writing fast. After finishing a piece, a careful writer reads it slowly at least once, marking out some words and scribbling in substitutes. Is a frail person described as "puny"? Yes, but "delicate" better suggests the person's appearance. In typing the piece again, the writer is likely to find other imprecisions that he can change while typing, and another reading usually turns up other imprecise words and leads to more scribbling, more typing. Such care creates precise writing.

PRECISION AND THE AUDIENCE

The central problems in writing with precision are that word meanings are different depending on the context, new meanings become attached to old words, and many words have different meanings for different audiences.

George Bernard Shaw said, "England and the United States are divided by a common language." So is the United States itself. For example, a *stob* in the South is a *stake* in the North. This division, however, is not just geographic. Wherever a middle-class American lives, he is likely to think of *work* as an opportunity to realize his talents and enhance his prestige. To a lower-class American, *work* may symbolize nothing more than a grinding necessity. The experiences of most men and women in our culture are so different, Margaret Mead has pointed out, that *mother, love,* and *marriage* have many different meanings.

A word that excites emotion is the most difficult to use with precision. Its denotation, or specific meaning, always carries a heavier freight of connotations, or associated meanings, than other words carry. *Love* is burdened with connotations when standing alone, then (like other words) takes on other connotations when it is used in different contexts. It may have no specific meaning. Not only do we "love that soap" and "love to watch basketball," psychiatrist Joost Meerls suggests in the following that *love* as an expression of romantic interest may not even have a precise meaning to one who uses it:

> Sometimes it means: *I desire you* or *I want you sexually.* It may mean: *I hope you love me* or *I hope that I will be able to love you.* Often it means: *It may be that a love relationship can develop between us* or even *I hate you.* Often it is a wish for emotional exchange: *I want your*

admiration in exchange for mine or *I give you my love in exchange for some passion* or *I want to feel cozy and at home with you* or *I admire some of your qualities.* A declaration of love is mostly a request: *I desire you* or *I want you to gratify me,* or *I want your protection* or *I want to be intimate with you* or *I want to exploit your loveliness.*

Sometimes it is the need for security and tenderness for parental treatment. It may mean: *My self-love goes out to you.* But it may also express submissiveness: *Please take me as I am,* or *I feel guilty about you, I want, through you, to correct the mistakes I have made in human relations.* It may be self-sacrifice and a masochistic wish for dependency. However, it may also be a full affirmation of the other, taking the responsibility for mutual exchange of feelings. It may be a weak feeling of friendliness, it may be the scarcely even whispered expression of ecstasy. *"I love you"*—wish, desire, submission, conquest; it is never the word itself that tells the real meaning here.

If a word can be so elastic, how can we make the meaning precise? We can only place emotional words in *contexts* that should make the meaning clear. If we write *work, marriage,* and *love* in a paragraph that reflects high regard for them, most readers will understand what we intend to say about them. We can do nothing about the reader who hates his work, has bitter memories of a broken marriage, and is cynical about romantic love.

Fortunately, we can cope more successfully with other problems of writing with precision.

Jargon as Precision and as Gibberish

Even if you have long detested jargon, you are likely to become a jargonist. In fact, if you now refer to a course or a department as "Psych" or "Eco," you already are. We can think of jargon as the special terminology of a group—or we can think of it as language reduced to gibberish. A story and the continuing controversy the story symbolizes may help you appreciate the difference.

A teacher who was critical of the social sciences devised for the amusement of his students a game that he called "Three-Digit Language." He would list and number words in three columns like this:

0.	evaluative	0.	coalition	0.	equilibrium
1.	functional	1.	power	1.	relation
2.	hyperbolic	2.	influence	2.	attrition
3.	intuitive	3.	communication	3.	contingency
4.	interactive	4.	sociometric	4.	gradient

5. reciprocal	5. role	5. structure
6. negative	6. activity	6. decision
7. operational	7. task	7. network
8. centralized	8. status	8. matrix
9. interdependent	9. interpersonal	9. index

Then the teacher would invite the students to think of any three-digit number—457, for example—and produce a phrase by reading the words beside each number: "interactive role network." Any combination the students chose (510 yields "reciprocal power equilibrium") would sound like social science. "That," he would say, "is how social science jargon is ruining our language, destroying meaning."

Is it? Most social scientists argue that their special language, or jargon, makes communication *more* precise. They point out that when a layman says, "I have a theory," he may mean that he has a vague notion, that a small thought has come to him, that he has a full-fledged idea, or perhaps even that he has developed a sweeping concept. But "theory" in the social sciences means a relationship between or among facts, or an ordering of facts in some meaningful form. No one can really *know* what the layman means, the social scientists contend, but *theory* and many other words that laymen use loosely have a precise meaning in the social sciences.

The language of the social sciences *is* precise—among social scientists (or most of them; the language is still developing, and some social scientists define special terms, including *theory*, differently). But for laymen, the language of social science is jargon as gibberish. Some social scientists who are proud of their special language pile special term upon special term in an offensive way.

This is a special problem in the classroom. Nearly every student has had the depressing experience of listening to a lecture that he does not comprehend, while other students seem to follow it easily. Is everyone smarter than I am? Am I really *that* stupid? Such questions are likely to occur to anyone who has already suffered similar defeats. The student may be in a course that is too advanced for him, or he may actually be less intelligent than most of his classmates. (Unknown to him, however, others who seem to comprehend may also be deep in self-doubt.) Far more often, however, such a student simply does not understand special terms. One who does not know the definitions of "dependent variable" and "independent variable" cannot follow the reasoning of a lecturer who assumes that everyone is aware of them.

Nor is the problem of jargon limited to the social sciences. In a literature class, what are you to make of a fast-paced lecture studded with words such as *Aristotelian, Jamesian,* and *mythic* if they are foreign to you? Ordinarily, you can learn the terms of almost any field by doing the prescribed reading. But even if you memorize definitions and work to understand the assigned reading, you can lose the thread of meaning when *Kafkaesque symbols* turns up in a lecture. You may have had the experience of searching your memory for a meaning, finding it, then discovering that you are lost because the lecturer is five sentences further along—and that he is now using *another* term for which you must search your memory.

Classroom and reading experiences make you aware of others who are jargonists. Using special terms makes *you* a jargonist—not an offensive one if you talk only to those who know the terms (but perhaps offensive even to them if you use terms for show rather than communication). Thinking of yourself as jargonist should help you decide whether a particular audience will understand the special terms you use in writing. Even if they will, consider your own motives. If you are about to use a term primarily to demonstrate that you are a member of an in-group, shun it.

Never assume that jargon is more defensible in writing than it is in speaking. True, those who must listen to lectures filled with special terms can seldom stop the flow of words long enough to learn or remember definitions; readers, on the other hand, can look up definitions. But will they? Using language readers do not understand invites them to stop reading. Unless they are compelled to continue (as many students are compelled to read textbooks), they will probably accept the invitation.

Pomposity vs. Precision

A plumber once wrote to the National Bureau of Standards to say that he had found hydrochloric acid useful in cleaning drains. Is it harmless? he asked. An official wrote in reply: "The efficacy of hydrochloric acid is indisputable, but the chlorine residue is incompatible with metallic permanence." The plumber replied that he was happy to hear that hydrochloric acid was all right. The official responded again in pompous language, and the plumber wrote back that he was still happy that the official agreed. Then the official wrote: "Don't use hydrochloric acid. It eats hell out of the pipes!"

The story may be fiction, but it points up the problem of writing pompously, which is not a problem limited to bureaucrats. Pomposity afflicts some students. F. Peter Woodford of Rockefeller University laments that students may write clearly and directly when they enter graduate school, but their writing soon changes. At first, they may write prose that scientists consider precise and concise, like this:

In order to determine the molecular size and shape of A and B, I measured their sedimentation and diffusion constants. The results are given in Table 1. They show that A is a roughly spherical molecule of molecular weight 36,000. The molecular weight of B remains uncertain since the sample seems to be impure. This is being further investigated.

To scientists, who know about such things as sedimentation and diffusion constants, this writing is clear and direct. Woodford says, however, that after two years in graduate school, a student probably writes something like this:

In order to evaluate the possible significance of certain molecular parameters at the subcellular level, and to shed light on the conceivable role of structural configuration in spatial relationship of intracellular macromolecules, an integrated approach (see 1) to the problem of cell diffusivity has been devised and developed. The results, which are in a preliminary stage, are discussed here in some detail because of their possible implication in mechanisms of diffusivity in a wider sphere.

You need not become a graduate student to become this pompous. The more you learn about a subject, the greater the danger. You may try to make your writing more significant with such hollow sounds, not knowing that they prevent readers from understanding what you have to say. As Wilbur Schramm said, "Have the courage to write simply."

General Words vs. Precision

Because we seldom remember exact figures, we become accustomed to using general words such as *few, several,* and *many,* sometimes because there is no way of knowing exact figures. I refer often in this book to "many writers" and "many readers." No amount of research could enable me to determine exactly how many. But writing should usually be as precise as the writer can make it, for what he implies with a vague word is seldom what all of his readers infer. When sixty-five students in a college class filled out the questionnaire in the left and middle columns below, their answers covered the wide range in the right column:

1. "The senator was elected by an overwhelming majority."	What percentage of the vote did he receive?	Lowest, 54 percent; highest, 75 percent.
2. "My 17-year-old son is of average height."	How tall is he?	Lowest, 5 feet, 8 inches; highest, 6 feet, 1 inch.
3. "Uncle Ned is a moderate smoker."	How many cigarettes does he smoke a day?	Least, ½ pack a day; most, 1½ packs a day.

4. "Jane really isn't a 'brain,' but she makes good grades."	What is her scholastic average (in %)?	Lowest, 75%; highest 90%.
5. "Although my friend isn't wealthy, he makes a comfortable living."	How much does he make a year?	Least, $8,000 yearly; most, $30,000 yearly.
6. "I read several books last summer."	How many books did I read?	Least, two; most, thirteen.
7. "Mrs. Jensen is middle-aged."	How old is she?	Youngest, 35; oldest 55.

Obviously, words such as *average, moderate,* and *several* are too feeble to do much work. When we consider that the respondents were students, and were thus alike in that all were attending college (which set them apart from most Americans) and all were about the same age, we can imagine the scattershot responses that would have come from a cross-section of the population. Of course, such respondents would be even less likely to guess what was intended by the general words.

It should be obvious that the plain style of writing is different from speaking; although it uses familiar words easily understood, it is more precise. Plain style is idiomatic: the written version of the English spoken by reasonably well educated Americans. Euphemisms are tested to determine whether they contribute to decency. If they exist to mislead or evade, we avoid them. Slang is made up of fad words. Slang that is not passing into standard English, or is not likely to, has no place. That is the precision of plain style: informal and relaxed but not faddish.

CONCISE SENTENCES

Many people think that concise means only short. We should worry about sentences that run long but worry more about using only the number of words needed. When a good writer goes over his work, he does away with the repetitious words and phrases that inevitably crop up. When he finds that his writing wanders, he cuts into it, deflating language, usually making two sentences or more of a loose sentence, but preserving flavor and variety even as he works for conciseness.

Such revising depends on balance and taste, as well as on purpose and audience. Is the writer trying only to inform a diverse audience of readers who differ in knowledge and interest? If his main purpose is to transfer facts from one mind to others, especially in news stories, sentences should be short. Is the writer trying to explain *and* inform? The sentences may be longer, or at least a greater mixture of lengths. Or is the writer trying to create a reading experience? That is a more complicated matter.

The following experience illustrates how taste, purpose, and individuality cause us to vary our writing.

A student took careful notes during the first meeting of his 9 o'clock class in composition as the teacher emphasized the need for direct, concise writing. At 10 o'clock, he attended the first meeting of his class in American literature and was assigned to read some of the works of Thomas Wolfe and William Faulkner. That evening, he began to read Faulkner and was understandably confused. If direct, concise writing is the ideal, he thought, why didn't William Faulkner practice it? And how could one teacher applaud concise writing and another applaud Faulkner?

Such experiences lead many students to believe that they are taught contradictory rules for writing. Keep it simple, they are told, and a teacher is likely to delete words and phrases from their writing and suggest that they read the stories of Ernest Hemingway to feel the impact of terse sentences that strike like bullets, and read the essays of George Orwell and E. B. White to learn how to write simple words in simple structures. It certainly seems contradictory to be assigned to read Wolfe, Faulkner, or the literary essays that appear in the *New York Review of Books* (not to mention many other writers and publications that seem devoted to the difficult). Wolfe's rolling, twisting prose, Faulkner's winding sentences, the long-winded reasoning of many of those who write for the *New York Review*—all violate, or seem to violate, the principle of simplicity. Yet all are likely to be praised.

The contradiction might be explained by saying that the preferences of teachers (and others) differ. In a few cases, it can be explained that way. But the teacher who urges his students to strive for simplicity at 9 o'clock may also be the one who assigns them to read complex writing at 10.

Conciseness and Complexity

How can the teacher justify a seeming contradiction in his preferences?

First, complex phrasings and structures fit some kinds of writing and not others. At the risk of oversimplifying: Writing that appeals to the emotions can sometimes be expressed best by the rich, the complex, the unusual. Oversimplifying again: Writing that appeals primarily to the reason is best expressed simply.

However, some of the complexity in the work of the noted writers would be better if it were simpler. When Thomas Wolfe submitted his manuscripts to his publisher, some passages were dense thickets of words. Only laborious editing by Maxwell Perkins, who worked for Wolfe's publisher, made them comprehensible. He might have done more editing to good effect. Perhaps more of the passages in Faulkner's work, which was also edited, could have been improved by more vigorous editing. Certainly some of the essays in the *New York Review* could be pruned.

This does not mean that all writers should always imitate Hemingway, Orwell, and White. Wolfe often affected the emotions of his readers with long, cadenced sentences whose roll and rhythm were almost as important as the sense of the words. This sentence from *Look Homeward, Angel* indicates the power as well as the complexity of Wolfe's writing:

> He knew the inchoate sharp excitement of hot dandelions in young spring grass at noon; the smell of cellars, cobwebs, and built-on secret earth; in July, of watermelons bedded in sweet hay, inside a farmer's covered wagon; of cantaloupe and crated peaches; and the scent of orange rind, bittersweet, before a fire of coals.

Rhythm is almost as important as the sense of the words. The length and complexity of some of Faulkner's sentences—a few are chaotically formed —are themselves a value: the form is an echo of the sense. But this level of artistry is high up. Beginners who try to reach it usually fall.

Every beginning writer should master simple expression. If you are meant to be creatively different, your nature will force you to it, perhaps even force you to become a writer with the intricate genius of James Joyce. But you will be a better one if you master simplicity first. This does not mean that simplicity is a primitive form. It should certainly be the beginning, but most of the greatest writers have made it the end as well. Leo Tolstoy is a prime example. His *War and Peace* is itself a complex structure because of the many plots, subplots, and characters, but the prose is simple.

The experience of Tolstoy suggests yet another reason to work for simplicity. Toward the end of his life, Tolstoy became obsessed with the need to write for the peasants of Russia in the simple language they understood. You need not think of yourself as one who writes for peasants to learn the lesson this teaches: Remember the audience. To communicate complex ideas and paradoxical facts with a simplicity that any literate person can understand is to address the largest possible audience.

In short, consider simple writing the conventional form, worthy of the best efforts of any writer. You can write unconventionally to accomplish a certain purpose or to product a particular effect, but you must justify the unconventional.

Conciseness vs. Mere Brevity

To write concisely is to use as few words as possible to give the intended meaning or effect, not to reduce graceful expressions to choppy sentence units. But grace should be sacrificed if the extra words serve no purpose, as in this sentence:

Throwing modesty aside, he claims to be the world's greatest musician.

The teacher deleted the first three words, reasoning that the rest of the sentence makes it clear that the man threw modesty aside. The student argued that because the sentences immediately before the edited sentence and those immediately after it were short and in a subject-verb, subject-verb pattern, the deletion destroyed the balance of the passage. One cheer for the student, who had learned the value of variation. But only one cheer. Sentences must be balanced with substance, not ballast. We should balance passages by using sentences structured differently, not sentences carrying dead words.

The student who wrote the following news story for his college paper (in the right column) objected to the edited version, which deleted many words:

EDITED VERSION	ORIGINAL VERSION
Time is running out for the world. Our technological advances may destroy us, warned Barbara Ward.	The world is at a time this year where time is running out. The world can not long stand the problems caused by its technological advances, predicted Barbara Ward.
Miss Ward, the 56-year-old English economist, author of the widely known book "The Lopsided World," spoke before a capacity crowd in the Art Auditorium Friday on "A World Out of Balance."	Barbara Ward, the 56 year old English born economist and author of the well known book "The Lopsided World," spoke before a packed Art Auditorium Friday on the subject "A World Out of Balance."
Technological advances are causing a widening gulf between the "developed" nations and the "developing" nations. Persons she deemed "wasteful, filthy, and unconcerned" are overloading the environment.	Society's technological advances of late are causing the imbalance in two main areas: It is (1) causing a widening gulf between the "developed" nations and the "developing nations." (2) causing an overloading of the
Miss Ward said that the developed nations try to get everything for "us,"	

EDITED VERSION	ORIGINAL VERSION
and later think of "them." The un-concerned have. . . .	world's environment by persons she deemed as "wasteful, filthy, and un-concerned." In respect to problem (1) Barbara Ward said that the thought of the de-veloped nations is get everything for "us," and afterward think about "them." The unconcerned have. . . .

The student argued that the editing ruined the balance and rhythm of his sentences. The editor countered that although a straight news story should provide a reasonably balanced and rhythmic collection of sentences, its first purpose is to give information. Instead of expecting news stories to provide the pleasant reading experience they expect from feature stories, most readers seek facts from such writing. Moreover, the editor argued, even in a judgment of balance and rhythm, the edited version is better. Although the sentence structure of the original is a bit more varied, variation is achieved at the cost of repetitions that have no value.

Surely the editor was right. Although repetition can occasionally be used to good effect, using "time" twice in the first sentence is graceless, and "The world" is used at the beginning of each of the first two sentences to no purpose.

Note that in the second paragraph of the original version the writer says that Barbara Ward spoke "on the subject." To write that she spoke "on" says the same in two fewer words. Using two extra words is not a crime, of course, but a writer who does not know to delete such phrases is quite likely to do what this one did: use so many unneeded words in the next paragraph ("Society's," "of late," "causing . . . causing . . . causing," and others) that the reader must work to gather information.

Length and Conciseness

Because writing is not a science, there are no literary laws. We should listen to the great writers, not obey them blindly. Robert Southey, the poet, wrote that words are like sunbeams; "the more you condense them, the deeper they burn."

Sometimes, though, one can condense too much, as in "He is heterozygous for curly hair." If you write that in twenty words instead of six, all readers will understand: "He has received a gene for curly hair from one parent and a gene for straight hair from the other." For most readers, the twenty-word sentence is better. Too few know the meaning of heterozygous.

Writers also cause problems by making up symbols to replace words and by trying to force a few words to do the work of many. In a report on the costs of a volunteer army, the writer decided that wages for military service should be called "Wm," wages earned by civilians should be called "Wc." He wrote, "However, when one considers that a military aversion factor must be added to Wc or subtracted from Wm, assuming average aversion is positive. . . ." The sentence goes on, but few readers will. After pausing over Wc to try to recall what it means and pausing again over Wm, most readers will stop. In fact, they may stop even before that. Although "military aversion factor" is a concise way of saying that one must consider aversion to military life as well as wages, this is not the kind of condensing Southey would have approved.

Balance and Rhythm

Readers are attracted by balance, which is in the inner ear in reading just as it is in standing or walking a tightrope. The reader's ear is tuned to the parallel items in this sentence by Phyllis McGinley, writing about the unfair stereotype of the suburbanite:

> He is nearly as much a stock character as the old stage Irishman: "the man who spends his life riding to and from his wife," the eternal Babbit who knows all about Buicks and nothing about Picasso, whose sanctuary is the club locker room, whose ideas spring ready-made from the illiberal newspapers.

The reader's ear is also tuned to the rhythms of sentence variation. The sentence above appeared in this rhythmic paragraph:

> To condemn Suburbia has long been a literary cliché, anyhow. I have yet to read a book in which the suburban life was pictured as the good life or the commuter as a sympathetic figure. He is nearly as much a stock character as the old stage Irishman: the man who "spends his life riding to and from his wife," the eternal Babbit who knows all about Buicks and nothing about Picasso, whose sanctuary is the club locker room, whose ideas spring ready-made from the illiberal newspapers. His wife plays politics at the P.T.A. and keeps up with the Joneses. Or—if the scene is more gilded and less respectable—the commuter is the high-powered advertising executive with a station wagon, his wife a restless baggage given to too many cocktails in the afternoon.

Sometimes a very long sentence balances a passage, especially when it follows short sentences that have been building to a point. In an article in *Harper's* magazine protesting that Supreme Court decisions have nullified compulsory school attendance laws for the Amish, the writer ended with a bitter piling-up of arguments:

> Finally, is it not strange to be told now—after eighteen years of the effort to integrate the public schools, when one of the principal political issues appears to be whether there shall be busing to achieve a balance between the races; when the decision that gave rise to all this in 1954 held that "education is perhaps the most important function of state and local governments," that "compulsory school attendance laws . . . demonstrate our recognition of the importance of education to our democratic society," that, indeed, it is "the very foundation of good citizenship," that, in the famous statement that so troubled the logicians, "separate facilities are inherently unequal"—is it not strange to be told now that it is unconstitutional for a state to require children (or, at least, some children) even to go to high school?

Although it is necessary to read the rest of the article to judge the sentence fully and to appreciate its effect, this is enough to indicate that such a sentence can sweep the reader up in the writer's argument. A disciplined writer can send long sentences marching rhythmically, with words, phrases, and clauses carrying readers at a pace that would not be possible if he always restricted himself to short sentences.

We should seldom use such a technique, though, in part because repeated use of any bold technique reduces its impact. And when a writer stretches many words between two periods, he may become entangled in them. No matter how tangled the sentence, the writer probably knew what he wanted to say. His readers can only guess.

You can test for balance by reading your work with these principles in mind:

1   Any sentence that causes you to stumble, if only slightly, will probably make the readers stumble harder.
2   Any sentence that you must read more than once for understanding is probably not clear to readers.
3   Any sentence that begins, "In other words," "that is," or "That is to say" probably follows a sentence that should be rewritten.

Shortening Sentences

In writing designed primarily to give information, briefer is nearly always better. News writers usually see to it that most of their sentences are closer to twenty words than to thirty. Briefer is usually better in other kinds of writing, but one who fears writing should not use the principle of brevity to rationalize issuing cautious little sentences. Nor should those who have trouble expanding ideas and seeing variations in ideas think that "briefer is better" puts them on safe ground. We speak here of the brevity of sentences, not of thought and topic development.

The meaningful match in judging conciseness is a twenty-word sentence versus a fifteen-word sentence that says the same thing as clearly and gracefully, a forty-word sentence versus a thirty-word sentence that says the same thing as clearly and gracefully. In each case, the briefer version is better. This is because some sentences say in twenty words what could be said as well in fifteen. Constructing concise sentences often means condensing phrases. The messages in the left column are also carried by those in the right column.

dead body found	body found
new innovation	innovation
in the city of Boston	in Boston
cost the sum of $5	cost $5
future prospects	prospects
past history	history
past experience	experience
was of an oblong shape	was oblong
canary bird	canary
start off	start
throughout the entire day	throughout the day
perhaps it may happen	it may happen
in the year of 1975	in 1975
old traditions of the past	traditions
for a period of ten days	for ten days
during the course of the day	during the day
at the hour of noon	at noon
for the purpose of checking	to check
for a short space of time	briefly
reported to the effect that	reported
talk on the subject of charity	talk on charity

The words in the right column say everything that is said in the left column. To attach *new* to *innovation,* for example, is to tell the reader the same thing twice, for the definition of *innovation* includes "new." On rare occasions, redundancy is useful. To write "actual fact" is nearly always an error because all facts are actual. But we sometimes want to distinguish between a belief that was once widely held (Earth is flat) and one that was later proved to be factual (Earth is round). In such a case, we refer to the latter as the "actual fact" to emphasize the distinction. Ordinarily, it is also an error to write *new recruits;* all recruits are new. But it may sometimes be useful to distinguish between men recruited a month ago and those recruited yesterday. Perhaps *all* the redundant expressions in the left column above can be justified on such grounds, but so rarely that examples are not worth considering.

Words must justify themselves. Just as a talented architect does not design into buildings gewgaws that are neither ornamental nor functional, the writer does not include words that have no purpose.

It does not matter, of course, if a piece of writing has only a sentence or two including phrases like those above. If the writing is otherwise crisp, few if any readers will even notice the useless word in "The ROTC captain drilled the new recruits." But the writer who uses *new recruit* is quite likely to lard his work with similar sentences. If you train yourself to search for *new recruits,* you become aware of the need for conciseness.

Does it make any difference to readers that in a thousand-word essay seventy-five words serve no purpose? It does, even though few readers analyze writing, and few are even aware of superfluous words and phrases. They are affected nonetheless, as is suggested by a sentence composed largely of phrases taken from the left column above:

> The past experiences of the future prospects for employment in the city of Boston were brought out in interviews that were conducted throughout the entire day of June 12 in the year of 1975.

In contrast, that sentence might be written:

> The experiences of the prospects for employment in Boston were related in interviews conducted on June 12, 1975.

We have more trouble deleting modifiers that flavor sentences heavily. Voltaire said that "The adjective is the enemy of the noun." Like Flaubert, who said that there is only one right word, Voltaire exaggerated. Some adjectives are the friends of nouns, even indispensable partners. For example, it was necessary for me to write *"indispensable* partners" for emphasis. We must decide when an adjective helps emphasize or color or round out meaning. If it does not, it is an enemy. Unfortunately, many of those who write are so seized by the rich sounds of words that they pile up adjectives and adverbs to add color and intensity. In this sentence a writer tries to describe how a rich man protected the wealth of his company:

An elaborate and payrolled watchdog system was set to safeguard his interests, should any ambitiously piratical executive attempt a personal seduction of organizational assets.

This is a bad sentence for many reasons, especially because the reader must work to determine exactly what it says. The most obvious flaw is that the sentence is drunk with adjectives. The force of each is reduced because the reader must give his attention first to one adjective, then to another. The nouns are almost submerged by their enemies.

This is a common failing. In the days when the late J. Edgar Hoover was attacked for the way he operated the FBI, his supporters developed a widely quoted description of him: "a fearless fighter and implacable foe of the godless tyranny of cancerous Communism." Judging by the number of times this description was used by many speakers, they were proud of it. But it is too self-consciously flavorful. It tries too hard.

We might combine and paraphrase the statements by Voltaire and Flaubert: In most cases, the adjective is the enemy of the noun. If you must use an adjective, search for the right one—usually *only* one. Perhaps those who love words and delight in making phrases and sentences will remember the exceptions in this chapter: rhythm and balance, the value of the extended sentence that sweeps readers along, the danger of mere brevity. But the major message is simple: Be concise. Sir Ernest Gowers, author of *Plain Words,* makes the point this way:

> Use no more words than are necessary to express your meanings, for if you use more you are likely to obscure it and to tire your reader. In particular do not use superfluous adjectives and adverbs and do not use roundabout phrases where single words would serve.

PROJECTS

1   The word *say* means "to express in words." List the following on one page and write beside each a few words that explain the meaning.

report
reveal
point out
charge
assert
suggest
comment

maintain

remark

claim

2   Type the seven-item exercise that appears in the "General Words vs. Precision" section of this chapter. Distribute ten copies to other students who are not members of the class and ask them to fill in the blanks. Write a summary of the results.

3   Find in one of your textbooks ten words or phrases that you consider jargon. List them and write the meaning of each in words that would be understandable to high school students.

4   Write these statements concisely:
   · tendered his resignation
   · completely destroyed by fire
   · made an investigation of
   · at regular intervals of time
   · students who are regularly enrolled
   · once in a great while
   · is of the opinion that
   · continued on
   · went on to say
   · concluded his talk to the assembled audience with the following words

5   Write these sentences concisely:
   · He was wearing a suit that was made of tweed and that had been bought in a clothing store in the city of Dallas.
   · Sociology, which is generally considered by most people to be one of the social science subjects, is a requirement for all students who are candidates for graduation.
   · Baseball is a sport which continues to keep on growing in its popularity to attract more and more people to the diamond contests to see the game.

6   Write this concisely:
   U.S. Senator Tom Johnson, who spoke to a joint, combined meeting that was convened here last Tuesday evening, in summing up the gist of the work of the United States Congress in the recent session that has just passed, pointed to the improvement of foreign relations as one of the bright spots in the general picture. This, the U.S. Senator said, was because there was cooperative action between the President, who is a Republican, and the principal leaders of the United States Congress, who are Democrats. It came in spite of the many prophecies of doom that had been emanating from some quarters for some time.

7   Use the principles of conciseness to edit or to evaluate any short piece of writing, preferably something you wrote long ago.

8   Read two or three articles in the New York Review of Books, two or three

articles in the *American Sociological Review* or the *American Journal of Psychology,* and several passages from one of the books by Tom Wolfe (*Radical Chic and Mau-Mauing the Flak-Catchers, The Electric Kool-Aid Acid Test,* and *The Kandy-Kolored Tangerine Flake Streamline Baby*). Does the *New York Review of Books* seem to deserve the name that John Fischer gives it, Long-Winded Profound? Are the articles in the scholarly journals appropriately described by "Murky Academic"? Does Wolfe's writing seem to you to deserve to be called Rococo Breathless? In answering, consider two questions: (a) Is the style in each case appropriate as a *general style,* one that might be used in any writing? (b) Is each style justified by the audience each writer is addressing?

Using Techniques:
Voice, Tone, and Flow

When we speak of technique, we speak of nearly everything. Technique is the only means the writer has of discovering, exploring, and developing his subject, conveying its meaning, and finally, evaluating it.—MARK SCHORER

3 Using precise words in concise, informal sentences is central, but there is much more to plain style. It is plain but not lifeless. This chapter focuses on some of the techniques that give writing life and color. Much depends on voice and tone, and especially on making sentences and paragraphs flow so that they carry readers along with them.

CHOOSING A VOICE

The late Harold Ross of the *New Yorker* was a great editor primarily because he read everything submitted to his magazine as though he were a subscriber. He sometimes carried the reader's point of view almost to absurdity. At one weekly staff meeting, he looked with bewilderment at a cartoon other editors were chuckling over and asked, "Where am *I* in this?" That was his blunt way of saying: "Imagine that this is a real scene the reader is watching. Exactly where is he standing?"

That is closely related to questions writers must ask themselves: Where do I want the reader to focus? On me? On his own involvement in my topic? On something or someone distant from both of us? Answering such questions helps determine which voice to use.

I use *I* infrequently in this book—perhaps twenty-five times—for rea-

sons outlined under "Be Careful With *I*." *You* appears more often because that voice lends itself easily to instructional writing. *We* appears
almost as often as *you* because you and I and others are together in a community of writers. (An author may also use what is called "the editorial
we" to refer only to himself.) This book refers most often to "the reader"
and "readers" because a writer must always think of them. "One" appears
only occasionally; it is impersonal, and many uses of "one" sound stilted
(One must consider one's future when one . . .).

Here are some guidelines for choosing a voice.

Be Careful with *I*

When you are writing about yourself, *I* is natural. Ordinarily, we
need only edit first-person writing carefully to make certain that every
sentence is not dotted with *I*. In writing about someone else, however,
we must remember that most of us are so self-centered that we insert *I*,
often unconsciously, into almost everything. Here a male student who set
out to write about a girl writes too much about himself:

> I'm quiet. Shy, retiring. I'm the one who sits in the back of the class in
> constant fear of being called upon.
> Perhaps, then, you can appreciate the perplexity I felt meeting a par-
> ticular girl last year.
> The scene: a Christmas party in one of the college dormitories. Most of
> the people were clustered around a bowl of warm wine. Others were mak-
> ing decorations for the tree. I had stationed myself next to the stereo,
> which was tuned to a local FM station. I had taken it upon myself . . . .

He is shy, quiet, retiring—and self-indulgent. He wrote a total of
700 words, 300 of them about himself, before he got around to showing
readers the girl. Then he gave himself equal space with her to the end.

An adroit writer can, of course, show us someone else by sketching
his own reactions to the other person. James Thurber began a piece titled
"Something to Say": "Elliot Vereker was always coming into and going
out of my life. He was the only man who ever continuously stimulated me
to the point of a nervous breakdown." Thurber's piece is dotted with "I"
in many places, but the focus is always on Vereker. Thurber reported his
own reactions to reveal Vereker.

Many of us sprinkle the perpendicular pronoun through our writing. We should not always avoid using it. Personal experiences can seldom
be written well except in first person. Some journalists avoid using *I* by
giving themselves another name, or by referring to themselves as "the
reporter" or "this reporter," which helps create the image of the journalist
as a bloodless, detached observer, but which sometimes sounds ridiculous.

A writer can intensify and personalize certain other pieces by including himself. But self-indulgence is always lurking about. To avoid it, pose these questions in trying to decide whether to write in first person:

> Why *should* I put myself in this? Am I essential? Can the points be made as well without me? Can they be made *better* without me?

The answers usually pivot on whether the topic is a concept or an experience. If a writer only conceives of his topic—knows about it because he has studied or heard about it, or has seen it—he should probably stand away from it in writing as he did in life. But if the topic is based on an experience, a writer may be able to involve his readers by showing his own involvement, as poet Dylan Thomas did in writing about a memorable day in his youth:

> It was on the afternoon of the day of Christmas Eve, and I was in Mrs. Prothero's garden, waiting for cats, with her son Jim. It was snowing. It was always snowing at Christmas. December, in my memory, is white as Lapland, though there were no reindeers. But there were cats. Patient, cold and callous, our hands wrapped in socks, we waited to snowball the cats. Sleek and long as jaguars and horrible-whiskered, spitting and snarling, they would slink and sidle over the white back-garden walls, and the lynx-eyed hunters, Jim and I, fur-capped and moccasined trappers from Hudson Bay, off Mumbles Road, would hurl our deadly snowballs at the green of their eyes. The wise cats never appeared. We were so still, Eskimo-footed arctic marksmen in the muffling silence of the eternal snows—eternal, ever since Wednesday—that we never heard Mrs. Prothero's first cry from her igloo at the bottom of the garden. Or, if we heard it at all, it was, to us, like the far-off challenge of our enemy and prey, the neighbour's polar cat. But soon the voice grew louder.
> "Fire!" cried Mrs. Prothero, and she beat the dinner-gong.
> And we ran down the garden, with the snowballs in our arms, toward the house; and smoke, indeed, was pouring out of the dining-room. Mrs. Prothero was announcing ruin like a town crier in Pompeii. This was better than all the cats in Wales standing on the wall in a row. We bounded into the house, laden with snowballs, and stopped at the open door of the smoke-filled room. Something was burning all right. . . .

Thomas is smiling at his own memory of himself ("trappers from Hudson Bay, off Mumbles Road," and "eternal snows—eternal, ever since Wednesday"); he does not appear in his writing merely to preen himself. His presence illuminates the subject for his readers rather than blocking their view of it.

Addressing *You*

George L. Dyer, the advertising manager of the clothing company Hart, Schaffner & Marx, often wrote long, word-packed advertisements. Max Hart, his employer, argued that short punchy ads with large pictures were more persuasive. Dyer told him, "I'll bet you ten dollars I can write a newspaper ad of solid type and you'll read every word of it." Hart laughed at him. Dyer responded, "I don't have to write a line of the ad to prove my point. I'll only tell you the headline: THIS PAGE IS ALL ABOUT MAX HART." Hart paid the bet.

We could easily attract and hold a reader's attention if we could always write about that reader, but we cannot. The greatly talented can seem to: a journalist in skillfully covering events that touch the lives of nearly everyone, a novelist in looking into the human condition with such sharp insight that he seems to address every reader personally while writing about only one. But they are enviable exceptions.

A writer who is sensitive to his readers' natural interest in themselves may try to speak directly to each reader by using the second person. Addressing the reader as "you" has a value obvious to anyone who recognizes the principle underlying THIS PAGE IS ALL ABOUT MAX HART. In advertising, in books and articles with titles beginning "How to," and in direct-mail appeals, the reader is attracted by an implied "you." In instructional writing, such as some textbooks, *you* may be natural. Writers who describe exotic places sometimes use it fairly effectively (You ride up the Nile, your vision filled with . . .).

You is affecting but often troublesome. Perhaps the power of the address, the constant you-you-you, makes readers too conscious that it is a technique. Most of us find it natural for only a short time to speak to another person about that person—"You would be sure to enjoy that movie because you have such an appreciation of. . . ." "You should fix your hair another way because you. . . ." A continuing *you* in print, like a continuing *you* in conversation, may eventually embarrass or exhaust both reader and writer. Of the three voices, *you* is the most difficult to keep to comfortably. A writer who begins with *you*, finds that he cannot sustain it gracefully, then switches to first or third person leaves the reader wondering, "Whatever happened to me?"

The Useful Third Person

It may seem ironic that the two personal forms of address, *I* and *you*, should be almost useless for so many kinds of writing. That seems to leave only a detached third person, which places both reader and writer at arm's length from one another. But is it detached and distant?

Actually, the third person both avoids the dangers of *I* and *you* and is the most flexible of the three forms of address. A skillful writer can use it to create much the same effects created by the others. Consider this passage from *The Kingdom and the Power,* in which author Gay Talese describes the managing editor of the *New York Times:*

> He is a most interesting-looking man but difficult to describe because the words that quickly catch him best initially seem entirely inappropriate for any man who is a man. But the impression persists. Clifton Daniel is almost lovely. It is his face, which is long and pale and soft and dominated by large dark eyes and very long lashes, and his exquisitely groomed, wavy hair that makes him seem almost lovely. His suits are very Savile Row, his hands and nails immaculate, his voice a soft, smooth blend of North Carolina, where he was born in a tiny tobacco town, and England, where he came of age as a journalist and squire of fashionable women and was sometimes referred to as the Sheik of Fleet Street.

Talese might have begun this passage with, "As I looked at him, it occurred to me that he is a most interesting-looking. . . ." Talese might also have begun, "If you were to see him in his office at the *Times,* it might occur to you to think that he is a most interesting-looking. . . ." But in both cases, why? Readers are aware that Talese has looked at Daniel; it isn't necessary to make that clear. Most readers would probably dismiss the likelihood of their visiting Daniel in his office, which suggests that *you* wouldn't fit. By describing Daniel carefully and imaginatively, Talese has, in effect, placed both himself and his readers with Daniel in the office.

That example is sharp-focus third person; the writer fixes unrelentingly on the small details that flesh out one person or object. A writer can also use an omniscient third person, sketching a panoramic view that sweeps both the field of vision open to any one person and far beyond it. And, of course, a writer who organizes his work carefully can leap from sharp-focus to panoramic views and back again.

If this appreciation of third-person address seems to overemphasize its flexibility and force, remember the power of first- and second-person writing. Whatever the choice, the ultimate effect also depends on using other techniques imaginatively.

CHOOSING A TONE

Our lives are so pervaded by the work of journalists, most of whom aim at dispassionate reports, that most writing may seem straightforward and relatively toneless. But straightforwardness is itself a tone. We are warm-blooded and changeable, and have to work to keep our writing at a single temperature. Chapter 5 covers writing that aims at straightforward explanation; we can consider other kinds here. For example, a student tried in writing the following paragraphs to involve her readers in a concert:

> Becoming.
> The whole day was a process of becoming. For thousands of members of the subculture—the hippie-longhair-pot smoking-revolutionary subculture—the day was becoming the Rolling Stones concert.
> The Rolling Stones.
> Five years ago the Stones made their first American appearance on the Ed Sullivan Show. A Sunday night like any other, it was invaded by strange creatures who suddenly leapt into millions of living rooms.
> The Rolling Stones were dirty. Mick Jagger's hair was longer than anyone else's and greasy. Actually greasy. If people had been using the phrase "far out" in 1964, that's what they would have called the Stones. Weird. Not people that folks in front of the tube could identify with.
> Now the Rolling Stones are a legend.
> One hour before the second show at the Coliseum thousands of people line the ramp outside the surreal circular building. Beaded. Belled. Smelling of incense and grass.

The writer began at such a pitch, using brief sentence fragments for impact, that she might have exhausted her readers if she continued it but might have let them down too quickly if she had not. She decided to mix conventional sentences with the fragments gradually. By the time she reached the last few paragraphs, she was writing conventionally, but still with verve:

> The crowd rests for a minute between songs, then reacts to what has become a theme song, "Street Fighting Man." Bouncing up and down with clenched fists and V signs, sweat and tears on their faces, the crowd worships the Stones and themselves.
> "What can a poor boy do, 'cept to play for a rock and roll band? It just ain't no place for a street fighting man." Just to be close to Jagger, to each other, is all they want at that moment.
> At four A.M. they straggle out. Spent with celebrating their culture, they pile into psychedelic buses and cars and crowd promising hitch-hiking corners.
> They had become part of the mythological beast they had created, the Rolling Stones concert.

The pitch of the entire piece may be shrill, but it reflected the mood of the crowd. Whether the writing is effective is up to its readers, which underscores again that one writes for an audience.

The circumstances and the audience are always pivotal in helping writers decide whether to use the tones that seem to give us the most trouble, which are described in the following section.

Exhortation, Invective, Scorn

To exhort is to urge strongly. To use invective is to abuse. To scorn is to treat with contempt. Although the meanings are different, we consider them together because a writer who attempts exhortation is sometimes in danger of drifting into invective and scorn, which are usually ineffective or worse. In this passage scientist George Wald exhorts his readers to work for peace, but in a reasoning tone:

> I think we've reached a point of great decision, not just for our nation, not only for all humanity, but for life upon the Earth. . . . The thought that we're in competition with Russians or with Chinese is all a mistake, and trivial. Only mutual destruction lies that way. We are one species, with a world to win. There's life all over this universe, but in the universe we are the only men.
> Our business is with life, not death. Our challenge is to give what account we can of what becomes of life in the solar system, this corner of the universe that is our home, and, most of all, what becomes of men—all men of all nations, colors, and creeds. It has become one world, a world for all men. It is only such a world that now can offer us life and the chance to go on.

Only in extreme cases should one use invective and scorn. Such a case grew out of an open meeting of the San Francisco Board of Education, which was held to discuss busing integration. Several men appeared at the meeting and attacked and injured a number of those who spoke for busing, then escaped unidentified. The executive editor of the *San Francisco Chronicle* wrote an editorial that called the men "self-appointed heirs of Hitler's brownshirts," "professional thugs," and "intellectually underprivileged apes." He concluded with a challenge:

> The members of this band of social neanderthals are obviously too insecure and too frightened to come forward and identify themselves. . . . If this phantom squad of bullies cares to take umbrage at these remarks and wishes to continue its cowardly and disgraceful activities, it can catch the executive editor of this paper almost any week night on the darkened Fifth Street sidewalk at the side entrance of the *Chronicle*. He leaves the building at approximately 8 P.M. on his way home.

No doubt the invective and scorn in this editorial pleased many readers who shared the writer's anger, perhaps more effectively because of the challenge. Issuing challenges is not customary, but most invective sounds as though the writer is pugnacious—from a safe distance.

Satire and Irony

Satire, which makes fun of folly, is gentler and more often useful than invective or scorn. The satirist usually attacks indirectly, sometimes by seeming to defend, as in these paragraphs about television:

> It is time to defend television, which has been criticized for presenting too much frivolity and not enough education for younger viewers. The critics say commercial TV is all entertainment, most of it uninspired.
> But there is documentary evidence to the contrary. Consider the following statistics compiled by a survey team:
>
> 167 murders
> 112 justifiable homicides
> 356 attempted murders
>
> This casualty list is not a record of all the mayhem on television since the medium was invented. It is a summary of the mortality rate during one week of those carefree, light-hearted goings-on in televisionland.
> The figures refute the criticism neatly. What could be less frivolous than a waterfront dive raked by machine gun bullets? Or a dum-dum bullet in the belly?
> No, television is many other things, but it is not one long lark, unless you were brought up in the Mafia. When 279 people die in everybody's living room and another 356 would have died but for some happenstance, "frivolous" is not the word.
> We can mourn and wear black for those who are gone, but if we think of their passing as serious education for the kiddies, they will not have died in vain.

This is not the direct assault of sarcasm, but it is much like irony, which is a subtle way of saying one thing and meaning the opposite. E. B. White, a gentle ironist, used the technique in a wartime piece published in the *New Yorker:*

> We received a letter from the Writers' War Board the other day asking for a statement on "The Meaning of Democracy."
> It presumably is our duty to comply with such a request, and it is certainly our pleasure.
> Surely the Board knows what democracy is. It is the line that forms on the right . . .

After giving many other illustrations, White concluded:

> Democracy is a request from a War Board, in the middle of a morning in the middle of a war, wanting to know what democracy is.

All the tones described in this section are occasionally in order. Invective and scorn are effective only rarely, and two tones at opposite extremes, flippancy and sentimentality, should never be used. We ordinarily find fewer good opportunities for exhortation than for satire and irony, and all three should be written deftly or not at all.

Keeping to a tone, especially in writing lengthy pieces, usually requires that we look back while writing, to the preceding sentence, to the preceding paragraph, even back to the beginning. Many writers find that putting a piece aside and reading it later helps them decide whether the temperature is the same throughout. A later reading of high-temperature writing may convince a writer to use a cooler tone.

MAKING IT FLOW

Some of the techniques used to make writing flow smoothly from point to point are so subtle and so important that few readers are aware that they enjoy the work of some writers at least partly because it is coherent. Readers usually praise writers for other qualities: "She puts things so well." "He says exactly what I've been thinking but didn't know how to say." "Her writing is so colorful." "The phrases are so clever." "He really knows what he's talking about." And so on.

Failing to think of the orderly flow of facts and ideas is understandable. Readers expect coherence. If a piece is wildly disorganized, they will almost surely dislike it and probably throw it aside after reading a few paragraphs. Readers interested in a topic may suffer their way through some disorder. When they discover a piece that moves so logically from point to point that it is seamless, they are pleased without knowing why.

Coherence in writing comes from sequential thought, which attaches one frame of fact and idea to another so that they fit together without rattling or falling apart. Thinking in sequence is difficult even when we are not writing. Norman Cousins, editor of *Saturday Review/World,* points out that it calls for a staggering number of mental operations:

> The route must be anticipated between the present location of an idea and where it is supposed to go. Memory must be raked for relevant material. Facts or notions must be sorted out, put in their proper places, then supplied with connective tissue. Then come the problems of weighting and emphasis.

Writing sequentially requires another complex operation: anticipating how readers' thoughts will move. The following passage shows how easy it is to forget readers:

> "Astrology, palmistry, phrenology, life reading, fortune telling, cartomancy, clairvoyance, clairaudience, crystal gazing, hypnotism, mediumship, prophecy, augury, divination, magic or necromancy" for money are illegal activities in Palo Alto and licensed businesses in Menlo Park. Both laws have been on the books for forty years and read as though they came from a Model Government Game, with blanks to fill in, permitted or not permitted.

"Both laws"? When the reader comes upon those words, his mind says that no law has been mentioned. The long series of unusual words in the first sentence makes him concentrate on them (while puzzling over a quotation attributed to no one); he cannot think of "illegal activities" and "licensed businesses" in terms of law. He probably would not have thought of them as laws anyway. An activity is illegal as a result of a law, a business is licensed because of a law; neither is a law. Moreover, the analogy of the "Modern Government Game" in the second sentence makes the reader use his imagination, which he can't do while puzzling over "Both laws." To understand "Both laws," the reader must look back at the first sentence to trace the meaning, which halts his reading and irritates him.

This error can be corrected by treating "illegal activities" and "licensed businesses" in terms of laws in the first sentence: ". . . illegal in Palo Alto and permitted by law in Menlo Park." The ease of correcting may make the principle seem unimportant, but if we do not think sequentially in small matters, we may be powerless with larger ones.

The largest problem in writing coherently grows out of the infinite number of ways we can combine the two basic kinds of order, chronological and subtopical. We can arrange the parts of a topic according to the time certain events occurred. We can arrange them according to the way subtopics fit together. In most cases, the topic itself helps us decide which kind of order should dominate. For example, the need for more opportunities for women to participate in campus athletics is likely to require arrangement by subtopic; it is focused on the present. A section of the piece could be chronological—perhaps recent actions by the administration to help satisfy the need—but arrangement by subtopic would dominate. If the topic, though, is the growing need, the piece would lend itself to a chronological account, probably with the first few sentences focused on the present, then a flashback.

Writing about a person usually calls for arrangement by subtopic, with a section devoted to the person's past related chronologically. If the topic idea is to show what a person has become, though—perhaps a profile of success that grew out of small beginnings—time elements should dominate.

Deciding the basic order of a topic is essential, of course, but that does not solve other problems. We must also arrange smaller units such as time and space sequences and link them with transitions.

Sequence of Time

The simplest chronological order is obvious: One thing happens, then another. But when we are writing a piece based on subtopical order that contains time sequences, we sometimes focus so strongly on arranging the subtopics and on reasoning from cause to effect and evidence to conclusion that we confuse the sequence of time. In the middle of a piece on a controversy involving black film-makers, a student wrote:

> Prior to this turn of events, a group of Black artists who work in the film industry decided to enter the controversy. Previously, groups such as Blackploitation and the Beverly Hills chapter of the NAACP Rating Committee for Black Films had approached the problem from the standpoint of censorship. They believe that only the positive aspects of Blackness are acceptable. The negative side must not be seen at all. The Black Artists Alliance was created to challenge institutional racism in the film industry and other media.

"Prior to this," then "previously"—twice the reader is pushed backward in time. He first absorbs the information about the group of black artists and fixes in his mind that the group began its work before the events just described. He can do that fairly easily. But then he must place himself in an even earlier time, take on information about two other groups, and learn their purpose. At the end of the paragraph, he must return to the first group to learn its purpose. Even if the reader is not confused, he must work to follow the sense.

This is a better arrangement:

> Groups such as Blackploitation and the Beverly Hills chapter of the NAACP Rating Committee had long before approached the problem as censors. They believe that only the positive aspects of Blackness are acceptable. Then a group of Black artists who work in the film industry entered the controversy, challenging institutional racism in films and other media.

When one action follows another in time like this, the reader is attracted. Sometimes whole paragraphs must be rearranged, as in this case:

Friday has finally arrived. Midterm week is history. But before the week turns into recorded grades, the weekend is before you, and it's time to get away. The beaches of the Pacific Coast provide an escape from the hassles and pressures of college life.

Thoughts of differential equations, iambic pentameter, and amino acids drift from your mind as you bask in the sun and listen to the waves. The wind may chap your skin and whip through your hair like a savage current, but a relaxing day at the seashore brings inner peace.

The only requisites for this excursion are a free day and a car or bike to take you to the water. But you should also take with you. . . .

Smooth as this may seem, it mixes time elements. In the first paragraph, readers think about the beach. In the second, they are on it. In the third, they are back in the dormitory getting ready for the trip. It is not essential to arrange the paragraphs in chronological order—readers need not work to understand the passage, as they must work to understand the passage about the black groups—but a writer should be aware of such minor faults. He should write sequences of time that are logical and, in addition, he should try to arrange them for the positive effects that grow out of passages that move smoothly from one moment to the next.

Sequence of Space

Sequences of space can also be written to produce subtle effects. At the beginning of one of his best short stories, Joseph Conrad shows a man at the bow of a boat that is making its way upriver. The passage is narrow; the shore thick with trees. The man's vision is constricted. So is the vision of the reader. Then the river widens, the man can see more, and suddenly, so can the reader. It does not matter that readers do not analyze the technique. They are affected by it.

Readers are affected negatively by faulty use of space, as in the following:

Wave after wave of organ-launched tones charge the vaulted cavern of the church, crowding and jostling and invading every recess, resounding to assault each person from all sides. The congregation at the church's depths populates rows of parallel pews in a multicolored array, arranged in mysteriously random groups of different sizes.

The people had gathered for the Sunday 11 o'clock service to hear John Hamerton Kingsley preach. Three domed sections of the church joined a fourth elongated section to form a hollow crucifix. The junction, bordered by four cement-cylinder arches connecting corner pillars, draws sunlight through a cloudy skylight capping the central dome. Far below, in the twilight of the filtered sunlight, stands a figure robed in black satin and velvet, a brilliant red stole over his shoulders. The music evaporates. With a sweep of his hand, the congregation shuffles to its collective feet. His voice. . . .

This passage contains far too many forceful adjectives and adverbs, but a worse flaw is the zigzag effect. The writer describes the church in the first sentence, the congregation in the second. The second paragraph starts smoothly: The congregation is mentioned, which provides a link to the preceding sentence, and the focus narrows to the preacher. Then, unaccountably, the writer describes the church again, then the preacher again. The writing leaps about. The readers must try to follow him.

A writer should look carefully for flaws in what he has written; beyond that, he can improve his writing by thinking positively about sequences of time and space. Ask yourself: How can I arrange time and space so that readers can move smoothly?

Transitions: Value and Danger

Nearly everyone has been taught that transitions are vital links that help make writing flow. But knowing what transitions are is not enough. We must also have enough information to make the parts of a piece fit together. The writer of the following passage, which is part of a long profile of a history professor, had too little information to unify the passage:

. . . Although preliminary copies will be available sooner, the book will be officially released on March 15.

A man of many talents, Dr. Mann is a former chess fiend. "A young man's game," he gave it up after he reached the age of 40 ("and I'm not telling how long ago that was").

Dr. Mann's favorite hobbies are typing and carpentry. His office is filled with cabinets which he designed and built. A self-taught typist, he typed every word of his manuscript himself. ("I may not be able to ride a horse, but I certainly know how to ride a typewriter.")

When he finds time, Dr. Mann also enjoys puttering around in his mango grove "to unkink the kinks of academic kinkery."

The three sounds he likes best are good conversation, music, and the crackle of folding money.

A member of the faculty since 1946, Dr. Mann was a trouble shooter during World War II for the Red Cross in the New England area as well as a ground school navigation instructor. . . .

This passage reads as though it had been written from answers to a questionnaire, which at first makes it seem that the writer merely failed to use transitions to link sentences and paragraphs to one another. Transitions are almost nonexistent, but they are much too weak to do all the work needed here. Transitions should be used to link elements that belong together. Inserting words and phrases to link foreign elements is like penning up chickens with giraffes.

We can do only a little to rearrange parts of the passage and link them with transitions. For example, the first paragraph quoted above is about Dr. Mann's book and falls naturally into place with the third paragraph, which is primarily about typing the manuscript. It is not possible, however, to rearrange all the parts and expect to use transitions to do the rest of the work of unifying. The wide gulf between the first paragraph and the last should be bridged, but too many pieces are missing.

The writer obviously needed more facts than he had when he wrote, but when he was gathering information he probably had no way of knowing that he would need to build this bridge. Inability to foresee such needs underlines a point made earlier: A writer must gather more information than he will need so that he can select the best from a wide array. Not having enough information tempts us to write around what is missing, leaving gaps. And not having needed information leaves us powerless to use transitions except here and there.

The passage about Dr. Mann contrasts strikingly to this one about a Hollywood agent named Irving "Swifty" Lazar:

> . . . He is so busy that other agents cannot figure out how he can look after his clients. The answer, Moss Hart has said, is simple, "Other agents have outside interests. All Irving's got is his agency and a bottle of disinfectant."
>
> Hart was referring to Lazar's abnormal passion for cleanliness. He won't even enter his own car—a high, old-fashioned limousine, a gift from Mrs. William Goetz—without making certain that it has been sprayed with a perfumed antiseptic. He keeps his own bed linen in the hotels he usually patronizes. His scrupulous neatness is carried out in his clothes, which are all made to order and monogrammed; even his socks and underwear are monogrammed.
>
> "Swifty is so clean," says Lauren Bacall, "he'll never get married. No girl would be neat enough for him."
>
> Lazar wants to get married, nevertheless. He never goes anywhere without his personal telephone directory, which, in addition to containing his clients' and business associates' names and numbers . . . is also indexed: GIRLS—HOLLYWOOD, GIRLS—VEGAS, GIRLS—NEW YORK, and GIRLS—EUROPE.
>
> He seldom appears in public without a dazzling beauty on his arm. All these girls . . .

In this short passage the writer touched on Lazar's clients, cleanliness, and romantic interests. The writer could move smoothly from one of these to another because he had so much information that he could choose from among many items, primarily quotations, those that covered two subtopics. Moss Hart mentioned Lazar's work and cleanliness, Lauren Bacall his cleanliness and bachelorhood; the movement from one to another is natural.

Contrasting the quoted passages makes it obvious that a logical arrangement of facts is essential so that transitions can do their work.

Some simple words and phrases are standard transitions: *indeed, nevertheless, besides, but, then, therefore, and, also, on the other hand, for this reason, but then, after all,* and others. Using these words and phrases ordinarily makes an automatic link. Another standard technique is to mention at or near the beginning of one sentence or paragraph a word or phrase that has already appeared, or a synonym or a word close in meaning to one that has appeared.

Such transitions are useful, but writers who are over-conscious of the need for transitions sometimes overdo them. Here is an example:

> . . . After he gets his college degree, he would like to go into some form of education.
> But before education, his first goal is professional basketball. . . .

But is a strong bridge. It does not need the help of "before education," as this construction suggests: "But his first goal is professional basketball." Moreover, using too many transitional words makes readers back up a bit to take on information they already have. "Education" lingers in their minds from the preceding sentence. They need only one transitional word.

Pronouns can often be substituted for repeated words to make sentences move swiftly, as in this case:

> The maladies are characterized by heightened sensitivity to darkness.
> Due to this heightened sensitivity. . . .

The five words at the beginning of the second sentence could be reduced to two: "It causes." As above, the effect is to move readers swiftly from point to point instead of requiring that they read, then pause while reading the same thing. When many sentences that carry many transitional words are sprinkled through an essay, readers become irritated.

There are three dangers in using transitions. This section has covered two of them. The discussion of the passage about Dr. Mann shows that a writer cannot expect transitions to do all the work of unifying. A writer who is too careful, however, may slow readers by repeating a transition unnecessarily or by writing one too heavily. The third danger is the most threatening to coherence: transitions can pull a topic in a direction it should not go.

Such a transition is usually written at the beginning of a paragraph. Having just written the last sentence of one paragraph, the writer has that sentence in mind, or looks to it, in making a transition. He is usually safe in so doing, but if the sentence fails to express or refer to the essence of the paragraph, the transition he makes may send the new paragraph off at a tangent from the old one.

In one instance, a student who was writing about a beautiful woman ended a paragraph with a sentence about concepts of beauty, then used that sentence in making a transition at the beginning of the next paragraph. Gradually, as paragraph grew out of paragraph, he found himself far afield. He lurched back by writing one paragraph about the woman, then another and another. The wandering middle of the piece made the whole incoherent.

A writer can use three methods to avoid such wandering. First, he can skim the preceding paragraph to find its essence, then begin his transition from the last sentence if that sentence expresses the essence of the paragraph. If it does not, he can use a transition from another sentence in the paragraph. Second, he can look back to other paragraphs, all the way back to the first paragraph if necessary, to make certain that one paragraph grows out of another and develops the topic. (It is wise to look back at the beginning fairly frequently even when one need not fear wandering.) Finally, the writer can check his outline, or whatever plan of organization he developed before beginning to write, to make certain that he is staying on course (which indicates one of the central values of planning).

Speeding the Pace of Sentences and Paragraphs

Writing each sentence so that the reader moves from one point to another speeds the pace of each paragraph. The second paragraph from this description of students in a beginning tennis course needs a bit of editing to give readers a sense of movement:

> They relax arms and shoulders with broad, slow arcs in the air. Each scrambles for a ball and consciously adjusts his psyche. They serve in threes. "Weight back—push your racquets down, toss, come up, and hit," the instructor intones. Three balls wobble up and are knocked from their paths. Three more, three more, and three more fly up together, separate on contact with the racquets, and go up, over, down, or nowhere,

according to the server's skill. The drill is repeated with little more
success.

The instructor demonstrates. He steps in front of the class and executes
the exercise. The ball performs admirably, sizzling a quarter-inch over
the net. The next serve easily floats away, accurate again.

Note that each sentence in the first paragraph carries the reader forward. The beginning of the second paragraph, however, is halting: "The
instructor demonstrates. He steps in front of the class and executes the
exercise." Although different words are used, the second sentence says
little more than the first. (If the writer were describing complex action,
the classic device of restatement in different words might be useful.) In
effect, the reader is marking time instead of marching. The writer can
speed the pace by combining sentences like this: "The instructor steps
in front of the class and demonstrates." That enables the reader to move
into the sentence beginning "The ball performs" with a sense of a fast
pace.

Except when the writer is trying to produce a special staccato effect,
short sentences should ordinarily be combined to help speed the pace.
Here is an example of a paragraph that seems a bit halting because all
of its six sentences are short and approximately the same length:

To Texas students, a football game is many things. To some, it is an
all-day party. To others, it is an opportunity to socialize. To still others,
it is a great place to get a tan. Some come primarily to watch the band
perform. A few even come to watch the game.

Each sentence moves a bit because each offers new information. But
the pace is slow between the first sentence and the last. Perhaps the
paragraph should read:

To Texas students, a football game is many things: an all-day party, an
opportunity to socialize, or a great place to get a tan. Some come
primarily to watch the band perform. A few even come to watch the game.

The first four sentences were combined to speed the pace. The fifth
was not changed because a different rhythm sets up the sentence at the
end.

If the Texas students had been in action in the stands, that paragraph might have been written at greater length to include action and
might also have been written as one or two sentences to make the prose
move as fast as the action. Hemingway, who usually wrote short sentences,
sometimes wrote long ones to give a sense of action, as in the sentence at
the end of his story "The Short Happy Life of Francis Macomber":

"He's dead in there," Wilson said. "Good work," and he turned to grip Macomber's hand and as they shook hands, grinning at each other, the gunbearer shouted wildly and they saw him coming out of the bush sideways, fast as a crab, and the bull coming, nose out, mouth tight closed, blood dripping, massive head straight out, coming in a charge, his little pig eyes blood-shot as he looked at them. Wilson, who was ahead, was kneeling shooting, and Macomber, as he fired, unhearing his shot in the roaring of Wilson's gun, saw fragments like slate burst from the huge boss of the horns, and the head jerked, he shot again at the wide nostrils and saw the horns jolt again and fragments fly, and he did not see Wilson now and, aiming carefully, shot again with the buffalo's huge bulk almost on him and his rifle almost level with the oncoming head, nose out, and he could see the little wicked eyes and the head started to lower and he felt a sudden whitehot, blinding flash explode inside his head and that was all he ever felt.

This is hurry-up language that carries the reader along as it runs to keep pace with the bull. Mastering this technique is usually a long process of trial and error.

If you discover that you are starting nearly every sentence with subject, then verb, you can be certain that the pace of reading will be slow. This paragraph was preceded and followed by many sentences beginning in that conventional form:

I first saw Huahine in 1968 from a DC-3 enroute from Tahiti to Bora Bora. I was visiting the islands for a three-week period. The island looked startlingly pristine. The vegetation looked unbelievably thick. The island, divided into two parts by an inland bay, was surrounded by one common barrier reef which was spectacular in its colorful variations of blues and greens.

The paragraph could be revised in many ways to speed the pace. Consider this revision:

I first saw Huahine during a three-week trip in 1968 from a DC-3 enroute from Tahiti to Bora Bora. The island looked startlingly pristine, the vegetation unbelievably thick. Divided by an inland bay, it was surrounded by a common barrier reef which was spectacular in its colorful variations of blues and greens.

To summarize the principles that help in speeding the pace of paragraphs:

1 If short sentences are not written for a particular effect and reading them is monotonous, combine a few sentences.

2 Language can be made to keep pace with action by writing long sentences, but using this technique at first is likely to produce a tangle.

3 For variety in sentence structure, invert some sentences, especially to avoid a monotonous subject-verb, subject-verb structure.

Coherence enables readers to go faster, but the actual time spent in reading is not as important as their sense of speed. You can understand that sense if you have ever become so absorbed in reading that you wondered later where the time went. The pace may have seemed fast because you were caught up in the story or topic, but reading also seems swift when one sentence grows out of another and one paragraph out of another in a tight structure that might be represented graphically by a line running straight from the first word to the last. Carefully written sequences and transitions both draw that line and lead readers along it. A writer can lead his readers faster by making certain that each sentence moves.

Shaping Paragraphs

The concept of the paragraph has changed somewhat in recent years. Perhaps the change began, or became most visible, fifty years ago when Henry W. Fowler wrote *Modern English Usage,* which is considered by many writers and teachers of writing to be the best book of its kind. "The purpose of the paragraph is to give the reader a rest," Fowler wrote. The kind of rest provided by the end of a paragraph does not slow the pace of reading but quickens it. Instead of feeling as though a paragraph will never end, the reader becomes aware of frequent intervals and moves more swiftly toward them—or thinks he does.

Before the publication of Fowler's book, and among some teachers and writers for a long time afterward, the paragraph was conceived as a well-defined structure: a topic sentence that set the direction and the boundaries followed by sentences that developed it, the whole a small essay that was a well-defined part of the piece. The concept has not disappeared, but it is no longer so neat or so widely held.

Other influences have changed our concept of paragraph structure, among them the practices of the journalists and authors who keep paragraphs short to give many rest stops. Newspaper journalists write brief paragraphs, some only a sentence or two in length, because narrow newspaper columns make a sea of grey when paragraphs are composed of several sentences. Most magazine journalists favor relatively short paragraphs, but not as short as those that are common in many newspapers.

The newspaper paragraph is influential because readers become accustomed to the brevity and clarity that usually characterize it. But newspaper paragraphing carries a danger as well as the benefit of freeing reporters from the formula paragraph. Making one- and two-sentence paragraphs is relatively easy; a reporter may become accustomed to writing sentences that touch one another rather than grow out of one another. The danger becomes apparent to many newspaper reporters when they write magazine articles and books. After years of writing one- and two-sentence paragraphs, bringing sentences together in a paragraph that makes a fairly complex point may be difficult. That seems, however, to be less often the case now that many newspapers are being published with fewer and wider columns, which permit longer paragraphs. And fewer news stories are written as a series of bare facts now that interpretive reporting is taking a firmer hold on newspaper journalism; the interpretive form also tends to lengthen paragraphs.

Analyzing the work of respected writers makes it clear that a unified structure of sentences still identifies the paragraph. Many writers are experimenting with paragraphs much as they do with punctuation: using paragraph size and structure to steer readers as well as give them a rest. The paragraph at the beginning of a piece quoted in part in the Introduction illustrates one technique by starting with one word and ending with one other: "It hurts." Such a technique, which pulls readers into the next paragraph and thus commits them to reading, yields nothing resembling the traditional paragraph, of course. Like all manipulative techniques, however, it must be used infrequently and cautiously. Generally, most good writers make paragraphs that are unified statements of one point. The more complex the point, the longer the paragraph—like this one.

Except that a writer must occasionally give his readers a rest.

Using and Avoiding Repetition

Repetition usually makes reading monotonous, and thus slower. Ordinarily, we should avoid repeating words often within the space of a few sentences. To use one person's name four times in four sentences, or even in seven or eight sentences—Carolyn Nelson, Carolyn Nelson, Carolyn Nelson, Carolyn Nelson—bores everyone except Carolyn Nelson and her mother. It is better to refer to "she," "her," or "the woman" on occasion. A basketball can be called a basketball once or twice, but then "it" or "the ball" provides needed variation. We should avoid elegant variations, too-cute references such as "Mrs. Nelson's little girl Carolyn," and the hack sportswriter's trick of trying so hard for variety that he creates substitutes for "basketball" such as "spheroid" or "leather sphere" or "roundball." The obvious is better than the obvious avoidance of it.

We can sometimes use repetition for emphasis, which pleases

readers unless the writer falls in love with the technique. The first paragraph below uses repetition well. The second probably takes it too far:

> Meredith Wheeler is only 21, yet she teaches a section of a college broadcasting course. Meredith Wheeler is only 21, yet she has worked in New York for NBC News, hosted her own program on the campus radio station, and is writing a handbook about public affairs broadcasting. Meredith Wheeler is only 21, yet she knows where she is going.
>
> Where "Meredi" is going is into broadcasting. She has chosen an indirect and ambitious route. She is not entering broadcasting when she completes her senior year in June. Despite her experience and achievements, she thinks the broadcasting world would consider her "just another bright-eyed, eager graduate." Meredi wants "more upward mobility, and a chance to influence, to make a dent in the system." So Meredi is applying to law schools: Harvard, Yale, Stanford, and Columbia.

In the first paragraph, the repetition of name and age was valuable. Each sentence beginning "Meredith Wheeler" ticked off one of her accomplishments. Because she had accomplished so much at an early age, the writer wisely emphasized it.

But by the end of the second paragraph, the name has become a bit monotonous. The writer sensed that was the case and occasionally used "she" and "her" for variation, but it might have been better not to use "Meredi" in the last sentence. The writer might have made the name a framing device by using it as she has in the first paragraph, then using only "she" and "her" in the first five sentences of the second paragraph, and finally using the name again in the last sentence.

In unusual cases, a paragraph can be emphasized well by repeating a word so that it strikes one point from a different angle with each repetition. Here is an example:

> This means that parents need to be able to contribute their skills to the schools. . . . It means that teachers need to be able to draw on the whole community as a teaching resource. It means that students need to be able to perceive themselves as participating simultaneously in the general life of the community as well as in the special, hived-off life of the school. And it means . . . .

Hammering "means" over and over emphasized the value of the writer's plan for educational reform. No reader could doubt the meaning of his message. None could read that paragraph casually.

These guidelines summarize the main points about repeating words and phrases:

1   In ordinary cases, avoid repetition.

2 In avoiding repetition, do not drift into elegant variation.

3 Repetition is sometimes useful for emphasis.

Manipulating Punctuation

Tom Wolfe sometimes seems to be in love with typographic devices. In an article about Marshall McLuhan, who often theorizes wildly about the effects of the mass media, Wolfe wrote:

> What if he's right. What . . . if . . . he . . . is . . . right. W-h-a-t i-f h-e i-s r-i-g-h-t

	R		
W		I	
H	IF	G	
			?
A	HE	H	
T	IS	T	

Such extravagance suggests why many writers dislike the style Fischer calls "Rococo Breathless." Few of them will use devices that send words sprawling across the page or dribbling down it. But most professional writers are more imaginative than to use punctuation only in the way that seems to be prescribed by rules and conventions. They learned the rules and conventions in school, then learned to manipulate punctuation subtly to guide readers.

And why not? Punctuation, which seems to so many of us to be a fearsome mass of rules, is actually a reading guide. When speech was adapted to writing, it became necessary to develop punctuation to show various points of pause and stress. Pauses and changes of pitch had to be shown so that readers would not run at one pace through a long course of words, giving each word and phrase the same emphasis. The need to show slight pauses and changes led to the comma; the need for a heavier pause at the end of the group of words that we call a sentence led to the period.

Over centuries, the punctuation practices of writers who were attuned to pauses and changes of pitch seemed to be generally useful and have become rules that determine what is meant by various expressions. The need for exact meanings expressed by punctuation is such that to violate some rules now that they are generally accepted is to change meaning. For example, in 1973 the California Legislature voted itself a raise in retirement benefits but lost it because those who drafted the legislation left out two commas. The legislation was intended to increase total benefits for any legislator who retired in 1973 or 1974. But the language of the legislation said that allowances payable "with respect to service during the years 1973 and 1974 shall be computed on the basis of 5.5 percent (in 1973) and 3.3 percent (on the combined total for 1974)." Because no commas separated "during the years 1973 and 1974" from the rest of the sentence, the language made the increase payable only for those two years, not for the legislators' total time of service.

Many of the other punctuation practices of respected writers did not establish meaning but were useful enough to become conventional. Some conventions change as fashions in language change. As anyone knows who has read a nineteenth century novel, our language has become less formal. Speech is less formal, writing has changed with speech, and punctuation has changed as much as either. Perhaps punctuation has changed more. Many writers try increasingly to make words on paper resemble speech. But the resemblance can be increased relatively little by making the words used in writing the same as those used in speaking. Because pauses and changes of pitch must be shown by punctuation, writers experiment, most of them more subtly than Tom Wolfe does.

If we could persuade a large group of respected writers to give their thoughts on punctuation, they might say this: We keep in mind as we write the many rules and conventions that remain useful. They are reliable guides in most cases; many are flexible and some leave decisions to the taste of the writer. But there are many millions of possible word combinations and many millions of contexts for sentences. We must also consider the many inflections. Each of us must look beyond rules and conventions fairly often and ask: How do I want my readers to read this sentence? What effect do I want to produce?

Such thoughts should suggest a strategy for punctuating. Think of yourself as trying to talk to readers through words on paper. Use the rules and conventions as guidelines; they will enable you to talk understandably in nearly everything you write. But when you want to produce effects that do not seem to be covered by the guidelines, think of your readers as reacting to signals.

PUNCTUATION MARK	SIGNAL TO READERS
self-reliant	these words should be read as one word
,	pause slightly or change pitch
;	pause a bit longer
—perhaps an even greater feat—	this is an emphatic interruption
—all to no avail	pause, then emphasize the words after the dash

PUNCTUATION MARK	SIGNAL TO READERS
(his last novel)	de-emphasize these words
:	the words before this introduce those after it
?	What do you think?
. . .	I'm leaving out words
.	stop
!	stop in astonishment! (I won't make you do this often)

Most of the marks give other signals, of course, that are suggested by rules and conventions. But the signals listed above are the strongest. Using them, you can move readers at will: nudging, steering, pushing, pulling, and stopping. You have been signaling with these marks since the first time you wrote. If you think what the signals mean, you can move beyond using them automatically.

You can use most of the techniques outlined in this chapter to improve your writing, but they must be practiced almost endlessly before you can fit them into your style. The best test is to read your writing aloud, especially after you have put it aside for a time. Do you like a particular passage because you have used a technique adroitly? If so, consider revising. A technique that stands out as a technique dominates. Instead of bowing to techniques, use them to help you say what you want to say.

PROJECTS

1 Part of this chapter argues that one should consider carefully whether to use *I* in writing pieces that do not report on the writer's own experiences. The May/June 1971 issue of *Columbia Journalism Review* carries a long article about the underground press, heavily dotted with *I*. Read the first five paragraphs of the article which follow and rewrite it without using *I*. Compare the two versions and decide which you prefer.

Anyone who is guilty of being forty-five years old, as I am, is probably so afflicted with the tunnel vision of his generation that he can judge other generations only by his standards rather than theirs. Thus, for a long time I dismissed the underground press because it seemed to have all the stability of a floating crap game. My opinion began to change because of these events:

• The Los Angeles *Free Press* installed a time clock. I didn't like time clocks when I had to punch one twenty years ago, and I wouldn't like to punch one now. But an underground paper that begins to check on the comings and goings of its staff members takes on a businesslike aura that might lure a smile from William Randolph Hearst.

• The owner of the Berkeley *Barb,* Max Scherr, and his staff began to fight over money. The staff wanted to buy out Scherr and cited evidence that he had been making $5,000 a week from the paper. Although reading the *Barb* fairly regularly persuades me that I do not share many values of Scherr and his staff members, this financial wrangle suggests that they share at least one of mine.

• Citizen Zenger Company, publishers, of Fairfax, Calif., has issued a prospectus for a kind of *Reader's Digest* of the underground press. In keeping with the casual underground spirit, some of the pages are numbered and some are not. But the prospectus is thick, it seems to cover all the factors that might bear on the success of the venture, and it reflects a serious effort to raise $100,000 to start the *Underground Digest.* Reading these plans sets me to wondering whether, like these entrepreneurs, DeWitt Wallace was foresighted enough to copyright *his* prospectus.

2 The following paragraphs are taken from the middle of an article about a student. Rewrite them in a different order that places like paragraphs together, then write a paragraph explaining why you changed the order as you did.

She is very active during dinner, especially when there is an extra spoon on the table. She uses it as leverage. After calculating the right momentum, she places a pack of sugar on the end and Wham! the sugar lands in someone's lap. She has almost reached the point of starting a food fight with the adjoining table.

When she doesn't feel like answering a question, she says, "I didn't come here to be insulted," or, "Aw, shucks." Such responses startle those who are not accustomed to her.

She has started a campaign against dirty plates. Every night at dinner, she insists that everyone who sees a speck of dust, dirt or dinginess on his plate take it to the kitchen and complain.

3 One of the passages quoted in this chapter shows how Hemingway used a long sentence to give readers a feeling of action. In the following passage he wrote a long sentence, but the action description is different; Hemingway is *talking about* an action, not describing one. Compare the two passages and decide which is more effective and why.

If the spectators know the matador is capable of executing a complete, consecutive series of passes with the muleta in which there will be valor, art, understanding and, above all, beauty and great emotion, they will put up with mediocre work, cowardly work, disastrous work because they have the hope sooner or later of seeing the complete faena; the faena that takes a man out of himself and makes him feel immortal while it is proceeding, that gives him an ecstasy, that is, while momentary, as profound as any religious ecstasy; moving all the people in the ring together and increasing in emotional intensity as it proceeds, carrying the bullfighter with it, he playing on the crowd through the bull and being moved as it responds in a growing ecstasy of ordered, formal, passionate, increasing disregard for death that leaves you, when it is over, and the death administered to the animal that has made it possible, as empty, as changed, and as sad as any major emotion will leave you.

Using Techniques: Visual Writing

4 Early in World War II, when the British were hard hit by German bombs and seemed on the verge of losing a war that had barely begun, Prime Minister Winston Churchill inspired his countrymen with a famous speech that included this sentence: "I have nothing to offer but blood, toil, tears, and sweat." We usually remember the address, and refer to it, as Churchill's "blood, sweat, and tears" speech. Why? Why do we leave out "toil"?

Perhaps the phrase is now "blood, sweat, and tears" because we tend to group things in threes; three items are easier to remember than four. But if so, why those three? Why not "blood, toil, and sweat"? Or "blood, toil, and tears"? The answer seems obvious: We forget "toil"—forgot it long ago—because it is not concrete. To put a fine point on it, blood and sweat and tears can be seen and touched—even held in the hand. Of the four words, only toil fails to represent something concrete, something we can see.

If there were nothing more to writing that enables us to see than choosing concrete words, anyone could learn to produce it the way the craftsman teaches himself to use precise words and make concise sentences: by keeping principles in mind while writing and revising. Up to a point, that method works for everybody. But one writer can choose concrete words and help us to see without deeply affecting us. Another can choose concrete words imaginatively, make memorable phrases, and create smooth and evocative sentences that come alive—art.

Whether everyone can learn to combine ideas creatively is certainly questionable. But we should note at least that before relaxing and depending on their subconscious, creative people work their conscious minds, which is the craftsman's method. Much of the rest of this chapter analyzes how craftsmen produce visual writing.

SPECIFIC AND GENERAL, CONCRETE AND ABSTRACT

"Be specific!" All of us have spoken these words and have heard them. They express our desire to be told *exactly* what is meant rather than some cloudy approximation of it. A man shot the president? What man? A term paper must be written for this course? What kind? How long?

The specific information these questions ask for is important in writing. But the specific and the general as qualities of writing mean that and more. A general word refers to a group or class. A specific word refers to a member of a class. *Building* is general. *House* is specific. *Five-bedroom house* is more specific. In most writing, the more specific the better.

The difference between concreteness and abstraction is much the same. Students who say, "That book is too abstract," usually mean that it seems to be removed from reality. Because "abstract" literally means "take away," this is reasonably accurate. Abstraction is usually a flaw in writing.

> You must have the means to develop coherent concepts that are sufficient to build up a conceptual structure which will be adequate to the experiential facts you want to describe, and which will not only allow you to characterize but also to manipulate possible relationships you had not previously seen.

The sentence is bad because of its woolly abstraction. No word in it pictures anything that can be touched or seen.

Bertrand Russell demonstrated in writing *The Scientific Outlook* how one who customarily analyzes the general and abstract can make them understandable to those who do not. In trying to persuade readers that "what is actually experienced is much less than one would naturally suppose," Russell used an everyday example to show the complexity of vision:

> You may say, for example, that you see your friend, Mr. Jones, walking along the street: but this is to go far beyond what you have any right to say. You see a succession of coloured patches, traversing a stationary background. These patches, by means of a Pavlov conditioned reflex, bring into your mind the word "Jones," and so you say you see Jones; but other people, looking out of their windows from different angles, will see

something different, owing to the laws of perspective: therefore, if they are all seeing Jones, there must be as many different Joneses as there are spectators, and if there is only one true Jones, the sight of him is not vouchsafed to anybody. If we assume for a moment the truth of the account which physics gives, we shall explain what you call "seeing Jones" in some such terms as the following. Little packets of light, called "light quanta," shoot out from the sun, and some of these reach a region where there are atoms of a certain kind, composing Jones's face, and hands, and clothes. These atoms do not themselves exist, but are merely a compendious way of alluding to possible occurrences. Some of the light quanta, when they reach Jones's atoms, upset their internal economy. This causes him to become sunburnt, and to manufacture vitamin D. Others are reflected, and of those that are reflected some enter your eye. They there cause a complicated disturbance of the rods and cones, which, in turn, send a current along the optic nerve. When this current reaches the brain, it produces an event. The event which it produces is that which you call "seeing Jones." As is evident from this account, the connection of "seeing Jones" with Jones is a remote, roundabout causal connection. Jones himself, meanwhile, remains wrapped in mystery. He may be thinking about his dinner, or about how his investments have gone to pieces, or about that umbrella he lost; these thoughts are Jones, but these are not what you see. . . .

Russell transformed the abstract into the concrete here by illustrating. He could have done less work merely by writing of the effects of light quanta reflecting from an object. But that would have been lazy, and laziness is the chief reason so much writing is marred by vague generalizations and abstractions. A writer must often search for an apt example. Then he may discover that he does not know enough to use it. If he should decide to illustrate vision by describing light reflecting from Mr. Jones, he may not know what happens to the reflected quanta when they enter the eye. Are the rods and cones involved? What happens in the optic nerve? Does a current move along it? Is *current* the right word? The writer could find the answers, but it is easier to write generally and abstractly.

Writing well is work, but the effort is necessary. In most cases, the more work we do, the less readers must do to understand. Ordinarily the more work we do to give specific and concrete examples, the greater the reading pleasure. The specific and the concrete move prose close to what Joseph Conrad considered the heart of effective writing, the visual.

VISUAL WORDS

One who hears that the visual is valuable in writing probably thinks first of using adjectives. But consider again the sentence quoted in Chapter 4:

An elaborate and payrolled watchdog system was set to safeguard his interest, should any ambitiously piratical executive attempt a personal seduction of organizational assets.

Piratical is the only adjective here that has visual power, the only one that enables readers to see. And *its* value is questionable. Because this sentence is about executives, who are far more likely to embezzle than to take wealth boldly, as pirates did, *piratical* calls up an image that does not quite fit.

To consider another point, however, assume that *piratical* does fit here. Then imagine that all the other adjectives in this sentence also have visual qualities. *Piratical* would lose some or all of its power, first because the sentence would strain for effects with so many visual words that the technique would call attention to itself (and the sentence become almost ludicrous), second because readers would react to a bombardment of visual words that would create an explosion rather than a picture.

One who detests Liberace, the pianist who has developed a classical pop-music technique, might describe him as "a giggling, fruit-flavored heap of mother-love." Now consider how a music critic actually described him several years ago:

A deadly, winking, sniggering, snuggling, giggling, fruit-flavored, mincing, ice-covered heap of mother-love, a sugary mountain of jingling clap-trap wrapped up in a preposterous clown.

Was the elaborate attack effective? It may have been—among those readers who shared the critic's loathing for Liberace. It may have been effective also among those who both disliked Liberace and considered the piling-up of adjectives a virtuoso writing performance. Almost certainly, though, many who read the critic's description, probably including some who disliked Liberace, were repelled by it. The writer seemed to be bludgeoning a butterfly.

Consider the adjectives, especially *deadly*. Anyone who has seen Liberace perform surely doubts that *deadly* describes him. Those who have not seen him probably wonder how he can be snuggling, giggling, mincing, and all the others, and at the same time be deadly. If Liberace is all these things at once, the writer should have made much of the paradox, probably by writing another sentence to point it up.

And if *ice-covered* was intended, like most of the other adjectives, to describe his manner, readers must have had trouble imagining how a performer who snuggles and giggles and minces can seem to be ice-covered as well. Iciness suggests aloofness. Liberace is not aloof. If, however, ice-covered was intended to describe Liberace's dress, it is accurate (his suits glitter with sequins). But it would have been more effective to limit the sentence to words describing his manner—especially because there are so many of them—and to write another about his dress. As the sentence was written, ice-covered probably confused readers who considered it a description of manner and divided the attention of those who did not between an adjective describing dress and many adjectives describing manner.

Should the writer have piled up in one sentence all the adjectives that do describe his manner? Probably not. Surely "winking, sniggering, snuggling, giggling, fruit-flavored, mincing, sugary, jingling, and preposterous" prevented most readers from savoring any adjective because there were so many. In a sense, the adjectives are complementary because they have different shades of meaning. "Snuggling" and "giggling," for example, are not synonyms and seem to complement one another. But if we are to judge only by this standard, where should a writer stop? Why should he not use seventy complementary adjectives? He should not because the sheer weight of so many—however valuable each might be—would make the sentence stagger.

Some might argue that the critic's very extravagance was valuable. Although in most cases a writer should orchestrate his techniques so that each works subtly, the critic wanted to assault his readers with his contempt for Liberace. But the critic's sentence seems too heavily packed with visual words to allow the readers' minds to do their own work of visualizing. The shorter version, "a giggling, fruit-flavored heap of mother-love," allows readers to fill out the picture the words evoke, to complete the creation the writer has started.

A much more affecting use of adjectives is apparent in this description of Liza Minelli by Clive Barnes, drama critic of the *New York Times:*

> It is probably her nervousness, those stretched-out moments of the spirit, that makes her performance so exciting. She seems to be playing a game with herself and with her audience. Sometimes she is coming on strong, doing a Jolson number as Miss Showbusiness of 1932, then she will be a little girl lost in a Lord Fauntleroy velvet suit, mourning in a tough way the tattered loss of innocence.

Barnes is content to let each adjective do its work. Although he is describing, which gives him more leeway than he might take in other writing, he uses few adjectives. The relative absence of others lends force to a visual adjective in the first sentence, *stretched-out,* and to another in the third, *tattered.*

When a writer chooses adjectives carefully and uses them sparingly, those with visual power affect us.

But the greatest power of visual writing is in nouns and verbs, especially verbs. In this passage from *Travels With Charley,* John Steinbeck uses strong verbs to show how it feels to change a tire in the mud:

> I lay on my stomach and edged my way, swam my way under the truck, holding my nostrils clear of the surface of the water. The jack handle was slippery with greasy mud. Mud balls formed in my beard. I lay panting like a wounded duck, quietly cursing as I inched the jack forward under an axle that I had to find by feel, since it was under water. Then, with superhuman gruntings and bubblings, my eyes starting from their sockets, I levered the great weight. I could feel my muscles tearing apart and separating from their anchoring bones. In actual time, not over an hour elapsed before I had the spare tire on. I was unrecognizable under many layers of yellow mud. My hands were cut and bleeding. I rolled the bad tire to a high place and inspected it. The whole side wall had blown out. Then I looked at the left rear tire, and to my horror saw a great rubber bubble on its side and, farther along, another. It was obvious that the other tire might go at any moment, and it was Sunday and it was raining and it was Oregon. If the other tire blew, there we were, on a wet and lonesome road, having no recourse except to burst into tears and wait for death. And perhaps some kind birds might cover us with leaves.

Steinbeck used few adjectives and adverbs. He did not write in the first sentence of his "suffering" or "straining" stomach muscles, or of his "wheezing" nostrils. He did not write of "tortuously" or "strainingly" making his way under the truck. He relied instead on verbs to show his actions and thus to draw a picture. The first verb, *lay,* is intended to give needed information. Then, he "edged" his way, and "swam" his way. He did not simply "make" his way; such a word shows the reader nothing. Nor did he say that he "kept" his nostrils clear of the water; "kept" shows nothing. Instead, he was "holding" them clear. And mud balls "formed" in his beard, which provides a small, sharp picture.

Comparing Steinbeck's passage to another that is written mockseriously shows the value of verbs. The student who wrote the following description of cafeteria food relied on adjectives and adverbs. The result is overwriting (a useful term that describes what usually happens when we lean heavily on strong modifiers).

> Cautiously, glancing suspiciously from side to side, the first eater passes through the threshold to stand beneath the obscene, flickering lights. What next? he wondered.
>
> Falteringly plucking at a knife, fork, and spoon, and arranging them clumsily on his tray, he steps forward into the unknown. One by one, others follow suit, arming themselves for the forthcoming assault on their senses.

A large bowl of semi-green lettuce, wilted with age, slowly dwindles under the unrelenting attack of stainless steel tongs, while the week-old dill pickles firmly stand their ground.

Penetrating red pimento eyes stare menacingly from dull green olives, threatening the health of those who dare to eat them. Butchered tomato slices await the sharp, piercing tines of Food Service forks.

Among the many flaws in this, the most obvious is the extravagant use of adverbs and adjectives. No doubt the writer reasoned conventionally: adverbs add intensity, adjectives add color. They do, but only when they are chosen carefully and used sparingly.

Analyzing the passage by Steinbeck and comparing it to the student's shows how often Steinbeck bypassed opportunities to overwrite. In a description of the kind Steinbeck wrote, an adjective could be attached to each noun. But to use so many would be to divide the readers' attention between the nouns, which are the bones of the sentences, and the adjectives that would modify them. Here and there, Steinbeck used an adjective to complete a meaning or a picture. He wrote of "greasy" mud not just to flavor the noun but because the mud was mixed with grease. He did not write of a "wounded" duck merely to flavor the noun. Ducks are comfortable in water (as Steinbeck, under the truck, was not) unless they are injured, ill, or wounded. Steinbeck also wrote of "superhuman" gruntings and bubblings, which seems at first to be overwriting. Certainly "gruntings and bubblings" are strong words that can do their own work. But "superhuman" may help prepare readers for the other exaggerations that lead to the large exaggeration of the last two sentences.

Steinbeck knew that the strong nouns are specific and concrete. Contrast his nouns (stomach, truck, nostrils, water, handle, mud) with the many general and abstract nouns in a sentence quoted earlier in this chapter: "You must have the *means* to develop coherent *concepts* that are sufficient to build up a conceptual *structure* which will be adequate to the experiential *facts* you want to describe, and which will not only allow you to characterize but also to manipulate possible *relationships* you had not previously seen." One need not always avoid such nouns. But a long sentence made up of many weak nouns limps from point to point, especially if the verbs and adjectives are lifeless.

Learning to purge adjectives and adverbs is hateful work because they are so rich and flavorful. How can one who loves words discard strong modifiers? The best way is to switch to expressive verbs, which are stronger. Their strength is shown in this comparison:

The student sat at his desk.
The student sprawled at his desk.

The verb in the first sentence describes hardly at all. The second is visual. The lover of words will choose the second and learn immediately the power of visual verbs. Moreover, if he will then read this sentence, "The lethargic student sprawled at his desk," he may begin to wonder whether the adjective is needed. If the preceding sentence said or hinted that the student was lethargic, surely the word does little but leech power from "sprawled."

Learning to use verbs that show is so important that you should overwrite strong verbs to fix them in your style. Where *is* or *was* appears —or *has* or *had* or any other verb that just sits there—substitute a visual verb. An editor can restrain a writer whose sentences are too strong. A writer can learn from such editing and strike a balance. But one who never uses the visual power of verbs resigns himself to sentences that plod.

VISUAL PHRASES AND SENTENCES

Anyone can learn to use visual words and make visual phrases and sentences. The making is not what counts, but the kind one makes. *Stretched-out,* for example, is a visual word that almost any drama critic might use in a phrase: stretched-out role, stretched-out play, stretched-out evening. Clive Barnes thought of "nervousness, those stretched-out moments of the spirit." Analogy and metaphor are the roots of such writing.

Analogies

The true test of intelligence, the philosopher William James believed, is whether one can make analogies—see basic similarities. John Ciardi, a former professor of English who is now a columnist for *Saturday Review/World,* has written:

> All mentality begins in analogy; in the act of recognizing essential likenesses and essential differences, and of discovering how such likenesses and differences illuminate the interrelation of things.

Analogies are ultimately false. An analogy cannot have the finality of a statistic because no one thing is exactly like another, especially the things artistic writers match to make the reader's imagination work.

Here is an expressive analogy James Thurber used in *The Years with Ross* to show how it was to work with Harold Ross, the editor of the *New Yorker:*

> Having a manuscript under Ross's scrutiny was like putting your car in

the hands of a skilled mechanic, not an automotive engineer with a bachelor of science degree, but a guy who knows what makes a motor go, and sputter, and wheeze, and sometimes come to a dead stop; a man with an ear for the faintest body squeak as well as the loudest engine rattle. When you first gazed, appalled, upon an uncorrected proof of one of your stories and articles, each margin had a thicket of queries and complaints—one writer got a hundred and forty-four on one profile. It was as though you beheld the works of your car spread all over the garage floor, and the job of getting the thing together again and making it work seemed impossible. Then you realized that Ross was trying to make your Model T or old Stutz Bearcat into a Cadillac or Rolls-Royce. He was at work with the tools of his unflagging perfectionism, and, after an exchange of growls or snarls, you set to work to join him in his enterprise.

Thurber was careful not to labor this witty analogy. The second sentence does not refer to Ross as a mechanic or to the manuscript as a car that needed work, and the last sentence barely touches the analogy by using *tools*. Analogies can be written at any length—even book-length —but the longer they run the defter the writer must be.

An analogy that was published in *Time* magazine twenty years ago illustrates how hard a writer himself must work when he pushes too far:

> The old man puffed into sight like a venerable battle-wagon steaming up over the horizon. First a smudge of smoke, then the long cigar, then the familiar, stoop-shouldered hulk that a generation had come to know as the silhouette of greatness. Prime Minister Winston Churchill scowled as he emerged from the *Queen Mary* and politely doffed his hat to official U.S. meeters and greeters.

The first sentence starts the analogy strikingly. Then, trying to complete it, the writer was stuck with the natural sequence of the image and pieced it out, but not convincingly. Churchill certainly was a hulking figure. But the first view of him disembarking from a ship would not be the smoke from his cigar, nor the second the cigar. The bulk of Churchill would come first, then the smoke and the cigar. Considering the trap that complete analogies always set, the writer did well. Perhaps the last sentence, which departs from the analogy, enabled him to escape uninjured.

Metaphors

We ordinarily use *metaphor* to mean the class of comparison that does at a stroke what analogies do at greater length: "Wine-dark sea" transfers a mental picture of wine to enrich the mental picture of the sea. To write of a sound that "cuts the silence" is to transfer a knife-like vision (and to inject action subtly). A simile differs from other metaphors only in transferring with *like* or *as:* "The old man puffed into sight like a venerable battle wagon," or "He looks like an English duke."

We do not know how to teach the making of artistic metaphors. We do know the picture is likely to be sharper when a metaphor has the same color as the rest of the writing. Thus, in a passage quoted earlier, Steinbeck wrote that he "lay panting like a wounded duck." Why not "lay panting like a long-distance runner"? The metaphor would clash with the setting; Steinbeck was working in water. Perhaps it would have been as fitting to write, "lay panting like a long-distance swimmer" (although "wounded duck" has the appeal of oddity), but "lay panting like a long-distance swimmer after a championship race" would drown the picture.

Conciseness sharpens by deleting words that are neither part of the picture nor necessary to frame it. A student who wrote a humorous piece that classified football game concessionaires unwittingly illustrated the need for conciseness in this paragraph:

> A similarly dangerous concessionaire is the fumbler. A novice, or one who is just basically maladroit, he stumbles through the stands leaving behind him a trail of sodden and lacerated bystanders.

"Behind him" says nothing that is not obvious. There is a less obvious flaw in "sodden and lacerated bystanders." Although the entire report is an exaggeration, the best exaggeration is the truth expanded. "Sodden" is apt because spectators have become wet from cold drinks at football games. But "lacerated"? The word is so far beyond ordinary experience that the writer seems to be trying too hard. The picture might be best drawn with:

> A similarly dangerous concessionaire is the fumbler. A novice, or one who is just basically maladroit, he stumbles through the stands leaving a trail of sodden spectators.*

To enable readers to see clearly, a writer must also use precise words. Imprecision in the following sentence about an industrial plant results in a blurred image:

> Its big smokestack spilled smoke, soot, and cinders.

---

* "Spectators" is better here than "bystanders" because "bystanders" are those who are not involved.

The picture of a smokestack *spilling* soot and cinders is apt. But smoke does not leave a smokestack in anything like the way solids such as soot and cinders spill from it.

Metaphors are worse than useless when a writer clangs two together. In a term paper on military justice, a student wrote: "It is an indictment because the isthmus of military law is the cutting edge of democratic society." As George Orwell reminded us: "The sole aim of a metaphor is to call up a visual image." The student called up one image, an isthmus, then asked that we see it as a sword. The metaphor was almost as mixed as Richard Nixon's "We have some cards to play, and we intend to play them to the hilt."

Clichés

The worst metaphors are the exhausted ones, especially those that run so long that they exhaust readers. When President Gerald Ford was a Republican congressman during the troubled presidency of Democrat Lyndon Johnson, Ford turned to his own use one of Johnson's metaphoric statements:

> The President's only explanation was, when a great ship cuts through the sea the water is always stirred and troubled. Apparently, the President has been standing on the stern, looking backward at the wake, wondering which of his officers to dump overboard next.

Ford was so pleased with this effect that he went on with it:

> His ship of state is wallowing in a storm-tossed sea, drifting toward the rocks of domestic disaster.

That was quite enough, but not for Ford:

> Beaten by the waves of worldwide financial crisis, the captain should return to the bridge. We need a captain who will seize the helm, call up full power, break out new charts, hold our course steadfast, and bring us through the storm. It's time for all hands to man their action stations. Let's not give up the ship. America has weathered many a terrible storm, rescued many a weaker vessel, and will do it again.

The threat of seasickness may be the greatest danger, but the basic metaphor fails because it is senile. Perhaps every politician since Cicero has referred to a nation as a ship and to a national leader as its captain. By stringing out an ancient metaphor until it became ridiculous, Ford emphasized the emptiness of clichés.

But if you have been told since junior high school to avoid clichés, do not fear that this is a preface to that familiar lesson. Clichés should be avoided, but they can teach us much about expressive phrases.

First, a definition by exclusion. A cliché is not merely a phrase used often during many years. "The narrow street" may have been written billions of times by millions of writers. But those words in that order are as useful now as they were the first time they were written. The same is true of most phrases; they merely give information and can be used endlessly.

In contrast, a cliché is a phrase that calls attention to itself. It was so expressive when it was coined that it was borrowed again and again by lesser writers and became exhausted. But how wonderful it must have been to be the first to write "light as a feather," "heavy as lead," and "hot as the hinges of hell"!

Not only should we applaud those who coined the expressions that have become clichés, we can applaud ourselves—but lightly—for borrowing them. We can think of ourselves as reaching into a literary junkyard when we use clichés, but we should also consider that using them shows that we want to express facts and ideas vividly. Clichés are visual phrases, and we demonstrate by using them our instinct for expressive language.

How can a writer turn this instinct from junk-shopping to creativity? First, he should consider the antiquity of many of the phrases he borrows. One who is tempted to write, "The proof of the pudding is in the eating," should know that its first recorded use was by Joseph Addison in 1714. The writer who uses "Don't look a gift horse in the mouth" should know that Saint Jerome wrote in 400 A.D., "Do not, as the common proverb has it, scrutinize the teeth of a gift horse" (and note that it was then a "common proverb"). "One foot in the grave" is attractive—and so Plutarch thought when he wrote it in 95 A.D. As for "One man's food is another man's poison," Lucretius wrote in 45 B.C.: "What to one man is food, to another is rank poison." Finally, anyone who is charmed by "chip off the old block" should know that Theocritus wrote "chip off the old flint" in 270 B.C.

What is wrong with using ancient phrases? Nothing—if the writer cares little for his readers. But the writer who wants to lure readers rather than repel them must shun clichés. And one who hopes to write unforgettably will try to create clichés: coin phrases so expressive that they will live beyond him. Theocritus wrote "chip off the old flint" in 270 B.C., expressing a striking thought visually. In the centuries since then, one visual word has replaced another (*block* for *flint*), but the expression is otherwise the same. Because it was useful and captivating, the phrase became immortal.

If you are not so bold as to seek immortality, try for another worthwhile goal: providing pleasure for a few readers by writing visual phrases. You may begin by remembering only an old phrase, a cliché. Instead of groaning because only a cliché comes to mind, you should consider it positively. You have, after all, tried to be expressive. Recognize that your instinct was right, your reach too short. Searching for a striking expression, you found only what was nearest at hand. That is the critical point. You must move beyond the cliché, but doing so calls for the most demanding kind of work, mental effort.

VISUAL DETAILS

Plutarch, who was one of the earliest as well as one of the greatest theorists about biography, reflected on his own work with:

> Sometimes a matter of less moment, an expression or a jest, informs us better of characters and inclinations than the most famous sieges, the greatest armaments or the bloodiest battles. . . . As portrait painters are more exact in the lines and features of the face, in which the character is seen, so I must give my attention to the marks and indications of the souls of men.

Details of many kinds have strong effects when writers use them imaginatively. The poet Antoine de Saint-Exupery wrote of Joseph Conrad's method:

> When Conrad described a typhoon he said very little about towering waves, or darkness, or the whistling of the wind in the shrouds. He knew better. Instead he took the reader down into the hold of the vessel, packed with emigrant coolies, where the rolling and the pitching of the ship had ripped up and scattered their bags and bundles, burst open their boxes, and flung their humble belongings into a crazy heap.
> Family treasures painfully collected in a lifetime of poverty, pitiful mementos so alike that nobody but their owners could have told them apart, had lost their identity and lapsed into chaos, into anonymity, into an amorphous magma.

Anyone who has read a book by Barbara Tuchman (among them are *The Guns of August, The Proud Tower,* and *The Zimmerman Telegram*) knows that she often uses small, intriguing details. Recognizing how sharply they flavor writing, she *works* to include them. A visible detail captivated her while she was writing *The Guns of August:* the Grand Duke Nicholas, who was six feet six inches tall, had an aide pin a fringe of white paper over the doorway of the railroad car in which he had established military headquarters so he wouldn't bump his head. "I was so charmed by the white paper fringe," she wrote, "that I constructed a whole paragraph describing Russian headquarters at Barovici in order to slip it in logically."

Time and *Newsweek* draw readers by the millions partly because their reporters search out the details that flavor news reports. In a manual for *Time* correspondents, the editors emphasize writing style, then add:

> Far more important is that you tell us all we need to know, not merely get the facts straight but to see, feel, hear—even smell—what has happened.
> What color and texture were the dress?
> How did the mayor enter the editor's office?
> Exactly what did the druggist say to the narcotics agent?
> Of what kind of wood was the doctor's table made?

Such details help draw readers to the news magazines. You can appeal to readers, too, by seeing, feeling, hearing—even smelling—details. If you are not accustomed to using them, you may at first use too many and repel readers. In time, if you match your use of detail against that in the writing of a professional, you can learn to pare details so that the flavor comes through. First, though, you must gather them—many more than you will need.

ANECDOTES AND ILLUSTRATIONS

Anecdotes show. We are too likely to think of them as amusing but frivolous—even as jokes. Many are funny, but the important matter is usually whether an anecdote has value apart from its humor. Instead of thinking of anecdotes in terms of punch lines, think of them as little stories that show memorably. A good anecdote both attracts and informs.

A student who sits and thinks about how to describe one of his teachers is likely to produce something like this:

> Professor Johnson listens thoughtfully to the many questions from his students. Sometimes he replies slowly and hesitantly. Sometimes, though, he reacts vigorously and even gets up and runs to the chalkboard. His words become more vigorous, too. He can be quite lively.

Contrast that ordinary description with one written after watching the teacher at work:

> Questions are hurled at Johnson, who receives them thoughtfully,

leaning back in his chair, fingertips aligned or interlocked. Occasionally, he'll gaze off, looking much the part of the poet in quiet contemplation.

Other moments offer a striking contrast. Johnson will react to some student with, "Now you're getting into it!" hit the table, and run to the chalkboard wih some sort of historical explanation, philosophical allusion or Latin derivation. His speech, characteristically flavored by the 18th Century (that is, polished, eloquent, and abounding in "albeit's," "thereunto's," and "henceforth's"), becomes more fluid. Sentences are uttered breathily and words become onomatopoeic. Thus the word "groping," in the act of groping, becomes "g-r-r-oping." A "sure" which is definite indeed, becomes the exaggerated "shu-wer."

He'll vehemently cast out an idea, direct it to a literary issue, and then play with it. He's totally animated and effervescent. Occasionally he'll exclaim to a student, "YES! I never saw it that way until this very moment!" His intense eyes dart around and he's on such a solitary mind trip with Jonathan Swift and Samuel Johnson that it wouldn't matter if the seminar room were whisked away.

This passage shows Johnson at work, and the explicit detailing of his actions makes him memorable. Readers might have trouble remembering the man described in the preceding passage; they are only told about him. They remember Johnson as he is described in the second passage because he is shown to them.

Because anecdotes must ordinarily be typical to be useful, we usually think of them as a class of illustration. But whether or not a good anecdote is typical, a writer is likely to use one that seems to fit his topic. In such a case, he should make it clear that the anecdote does not typify. All effective, and true, illustrations are typical because their function is to give an example of a class. If they are vivid, the flavor is stronger. The writer Phyllis McGinley wrote this to illustrate a particular kind of suburban town:

> Twenty miles east of New York City as the New Haven Railroad flies sits a village I shall call Spruce Manor. The Boston Post Road, there, for the length of two blocks, becomes Main Street, and on one side of that thundering thoroughfare are the grocery stores and the drugstores and the Village Spa where the teenagers gather of an afternoon to drink their cokes and speak their curious confidences. There one finds the shoe repairers and the dry cleaners and the secondhand stores which sell "antiques" and the stationery stores which dispense comic books to ten-year-olds, and greeting cards and lending library masterpieces to their mothers.

A Yiddish saying goes, "For instance isn't proof." But Phyllis McGinley's illustration of the suburban town has a solid ring—the details are presented in the wry tone of one who knows the territory—and is likely to be taken as better proof than a general statement. A generalization followed closely by a readable illustration nails down the point for readers.

DIRECT QUOTATIONS

If you use only your own words in writing about a person, readers may wonder whether they can rely on what you say. Quoting adds authority and allows readers to develop a sense of what the person quoted is like. Direct quotations are valuable, too, in writing that is not about a person. They enable you to lean on the authority of others, and they usually add a pleasing change of pace. When the words you quote are expressive, reader interest heightens.

A paragraph quoted earlier illustrates both the method and the value of using direct quotations:

> Where "Meredi" is going is into broadcasting. She has chosen an indirect and ambitious route. She is not entering broadcasting when she completes her senior year in June. Despite her experience and achievements, she thinks the broadcasting world would consider her "just another bright-eyed, eager graduate." Meredi wants "more upward mobility, and a chance to influence, to make a dent in the system." So Meredi is applying to law schools: Harvard, Yale, Stanford, and Columbia.

Note that the writer chose to quote these directly: "just another bright-eyed, eager undergraduate" and "more upward mobility, and a chance to influence, to make a dent in the system." Why quote those words and not others? The writer chose the quotations that were both readable and expressive—flavorful words that may help the reader to understand how Meredith Wheeler talks and thinks. The writer also took interview notes that included this sentence, "I'm a senior and will get my degree in June"—which merely gives information. Instead of quoting such sentences, the writer appropriately used the information in paraphrase. Readers focus on direct quotations and should not be made to focus on inexpressive words unless the authority of the person quoted is needed, as it often is in cases of controversy. (Note that in the first sentence the writer placed "Meredi" in quotation marks to indicate that it is a nickname. Having indicated that, the writer was free to drop the quotation marks.)

Four principles will help you in using quotations:

1 A direct quotation need not be an entire sentence or more. You may use

partial quotations (also known as "orphan" or "broken" quotations). But avoid using several partial quotations in one sentence or one paragraph. Because readers unconsciously bear down on short quotations, several partial quotations in a short space force them to bear down on the quoted words, let up for the writer's own words, bear down, let up, bear down, let. . . . Reading becomes exhausting.

2   In taking quotations from printed material, you are likely to quote too much. You may like the quoted material so well that you quote at length so your readers can share your pleasure. You may use a long quotation because it expresses important points better than you can. Or you may simply quote at great length so that you can fulfill an assignment with little more work than typing. Resist these lures by asking yourself exactly how much you need in order to illustrate or prove a point—and by reminding yourself that *you* are the writer.

3   Never use quotation marks to apologize for slang or clichés. For example, the writer is apologizing in this sentence:

> People who have "made it" in the entertainment world expect the "pot of gold at the end of the rainbow."

In putting quotation marks around "made it," the writer is saying, "See, *I* know it's slang." In putting quotation marks around "pot of gold at the end of the rainbow," the writer is signalling that readers should not think less of him; he knows it is a cliché and is proving it with the marks. If slang fits, as it seldom does, use it directly, without apology. Do not use clichés.

4   In quoting one person, then another, identify the second at the beginning of his quotation. Consider these sentences from an interview with several football players:

> "Maybe I'll know tomorrow, after I see the game movies," said Moore.
> "We were lined up strong to the left and Randy Vataha was my No. 1 target. But they put a good rush on me," said quarterback Jim Plunkett.

Readers cannot know as they begin the second quotation that Moore is no longer speaking. If they think he is continuing to speak, the quotation makes no sense. Moore is a receiver; so is Vataha. For Moore to say "my No. 1 target" of Vataha and "good rush on me" confuses readers who know that Moore is not a passer. Although readers understand when finally they are told that Plunkett, a passer, is speaking in the second paragraph, they are confused until they reach his name.

The principles in this chapter should help bring writing to life. Still, one writer who is guided by them may produce sentences that seem a bit mechanical, another may produce colorful, flavorful writing that entrances us. E. B. White confessed that the difference is a mystery: "Who can say what ignites a certain combination of words, causing them to explode in the mind?" We know only that most of the work of great writers is both alive and visual. The writer whose work has the clank of the mechanical should practice using the principles of visual writing—over and over and over.

PROJECTS

1 Four sets of visual words appear in the following paragraph, which is taken from "Shooting an Elephant" by George Orwell. Orwell used the middle word in each set. Write a short paragraph describing the different pictures drawn by each word in each set.

> He looked suddenly [shattered — stricken — smashed], [smaller — shrunken — lessened], immensely old, as though the frightful impact of the bullet had paralyzed him without knocking him down. At last, after what seemed a long time—it might have been five seconds—he [sank — sagged — drooped] flabbily to his knees. His mouth [drooled — slobbered — gushed]. An enormous senility seemed to have settled on him.

2 Write a short description of a campus building—perhaps the most prominent or the most ramshackle—that offers an opportunity for visual writing. Try to rely more on verbs and nouns than on adjectives.

3 The following passage is part of Tom Wolfe's description in the 1960s of the contrast in dress between a group led by the writer Ken Kesey and the FBI agents who arrested him. Write a similar paragraph that describes the difference between the youth culture today and the bureaucratic culture.

> The cops now know the whole scene, even the costumes, the jesuschrist strung-out hair, Indian beads, Indian headbands, donkey beads, temple bells, amulets, mandalas, god's-eyes, flourescent vests, unicorn horns, Errol Flynn dueling shirts—but they still don't know about the shoes. The worst are shiny black shoes with shoelaces in them. The hierarchy ascends from there although practically all low-cut shoes are unhip, from there on up to the boots the heads like, light, fanciful boots, English boots of the mod variety, if that is all they can get, but better something like hand-tooled Mexican boots with Caliente Dude Triple A toes on them. So see the FBI—black—shiny—laced up—FBI shoes—when the FBI finally grabbed Kesey.

4 Complete the following phrases as imaginatively as you can. It may help to decide first that your phrases will describe one kind of object, say, cars.

   a.   as fast as _____

b. as colorful as _____

c. as comfortable as _____

d. as relaxing as _____

e. like a _____

f. rides like a _____

g. corners like a _____

The following paragraph from Vladimir Nabokov's novel *Lolita* contains few details describing the men Lolita found attractive. Should Nabokov have described the men more fully?

Oh, I had to keep a very sharp eye on Lo, little limp Lo! Owing perhaps to constant amorous exercise, she radiated, despite her very childish appearance, some special languorous glow which threw garage fellows, hotel pages, vacationists, goons in luxurious cars, maroon morons near blued pools, into fits of concupiscence which might have tickled my pride, had it not incensed my jealousy. For little Lo was aware of that glow of hers, and I would often catch her coulant un regard in the direction of some amiable male, some grease monkey, with a sinewy golden-brown forearm and watch-braceleted wrist, and hardly had I turned my back to go and buy this very Lo a lollipop, than I would hear her and the fair mechanic burst into a perfect love song of wisecracks.

Writing to Inform and Explain: Exposition

Get your facts right first; that is the foundation of all style.
—GEORGE BERNARD SHAW

5 We live in a civilization so complicated that no one can understand all its complexities, but everyone must cope with many of them. The student who must try to understand a computerized registration form, the parent who struggles to put together a new toy for a child on Christmas Eve, almost anyone who tries to puzzle out the reasons for the latest economic crisis—all are impressed, if not irritated, by the problems of coping with the modern world. All must be given understandable information, which suggests why exposition—informing and explaining—is the most common form of writing. In many instances it is the most difficult, for the writer must often take complex events and issues and present them lucidly.

Clarity is at the center of exposition. Clarity, which grows mostly out of precise words in concise sentences, is also essential in the other forms of discourse: description, which depicts; narration, which tells stories and sketches events; and persuasion, which seeks to convince. We must try to frame all the forms of discourse in attractive phrases and sentences, using techniques that will make reading such a pleasure that we lure readers who have only a marginal interest in a topic. But clarity is central in expository writing.

What is the meaning of the politician's statement? How does this machine work? What is the use of that gadget? How did this come to be in that form? How is the object put together? When and why did that event occur? How important is this? What is it good for? How did it begin and develop? What are the roots of the controversy? Such questions are answered in expository writing.

STRUCTURES

The simplest and most common expository structure began with Aristotle, who set forth a beginning-middle-end design that is now more descriptively termed introduction-main body-conclusion. If you were to sketch it in outline, it would look like a football or a fat man, with the bulk in the middle.

One of the structures journalists use is similarly shaped. In writing an interpretive story, which explains and clarifies, journalists usually try to catch the interest of readers with an introduction, develop the explanation in the middle, and end by pointing up the meaning or the effect, or by looking to the future.

The straight news story in journalism is quite different. Usually written to inform, it presents the most interesting and important facts first. Toward the end, the information becomes less and less important. Readers who are in a hurry can probably learn everything they need to know from the first few paragraphs and ignore the details at or near the end. The straight news story, which resembles a funnel or an inverted pyramid, with the breadth at the top, is shown in Chapter 4 in the news story about a speech by Barbara Ward.

An expository structure often used by many writers is also shaped like a funnel, but for different reasons. The writer begins with a broad overview, then narrows his focus to show individual people or items in detail. In such cases, the end is as important as the beginning or the middle. In *The Decline and Fall of the Roman Empire,* Edward Gibbon wrote many paragraphs in structures that were like miniatures of the entire book. In this long paragraph Gibbon moves from the large to the small almost as though he were a cameraman focusing first on the broad sweep of a mural of a Roman legion, then rolling his camera in for a close-up to show the fine detail of each legionnaire's armament:

> . . . The heavy armed infantry, which composed its principal strength, was divided into ten cohorts, and fifty-five companies, under the orders of a correspondent number of tribunes and centurions. The first cohort, which always claimed the post of honour and the custody of the eagle, was formed of eleven hundred and five soldiers, the most approved for valour and fidelity. The remaining nine cohorts consisted each of five hundred and fifty-five; and the whole body of legionary infantry amounted to six thousand one hundred men.

Having given an overview of the infantry and its parts, Gibbon now describes the armament of each soldier:

Their arms were uniform, and admirably adapted to the nature of their service: an open helmet, with a lofty crest; a breast-plate, or coat of mail; greaves on their legs, and an ample buckler on their left arm. The buckler was of an oblong and concave figure, four feet in length, and two and a half in breadth, framed of a light wood, covered with a bull's hide, and strongly guarded with plates of brass. Besides a lighter spear, the legionary soldier grasped in his right hand the formidable *pilum, a* ponderous javelin, whose utmost length was about six feet, and which was terminated by a massy triangular point of steel of eighteen inches. This instrument was indeed much inferior to our modern firearms; since it was exhausted by a single discharge, at the distance of only ten or twelve paces. Yet when it was launched by a firm and skillful hand, there was not any cavalry that durst venture within its reach, nor any shield or corslet that could sustain the impetuosity of its weight. As soon as the Roman had darted his *pilum,* he drew his sword, and rushed forwards to close with the enemy. His sword was a short well-tempered Spanish blade, that carried a double edge, and was alike suited to the purpose of striking or of pushing; but the soldier was always instructed to prefer the latter use of his weapon, as his own body remained less exposed, whilst he inflicted a more dangerous wound on his adversary.

To show the placement of each soldier, Gibbon now finds it necessary to devote two sentences in this paragraph to the legion as a whole before returning to the individual soldiers:

The legion was usually drawn up eight deep; and the regular distance of three feet was left between the files as well as ranks. A body of troops, habituated to preserve this open order, in a long front and a rapid charge, found themselves prepared to execute every disposition which the circumstances of war, or the skill of their leader, might suggest. The soldier possessed a free space for his arms and motions, and sufficient intervals were allowed, through which seasonable reinforcements might be introduced to the relief of the exhausted combatants. The tactics of the Greeks and Macedonians were formed on very different principles. The strength of the phalanx depended on sixteen ranks of long pikes, wedged together in the closest array. But it was soon discovered by reflection as well as by the event, that the strength of the phalanx was unable to contend with the activity of the legion.

WRITING TO YOUR READERS

In an article about horse racing, a journalist wrote that a young woman jockey who had been racing for only two years had "captured 35 wins from the male jockeys." Then he went on to write about other matters, leaving it to his readers to try to puzzle out whether winning thirty-five races in two years was a modest record, a good record, or a great record.

Thirty-five victories would be remarkable if she had raced only fifty or sixty times—less so if she had raced two hundred times. And even though she was a woman competing in a sport that had long been barred to women, thirty-five victories in *two thousand* races would amount to only modest success; some jockeys who are considered to be only average riders sometimes win several races in a single day.

The point is that the journalist should have given the number of races in which the woman competed as well as the number she won. Readers who knew little about racing probably considered the woman jockey's record almost miraculous. It was not. Other women jockeys have been more successful. How many races did the leading jockeys win in the same period? How many did average jockeys win? How many did other women jockeys win?

All this points to one of the central questions in writing designed to inform and explain: Do facts speak for themselves? That can be answered only by considering a related question: To whom do what facts speak?

Obviously, you must know your readers before you can judge how much detailed information they need. You must also know them in order to judge whether they will understand technical terms. Consider this paragraph (the beginning of a long paper) written by a science student:

> No reliable and safe technique has yet been evolved for determining the myocardial blood flow in the human heart. Coronary arteriograms have been the standard technique for evaluating coronary blood flow for a number of years. This technique involves direct injection of a contrast medium—usually a radio-opaque dye—into the heart chambers or large vessels by catheterization and recording a moving film which shows the movement of the bolus in the heart.

To a specialist in the medical sciences, this paragraph is entirely understandable—even simple. It is, in fact, excellent for the purpose it is designed to serve. But to those who know little more than that blood must circulate through the heart to sustain human life, the paragraph is so dense that they can make their way through it only with the aid of a dictionary.

The following is a paragraph about the heart written for general readers rather than for specialists (by Louis I. Dublin in *The Problem of Heart Disease*):

> The heart is a complicated mechanism. Essentially it is a muscular pump composed of four chambers and their incoming and outgoing blood

vessels. The action of these chambers is coordinated and controlled by an intricate nervous mechanism. The chambers are paired into a right half and a left half. The upper chamber on each side is called the auricle, the lower, the ventricle. Each auricle is separated from its ventricle by a muscular valve which permits the flow of blood downward but prevents the leakage of blood backward.

The most obvious difference between these paragraphs is in choice of words. In the first, words such as "myocardial," "arteriograms," "radio-opaque," "catheterization," and "bolus" are used as though every reader will know what they mean. Although the second paragraph is not designed for elementary school reading (note "Essentially," "coordinated," and "intricate"), the writer recognizes by his choice of words that *his* readers know little. He is careful to make clear what is meant by *auricle* and *ventricle*.

An equally important difference is tone. In both cases, the writers are explaining. But the writer of the first paragraph seems to be discussing a problem with equals. The tone is that of a writer reviewing information familiar to his readers. In fact, he was doing exactly that: reviewing familiar information as an introduction to new findings—a valuable practice that enables readers to place the new in the context of the old. The tone of the writer of the second paragraph is that of the teacher: Let me tell you some things I know about the heart that you should learn. Although some of the words would not be understandable to children, the tone is a bit like that of the elementary school teacher. Note especially the simplicity of "The heart is a complicated mechanism" and "The chambers are paired into a right half and a left half." A writer should combine such sentences with others to avoid offending readers with sentences of Dick-and-Jane simplicity. One combination might be: "A complicated mechanism, the heart is a muscular pump composed of four chambers and their incoming and outgoing blood vessels."

In writing for those who are only vaguely acquainted with your topic, you must avoid technical terms, or define those that are essential. You can judge fairly accurately which terms must be avoided and which explained by recalling how much *you* knew before you began to do research on the topic. It is also important to avoid offending readers with a tone of Dick-and-Jane simplicity. Because nearly everyone knows that the heart is a complicated mechanism, such information should be given in a sentence that says much more.

Despite the differences, the paragraphs on the heart are alike in one important respect: They inform and explain soberly. Obviously, only those who have a deep interest in reading about the heart and those who must gather information about it for a purpose would be likely to read much writing on it presented in the style of either paragraph. Because they have an interest or a purpose, such readers are likely to prefer this style of straightforward, no-frills informing and explaining.

DEVELOPING AND FLAVORING EXPOSITION

There are six methods of developing a topic: identification, definition, classification, illustration, comparison and contrast, and analysis.

Identification is, of course, the simple placement of something or someone in a context: "Derek Bok is president of Harvard," or more fully, "Derek Bok, who was once dean of the Law School, is president of Harvard."

Definition sets limits of meaning, as is suggested by the two Latin words that make it up: *de* means "with relation to"; *finis* means "limit." One can define in the dictionary sense, but good writers seldom use such definitions. Writing is usually more effective when we define more imaginatively, as George Steiner does in this definition:

> A gentleman is one who cultivates disadvantage. He will not positively pursue it. But he takes little prudential or evasive action when it comes. There is laziness in your true gentleman, a streak of recumbency. But also fastidiousness: the dividends of the world—honors, power, earned fortune —come greasy. A man may win the game but stay grimy to his elbows. There is something about defeat, material setback, even personal betrayal by those one trusted that leaves one clean. At its purest, gentility is dated. It goes, perhaps unfairly, with camel's-hair coats and shooting sticks, with talc and loyal setters. The entire code was a feature of England before 1914, when caste was firm and private incomes were adequate to the many small defeats, impracticalities, covert ostentations, and boneheadednesses that made up a gentleman's non-career. Both the men and the manner were largely wiped out in the muck of world war. This was indeed the supreme imposition, the disadvantage least to be flinched from. But now and again the sandy mustaches, the pale, astonished eyes of the true gents still haunt the imagination.

Classification, as the word implies, means putting things in classes. Objects, animals, experiences—we classify everything without realizing that we are engaged in a formal process. Glimpsing a horse, we assign it to the appropriate classification: an animal whose qualities and characteristics we recognize. In expository writing, classifying is more studied and formal, but hardly ever as formal as a zoologist subdividing the animal kingdom: subkingdom, phylum, subphylum, class, order, suborder, superfamily, family, genus, and species. Instead, we usually touch on characteristics. The following paragraph is by the late H. L. Mencken, who was notable for classifying acidly:

> The average American judge, as everyone knows, is a mere rabbinical automaton, with no more give and take in his mind than you will find in the mind of a terrier watching a rathole. He converts the law into a series of rubber-stamps, and brings them down upon the scalped skulls of the just and unjust alike. The alternative to him, as commonly conceived, is quite as bad—an uplifter in a black robe, eagerly gulping every new brand of Peruna that comes out, and converting his pulpit into a sort of soap-box.

Illustration is the method of explaining with an example. In speaking and in writing we illustrate naturally—every time we use "for example" and "for instance." We need not use those words; in fact, when a writer generalizes, then offers an illustration immediately, "for example" or "for instance" usually wastes words. In the following paragraph, Vance Packard begins with a general statement, then illustrates:

> Roadside desecration takes form other than billboards. In the attractive rolling country near Vacaville, California, motorists are confronted with the question "WHERE'S HARVEY'S?" spelled out in thirty-foot-high letters. A few hundred yards down the road you learn the answer from another great sign blocked out on the verdant hillside: Harvey's is on Highway 50, near Lake Tahoe. It has apparently not dawned upon those responsible that these signs are atrocities in an otherwise beautiful region. Or to cite another example, a factory outside the pleasant rustic village of Monson, Massachusetts, is crowned by a vastly enlarged toilet seat. The display features this slogan: "Best Seat in the House."

Comparison and contrast calls for setting one item beside another to show likenesses and differences. The most common approaches are:

1   To present one item fully, then the other, referring throughout to points of likeness or difference or both. This is usually the best approach when the points are large-scale.
2   To present a part of one item and then a corresponding part of the other, gradually covering all the relevant parts. This is usually best for comparing and contrasting many details.
3   To present one item in full, then cover the second by referring to each of its parts in relation to the parts of the first item.

We can mix these approaches, of course, and perhaps we do mix them as often as not. In the following passage, the educator Harold Taylor contrasts two ways of reading books:

Schools and colleges . . . empty books of their true meaning, and addict their students to habits of thought that often last for the rest of their lives. Everything must be reduced to a summary, ideas are topic sentences, to read is to prepare for a distant test. This is why so many people do not know how to read. They have been taught to turn books into abstractions.

This goes against everything we know about what it means to read a book in real life, that is to say, which is uncorrupted by educational purpose. There is only one way to read a book, to give yourself up to it, alone, without instruction as to what you should be finding in it, without the necessity of making it into a series of points, but enjoying it, coming to know in personal terms what is in the mind of the writer. Only after that should there be discussion, criticism, comment by educators. Otherwise education becomes too much like another kind of real life, the kind in which nobody reads the book, everyone reads the reviews, and everyone talks as if he knew the book.

Analysis is the method of taking something apart to examine the parts or the whole structure. Here Sir James Jeans analyzes the constituents of sunlight to support his thesis that the sky is blue because the short blue light waves are diffused, unlike the long red ones:

Thus the different constituents of sunlight are treated in different ways as they struggle through the earth's atmosphere. A wave of blue light may be scattered by a dust particle, and turned out of its course. After a time a second dust particle again turns it out of its course, and so on, until finally it enters our eyes by a path as zigzag as that of a flash of lightning. Consequently the blue waves of the sunlight enter our eyes from all directions. And that is why the sky looks blue.

Here Loren Eiseley, in his famous book *The Immense Journey,* analyzes the increase of food sources as the earth developed:

That food came from three sources, all produced by the reproductive system of the flowering plants. There were the tantalizing nectars and pollens intended to draw insects for pollenizing purposes. . . . There were the juicy and enticing fruits to attract larger animals, and in which tough-coated seeds were concealed, as in the tomato, for example. Then, as if this were not enough, there was the food in the actual seed itself, the food intended to nourish the embryo. All over the world, like hot corn in a popper, these incredible elaborations of the flowering plants kept exploding.

Few pieces of expository writing use all six methods, but most exposition uses more than one, sometimes mixing the methods so that one merges into another.

Using these methods in exposition presented in precise words and concise sentences pleases readers who have a natural interest in your topic. You must do more to attract readers who have only a small interest. Think of the methods of exposition and think of precision and conciseness as the ingredients of a bland meal. Then think of the techniques sketched in Chapters 3 and 4 as flavors that will make it more enticing.

The following piece shows how a writer can develop exposition and add flavors that will attract readers who have only a marginal interest. Read the exposition straight through first. Then go back and read the comments in the left column, which explains how the topic was developed and how the writer (a student) added flavor:

COMMENTS

Beginning with a question is often effective—provided the question is written so interestingly (as this one is) that readers will not answer negatively. Note that this invites readers into the topic; the writer does not make an automatic assumption that they will be interested.

The writer is not yet focusing on the topic. This introduction (or lead) continues to invite readers to consider the broadest aspects.

Now the writer is defining the topic she will explain. Only the central word pheromones *is not known to most readers; the writer is careful not to use other technical terms.*

Note how deftly the writer uses history. She merely touches on it to provide readers with an overview. Her topic is not the history and development of scientific knowledge about pheromones; it is what scientists know now.

EXPOSITION

Have you ever wondered about that almost instant, electric attraction sometimes felt between men and women? There is increasing scientific evidence that there may be more going on than meets the eye. In fact, it's what meets the nose that researchers are looking at.

Everyone is familiar with the uncanny ability of a male dog to scent out a female in heat: even when the female is kept out of reach, the odoriferous news somehow spreads around. These sense cues, called pheromones, are chemical in nature and are perceived through the nose. Technically defined as "a substance secreted by an animal that affects the behavior of other animals of the same species," pheromones can be thought of as highly specific odors or a kind of airborne hormone.

Though observations of the dog-in-heat type have been noted for years, scientific interest in pheromones didn't begin in earnest until the late 1950's. The new era started with findings like the pheromonally induced pregnancy block in mice. If a newly impregnated female mouse is exposed to the odor of a strange male—a new man in town —her pregnancy is blocked, or ter-

COMMENTS

EXPOSITION

minated, and she becomes quickly receptive again, presumably to facilitate impregnation by the interloper. Since then, evidence has been piling up: more about mice and other mammals including rabbits, gerbils, sheep, and more; as well as much information about insects, including ants, who, it seems, mark their trails by pheromones.

Because this is not expository writing about research methods, the writer does not examine in detail how the research was conducted. She focuses on the findings. Then she signals readers that she will discuss the relevance to humans. Note the order in which she presents the findings: first, dogs and mice; then, in a compressed summary, other animals and insects, then animals that are closer to the human level. The story is developed in a way that assures increasing interest.

What does all this evidence about mice and cockroaches have to do with people? Not much, most scientists thought, until recently. New studies closer to the human level were done on Rhesus monkeys: British researchers proved the existence of and identified a sex attractant pheromone secreted by the female. One landmark study that braved the frontier between man and animal was done by a psychologist at Harvard University, Dr. Martha McClintock.

For most readers, this introduces the most interesting part—and the main body of the piece—because it treats human life.

She studied the menstrual cycles of college women living together in a dormitory and found that during a year the periods of women who spent the most time together became synchronized. Women who listed each other as close friends tended to have their periods about the same time during the months after an initial adjustment of several months. McClintock asserts that this is not unusual. Many women have noticed that their periods come at the same time as roommates, friends, mothers or other females they spend much time with.

Here the writer is making it clear that the study deserves to be taken seriously. It was not haphazard. In reporting on such research in a scholarly journal, the researcher must spell out in detail exactly how the study was controlled. The details usually cover several pages. In a theme such as this,

What is especially interesting about the McClintock study is that she carefully checked and controlled for other factors such as similar diet, life-style or stress patterns; knowledge of when the friend's period occurred; differing exposure to light (female monkeys at the equator are hypothesized to be attuned

COMMENTS

however, the writer need only assure her readers that the study she cites was carefully controlled so readers will know how much trust to place in the findings.

Only in these sentences does the writer use words that have a technical sound—hypothesized, maturational, and synchronization—and these words are used by so many specialists in so many kinds of writing that most readers know what they mean.

Although the writer is referring again to the experiments with mice, she has not deserted the human scene. Instead, the experiments are related to findings about humans, which keeps the focus on humans.

Look back at the beginnings of each paragraph, starting with the second. Note that each is tied to the one it succeeds. The paragraphs seem to grow out of one another, thus moving readers smoothly from point to point.

In writing that is designed to prove a case, it is often valuable to cite study after study of the same kind: This research proves the point, that one supports it, and so on. But in expository writing, one seeks primarily to inform and explain. To write here of another study of exactly the same kind would bore readers and make one point over and over again. Instead the writer cites

EXPOSITION

to the moon because of the light-dark patterns involved); maturational level —all of which have been suggested as possible explanations for the synchronization. She concluded that pheromones could well be responsible. At an animal level, experiments have shown the same synchronizing effect in female mice housed together.

She also discovered that the girls who spent more time with boys had more frequent and regular periods. This effect is also seen in mice: females caged together stop their cycles until a male is introduced, or a male scent is wafted their way. Then they all start up at once.

In relation to the effects of hormones, a study done with women on birth control pills also points to the possible existence of pheromones in humans. Researchers found that women on the pill were more likely to report that their husbands wanted intercourse during the luteal, or after-ovulation phase of their menstrual cycles than women not using the pill. The experimenters suggested that perhaps the women on the pill exuded a different odor or pheromone because of their different hormonal state. In the natural cycle, the hormone progesterone is produced by the ovaries after ovulation: women on birth control pills don't have this progesterone.

Another one of the few human studies was done by French biologist J. Le Magnen. He found that women varied tremendously in their ability to smell exaltolide, a synthetic substance used commercially in producing perfume. When they were ovulating, the women could smell the musk-like odor, which is similar in its chemical structure to sex hormones, at very slight concentra-

COMMENTS

another study of humans that adds to what she has already presented, and thus adds a level of explanation.

Having offered the findings of individual researchers, the writer moves to related information that has been proved by so many studies that it is generally accepted. Although the writer colors in this large picture with broad strokes, note that she has not yielded to the temptation to overwrite. She presents the information simply.

Here and elsewhere there are qualifying words: possible, *and in the next sentence,* probably. *Although the writer is not reporting in the specialist's jargon, she has adopted the specialist's habit of qualifying so that she will not state more than the findings will support.*

Again, the writer refers to research about other living things, but she keeps the focus on humans by starting and ending the paragraph with references to human life.

EXPOSITION

tions. When they were menstruating, much more was required before they detected the odor. Men and young girls were insensitive to the scent until they were given injections of estrogen, a female hormone. These cyclic differences in olfactory sensitivity may be linked to a human chemical communications system. Pheromones which provided information about the internal hormonal state would increase reproductive effectiveness by signaling the onset of fertile periods.

Biologists have long been aware of the correspondence between the nose and the sex organs. For example, the mucus membranes in the nose have erectile properties like the penis and clitoris. During sexual excitement and ovulation in the female, there is swelling of the nasal passages and a heightened sense of smell. In some male animals, castration causes decay of the nasal structures. Also, boys who are born without the ability to smell fail to mature sexually. All of this points to a nasal-genital linkage and the possible importance of chemical signals perceived through the sense of smell.

Pheromones are probably not often recognized as odors by humans, but take effect below the level of consciousness. Very minute amounts of pheromonal substance are sufficient to provoke a reaction. Some substances operate at the level of molecules, not milligrams. One female silkworm moth, for example, has enough sex attractant, if distributed efficiently, to excite one billion male moths. Though some animals have special glands for pheromone secretion, human pheromones are thought to be secreted to some degree in the pubic area, but mainly from under the arm.

COMMENTS

Without saying flatly, "Now I will consider what else could be done to investigate further," the writer is saying, gracefully, that she is turning to that aspect of the topic. Note especially that "These chemical signals" makes a smooth transition by relating this paragraph to the paragraph preceding it.

Note how deftly the writer defines "gas chromatography." Instead of devoting a sentence to the meaning of the term, which might insult those who know the meaning and make one who does not know the meaning feel the self-consciousness of one who must read a primer, the writer inserts the definition in a sentence that carries other information. Those who know the term can read the definition without bothering to focus on it, the others learn it without self-consciousness.

Just as the writer has used qualifying words such as "possibly" and "probably" so as not to mislead, here she makes it clear that readers should not assume that pheromones are necessarily as powerful in human life as some of the findings suggest.

The main body is already complete. Here the writer begins to develop a conclusion that, like the introduction,

EXPOSITION

These chemical signals are fruitful and fascinating topics for further research. An aggression-releasing pheromone is being analyzed in experiments with male mice, and some scientists have hypothesized the existence of a comparable pheromone in humans—a substance which makes a male scenting it attack. In line with this theory is the evidence which shows greater aggression in animals with higher levels of male hormone, or testosterone, in their blood.

Dr. Ray Clayton, a biochemist, says he has speculated about the possibilities of pheromones in humans. If there is an aggression-releasing pheromone, there might be a "maternal" one as the opposite—a signal which says, "I'm receptive, be nice to me."

Hypothesizing about the future of phermonal research, Dr. Alex Comfort, a noted British biologist and zoologist, suggested that pheromones might be used for birth control. With new scientific techniques such as gas chromatography—a method for determining the chemical structure of a substance—pheromones could be isolated and used as a controlling factor in reproductive functions.

The possibilities raised by the existence of human pheromones should be considered with some reservations: much or most human behavior, unlike that of animals, is determined by learning. Many scientists argue that although pheromones might once have been important in humans, they no longer really function to determine behavior.

These theories and recent findings, however, raise some questions about the way we deodorize and perfume

COMMENTS	EXPOSITION

offers a broad view designed to interest readers. She does not neatly summarize what she has explained—the explanation is clear and substantial enough to stand alone. Instead, she presents additional information closely related to the topic to help provide a satisfying reading experience.

ourselves. Americans are especially eager to rid themselves of any odor. Millions of dollars are spent on deodorants—underarm, foot, "intimate" —and millions more on perfumes. This is interesting when you realize for example that musk—one of the more popular new scents—is actually a scent secreted by animals as a sex attractant (musk means testicle in Sanskrit). In fact, musk closely resembles in structure the sex attractant or pheromone we might exude ourselves if we were not so carefully de-scented.

Had the writer presented the introduction or the main body in dry, plodding phrases and sentences, this last paragraph would be out of tune. But the tone of the whole is informal, which enables the writer to end on a light note that might otherwise seem flippant.

Definite conclusions as to the existence, type, and effect of human pheromones will be made only after many long and detailed scientific studies. But until we know a lot more, speculation is fun. Maybe that new man you met last night who seemed so sexy has a lot more going for him than his looks. . . . Or then again, the next time you forget your deodorant, don't panic. You may smell a lot better than you think you do.

Because the writer was careful to avoid technical terms and to use words precisely, we can understand her explanation. Because she wrote concisely, we did not have to wade through forty-word sentences to extract twenty words' worth of meaning. Although the piece is not as heavily flavored as descriptive writing—the purpose, after all, is to inform and explain—she did much more to attract readers than did either of the writers of the paragraphs on the heart.

You may argue, however, that the piece is interesting primarily because writing about pheromones is actually writing about sex—and many readers are interested in *that*. Can you add flavor to the exposition of a less appealing topic—even a dull topic?

The following piece is about linguistics, the nature and structure of human speech, which many students consider dull. It is different from the one on pheromones in two important respects: Most of it is devoted to defining the topic, and most of it is written chronologically. It is like the piece on pheromones in that the writer seeks to attract many readers, not just those who have a natural interest in the topic. Again, read the piece straight through first, then read the comments:

<table>
<tr><td>*COMMENTS*</td><td>EXPOSITION</td></tr>
</table>

Like the introductory paragraph that begins with a question, the anecdote introduction is often quite effective. But the anecdote cannot be merely interesting. It must provide a keynote for the rest of the piece. The writer who strains to make an anecdote fit the topic should begin with something else.

A black woman, intending to place a long distance telephone call, lifts her receiver and dials the operator. "Information," says a voice.

"Hey," says the caller, laughing softly.

"Hey," responds the operator, also chuckling.

When readers reach the second sentence in this paragraph, they become aware that the little story at the beginning is in tune with what follows.

The two women have exchanged a greeting and mutual recognition that they are soul sisters. On the basis of a single word, each has determined that the other is black.

This story, related by Shirley Lewis, a black graduate student, exemplifies what Mrs. Lewis calls a "very common phenomenon" among blacks. Something about the speech of many black Americans, she says, makes it different from the speech of whites. If this "something" puzzles Mrs. Lewis and others, it intrigues linguists, who are tackling with vigor the study of a dialect that has only recently gained recognition in this country—Black English.

By the end of this paragraph, the topic has been set forth—and much more interestingly than if the writer had begun: "There is a phenomenon known as 'Black English' that interests some linguists."

When the federally funded Project Head Start was instituted in 1966 as an educational program for culturally disadvantaged preschoolers, one of the recurrent themes was the need for helping black children overcome their "verbal deficit." Poor children were believed to be impoverished in communicative skills. Educators rationalized that poor people, mostly blacks, simply do not use verbal communication to the extent that middle-class people do, and that what ghetto children need is more verbal practice.

Here the writer is doing more than informing readers. She is sketching the intellectual conflict that has developed over Black English. Because conflict of all kinds attracts readers, it is too often contrived by writers. Clearly, though, this writer is not contriving conflict.

This information is not essential; the writer could have avoided mention-

Head Start classes placed heavy emphasis on forcing black children to

COMMENTS

ing Head Start and discussed immediately the difference between Black English and conventional English. But this groundwork—especially the examples of Black English in this paragraph—helps readers understand what Black English is. Like many complex terms, "Black English" does not lend itself easily to a short, simple definition. Most of this piece is a definition— one that promotes understanding in a way that a short definition could not.

Quotations by authorities are usually essential in this kind of writing. A writer can paraphrase, and should. But to present everything in paraphrase is to cause some readers to wonder: Is that true? Is that really what the authority said? Quotations establish confidence (even, in some cases, inaccurate quotations and quotations taken out of context).

The long passage that began with

EXPOSITION

eradicate "errors" like double negatives and the use of *dis* and *dey* for *this* and *they* from their speech and to replace such usages with "proper" English. If black children's speech differed from that of their white peers, teachers reasoned, it was only because they hadn't been exposed to enough good English.

This approach raised a furor among black leaders, who resented implications that blacks were somehow verbally inferior, and protested that things were not that simple. Their dissent led to a closer look at the language of ghetto children by linguists in the late Sixties. Many found what blacks had been saying all along; the language used is not merely a series of errors in "good" English, but a wholly different dialect with a complex grammatical structure and a strict set of pronunciation rules of its own. Black children learning standard English are in fact becoming bi-dialectal, linguists said. Teachers should be learning Black English, not castigating it, if they are to teach ghetto children effectively. They should master the dialect and use techniques employed by those who teach English as a second language; these methods have proved successful for children faced with a language—or dialect—barrier.

"The notion that black children are verbally deficient because of a lack of practice is nonsense," says linguist Joseph Politzer. "Speaking ability is valued very highly in the black community. If anything, black children have a speaking advantage over whites."

When linguists feverishly began to study the roots and structure of this "new" American dialect spoken in the black community, they immediately

COMMENTS	EXPOSITION

the first paragraph devoted to Head Start and extends through the next paragraph is a story. *In effect, the writer is using a form of narration to make her exposition effective.*

found that Black English is not new at all. It can be traced to the Sixteenth Century, when the English traders first ventured to the West African Coast. Most theorists hold that an examination of the pidgin languages—languages that develop for emergency communication by speakers of two different languages—between African speakers and the Portuguese, Dutch, French, and English traders all have several features in common. Most of these features were borrowed from the African languages.

After the first English settlement was formed in 1618 along the Gold Coast in Africa, an English-African pidgin developed and was exported to the New World. This language, which was carried over to later generations (or creolized, in linguistic terms), is called Gullah and is spoken today in Jamaica, the Caribbean and on several small islands off the coast of Georgia and the Carolinas. Gullah is an obvious combination of the West African languages and English.

Linguists argue the extent to which Black English now spoken in the United States has African features, and whether Gullah is a relic of the language once spoken by black slaves in the South. Some point to the fact that all the African pidgins—English, French, Dutch, and Portuguese—have a common structure and differ only in vocabulary. They argue that the features these pidgins share are part of the West African languages, and contend that this proves the African origin of Gullah and of Black English.

They have a powerful case. For example, all the pidgins lack inflection for person, as do the West African languages; *He go* replaces *He goes* in all of them. And all the languages omit

The examples the writer uses so often serve two purposes. They develop the definition in a way that enables readers to understand fully what Black

COMMENTS

English is and they enhance reader interest (nearly all apt examples do).

Like the writer of the piece on pheromones, this writer understands the value of providing a simple definition in a sentence that carries other information. If she had devoted a sentence to the definition of "decreolized," this passage would have taken on a primer quality.

Readers who have only a casual interest in Black English can easily skip this table. For those who want to get at the roots, the table is available for study. If the writer had placed this kind of information in the text instead of in a table, readers would have had to slow their pace to understand. Many readers who have only a casual interest might stop reading.

EXPOSITION

forms of the verb *to be* before adjectives; *He sick* is used instead of *He is sick.*

Particularly interesting is the necessity in all of the pidgins of distinguishing between *you* singular and *you* plural, a variance that leads to the English form *you-all.* Genteel white Southern speakers may well be using a form borrowed from black Africa.

The usages *okay, uh-huh* for yes and *uh-uh* for no, common in several languages, also have been traced to West African origins.

The pidgin language of the slaves in the South was slowly decreolized—brought closer to English—primarily by house slaves who worked close to English speakers. But the language retained much of its African influence. The product, today's Black English, has been examined by linguists, who have identified some twenty features that appear nearly universal among Black Americans, although there are certainly blacks who speak only standard English. The features seem to be general rules for Black English, although every feature appears in some other American dialect. Black English and Standard English contrast in these ways, among others:

STANDARD ENGLISH	BLACK ENGLISH
final consonant cluster pronounced costs, tests, walks	final consonant cluster simplified cosses, tesses, walk
regular past tense He walked I have started	irregular past tense He walk I done started, I been started

COMMENTS	EXPOSITION	
	third person marker	no third person marker
	He speaks	He speak
	He does	He do
	He is	He be
But the table must be placed here rather than at an earlier point. The earlier explanations enable readers to understand the table.	regular future tense	varied future tense
	I will go	I munna go,
	He'll miss you	I ma go,
		He miss you
Information in tables saves space. To make complete and understandable sentences of all the facts in the table might have consumed three times the space of the table. But because tables must be studied, *they should be used sparingly.*	Verb form *be*	deletion of verb *be*
	Fred is mad	Fred mad
	single negation	multiple negation
	Nobody knows anything	Nobody knows nothing
		Nobody don't know nothing
	possessive suffix	no possessive suffix
	Mary's book	Mary book
	distinct morphological plural	no distinct morphological plural
	two books	two book
	simple subject	pronominal apposition
	Ed is nice	Ed, he nice

This passage solves a problem in organization. In the paragraph above that begins "Particularly interesting" (the third paragraph up from the table), the writer mentions "you-all," which is used often by Southerners. Here, too, the writer focuses on the influence of Black English on Southern speech. An important principle in writing is to place comments on each part of the topic together. Obviously, scattering many points that treat one part of the topic confuses readers. Certainly the comment on "you-all" could have

Black English with its African influence has been absorbed to a great degree into the speech of some white Americans, especially in the South. Politzer cites examples in which Southern students going to Northern colleges were warned by their advisers to visit landlords in person, rather than telephoning, because they might otherwise be denied housing.

Linguist Raven McDavid cites experiments in Chicago in which middle-class Westerners consistently identified the voice of an educated urban white

COMMENTS

been placed in this section. But leaving "you-all" where it is makes this writing more orderly. That is because the comment on "you-all" is not so much about Southern speech as it is about the necessity to distinguish between "you" singular and "you" plural in pidgins.

Most writers are tempted in such cases to refer again to the point covered earlier. Such references can sometimes be written gracefully, but must usually be limited to a phrase or a clause, because an entire sentence calls attention to itself and points up the duplication. To introduce duplication with such words as "As noted earlier" ordinarily interrupts the flow of the writing.

Again, an example which is sometimes, as here, in the form of an anecdote, usually makes a point specifically in a way that enhances reader interest.

The writer wisely left this discussion to a point late in the piece. When readers are lured with devices such as anecdotes, they read a discussion with greater interest than if it had been

EXPOSITION

Southerner as that of an uneducated rural black, and many identified as Negro the voice of an educated white Chicagoan. McDavid says James Marchand, a middle-Tennesseean on the Cornell faculty, must carefully identify himself on the telephone as Professor Marchand if he wants a garageman to come and pick up his car.

Politzer says blacks in tests have regularly identified black speakers with more accuracy than whites, and Mrs. Lewis says that many blacks find the inability to hear differences between black and white speech both incredible and hilarious. Even without considering the twenty features that supposedly separate Black English from the standard variety, she says, Black English is markedly distinct to her. The telephone operator in her story, for instance, used none of the twenty features in the word "Information," yet the caller recognized her speech as "black."

How? By intonation, theorize some linguists; they maintain that Black English is spoken on three pitch levels, like many African languages, and English has four pitch levels.

Another black student, Mavis Taylor, says she had great difficulty learning French from a white teacher, but learned it easily when she lived in Africa with black French speakers. This might be explained, Politzer says, by proposing that the black French speakers used intonation levels that Mrs. Taylor could more easily imitate.

The study of intonation, however, is mostly speculation. Unlike grammatical and pronunciation traits, pitch is difficult to demonstrate and varies greatly among individuals. It is gram-

COMMENTS

placed at or near the beginning. To begin this theme with, "Sociolinguistic research shows that the systematic difference between Black and standard English is great enough to cause people to be clearly marked socially" would be to repel all readers except those who have a strong interest in the topic. Here, however, discussion is in order. Readers who have reached this point have probably developed an interest in the topic.

Although this passage discusses teaching methods, it is not designed to instruct. Expository writing that is designed to instruct is much more detailed; much of it describes methods step by step. Why, then, does the writer devote a fairly long passage to teaching methods? The answer is that, like the other passages, this is designed to provide a different perspective on Black English. To read of methods that have been adapted from methods developed for another purpose enables readers to approach the topic from another angle.

EXPOSITION

matical variance that causes problems for black school children. Sociolinguistic research shows that the systematic difference between Black and standard English is great enough to cause people to be clearly marked socially. Roger Shuy has demonstrated that the distinction is great enough to be a clear handicap to employment of blacks. Evidence shows that the difference affects the acquisition of reading skills. Thus educators, both black and white, have begun to develop new methods for teaching children who speak Black English.

The most popular method, developed by Irwin Feigenbaum, uses foreign language methodology to teach standard English by helping the child hear and see the differences between standard English and his own dialect. For example, using this method, a teacher might present pairs of words or sentences like *masks, masses* and *He work hard, He works hard,* and have the students say whether they are the same or different. The concept of appropriateness is stressed in this method; a teacher might present a list of sentences, and the class responds with "street" or "class" to tell where such usages as *She prefer movies* or *Robert plays guard* might be appropriate.

This method requires either that the teacher be a native speaker of Black English or that he at least become familiar with its rules and grammatical structures. He must be well-versed because, according to Politzer, it is probably more difficult both to teach and to learn standard English for a Black English speaker than Spanish or some other language, because the two are so similar that they are easily confused.

COMMENTS

Although the anecdote at the beginning may have made this piece seem as light in tone as the one on pheromones, this is clearly a more analytic examination. The writer wisely ends on a serious note.

In keeping with the roughly chronological structure—near the beginning the writer traces the history of Black English, then moves to the present— the piece ends with a note on the future. Readers are not likely to be conscious that they have covered past, present, and future in order—the piece is not obviously chronological—but they are nonetheless affected favorably by the orderly movement through time.

EXPOSITION

Educators have a long way to go before speakers of Black English will be educated on an equal footing with white standard English speakers, says linguist William Stewart, but they are finally at least beginning. "For the teacher," he says, "use of the different language patterns by blacks can no longer be ascribed to greater carelessness, laziness, or stupidity on the part of Negroes, but rather these patterns will be treated for what they really are —language patterns which have been in existence for generations and which their present users have acquired, for parent and peer, through a perfectly normal kind of language-learning process."

Like the piece on pheromones, this one has only a little flavor: the purpose is to inform and explain. Clarity comes first.

We do not suddenly leave clarity behind as we go on to consider the other forms of discourse. But we do begin in the next chapter to analyze the forms of discourse that rely much more heavily on the techniques that give writing its color and life. We also begin to consider writing that we are much more likely to think of as demanding the skill of the literary artist.

PROJECTS

1   Read again the six methods of exposition outlined in this chapter and study the piece on pheromones to determine how many of the methods the writer used. Do not assume that they will be easy to find. A good writer focuses on his topic and thinks of the best way to present it, seldom thinking of using a method. Write a short analysis of the piece on pheromones to point to the methods you find. End with a paragraph that considers whether the writer could have improved the piece by using an additional method.

2   Look back at Chapter 2 for the description of the plain style. Study the pieces on pheromones and Black English for evidence that the writers use the plain style or do not. Write several paragraphs citing the evidence.

3   Practice explanation by writing several paragraphs in the form of instruc-

tions for driving a car. Write as though you were teaching a college student who has often been a passenger but has never learned to drive.

4 Imagine that you have been given this assignment by the editor of the student newspaper: Cover a speech made on the campus, reporting its highlights in 500 to 700 words. Do it.

5 Choose from a textbook used in any course you are taking an important topic that you can explore in interviews and in other reading. Write a 1,000-word essay that you think will interest other students.

Writing to Depict: Description

My task is to make you hear, to make you feel—it is, before all, to make you see.—JOSEPH CONRAD

6 If you are like many other readers, the term "descriptive writing" probably makes you think of a sentence such as this one from *In Cold Blood* by Truman Capote: "Though mud abounded underfoot, the sun, so long shrouded by snow and cloud, seemed an object freshly made, and the trees were lightly veiled in a haze of virginal green." You may also think of a sentence describing a person, such as this one from a story titled "Hilda" by George Orwell: "She was a small, slim, rather timid girl, with dark hair, beautiful movements and—because of having very large eyes—a distinct resemblance to a hare."

Nearly everyone is so accustomed to such simple uses of description that you may not think of this paragraph from a student's profile of a teacher as descriptive writing:

> He uses many dramatic techniques. He speaks with a series of intonations and accents that seem to underline the student's notes right in the notebook. As he speaks, his hands follow appropriately: extended out front, stopping and then flowing rhythmically as though he were conducting an orchestra. When an idea is extremely important, he stands like a pointer, one foot behind on its toes, an arm extended to the front while the other is kept close to his body.

If you had read the *New York Times* story by Charlotte Curtis about a party at which the Museum of Modern Art celebrated its reopening, you probably would not have thought of the numbers she used as descriptive writing. She reported that the Museum served "80 cases of champagne—which amounted to 960 bottles, or 7,680 three-ounce drinks—to five thousand guests."

METHODS OF DESCRIBING: TELLING AND SHOWING

All these are examples of descriptive writing because all enable readers to see. The first three use the visual words and phrases analyzed in Chapter 4. The sentences by Capote and Orwell obviously enable us to see. But such descriptions are so common that we may be inclined to think of them only as descriptive writing. Consider, though, how vividly we can see the teacher. And although numbers are usually presented to inform and seem not to describe as well, imaginative writers use them to create strong images. Barbara Tuchman, who won the Pulitzer Price for history, wrote of Charlotte Curtis's report: "Somehow through this detail the Museum's party at once becomes alive; a fashionable New York occasion. One sees the crush, the women eyeing each other's clothes, the exchange of greetings, and feels the gratifying sense of elegance and importance—even if, at one and a half drinks per person, it was not on an exactly riotous scale."

The examples quoted above illustrate two kinds of description: *static showing* and *action showing*. In the sentences by Capote and Orwell, phrases such as "the trees were lightly veiled" and "a distinct resemblance to a hare" are static. They enable us to see (if a bit vaguely) because of their visual qualities. Static showing can create a sharp image, as in this sentence by William Faulkner: "Her eyes, lost in the fatty ridges of her face, looked like two small pieces of coal pressed into a lump of dough."

However deftly this kind of description creates images, we are likely to write too much of it. Truman Capote uses such descriptions so often that they sometimes become irritating. Stanley Kauffmann, a noted literary critic, wrote that the descriptive passages in Capote's *In Cold Blood* were "Reddiwhip writing—goo that gushes out under the force of compressed air." Quoting the last sentence of the book, "Then, starting home, he walked toward the trees, and under them, leaving behind him the big sky and the whisper of wind voices in the wind-bent wheat," Kauffmann sneered, "Presumably, he decided not to take the sky and the wind voices with him."

Action showing is represented by the student's description of the teacher: ". . . his hands follow appropriately: extended out front, stopping and then flowing rhythmically as though he were conducting an orchestra. When an idea is extremely important, he stands like a pointer, one foot behind on its toes, an arm extended. . . ." In effect, the writer has taken the readers to the classroom and shown them the teacher.

If the student had written only the first sentence of the paragraph quoted ("He uses many dramatic techniques") without showing how the teacher lectures dramatically, that would have been a third kind of description, *telling,* which is weaker than either static showing or action showing. Telling description does not contain visual words. The sentence by Orwell began with telling—"a small, slim, rather timid girl"—and became showing description only when it reached "a distinct resemblance to a hare."

(Charlotte Curtis's artistic use of numbers to describe probably should be classified as static showing, but the technique makes the example difficult to classify. By using one number after another in a single sentence that is surrounded by descriptive sentences, she gave the numbers themselves unusual descriptive power. Ordinarily, numbers are only technical description and are more appropriately classed as expository writing because they inform and help explain rather than create images.)

Which method of describing is better, telling, static showing, or action showing? Many novelists and New Journalists (whose methods are described in the next chapter) work hours and sometimes day to fashion a single scene of action showing. Some of them hardly ever use telling description because both static showing and action showing are more likely to affect readers. They are usually most proud of action showing, which requires more work.

The appropriate question, however, is not which of the three is better but when should we use each. All may be appropriate in different writing situations. Minor figures and scenes might occasionally be presented in telling description. It could be appropriate simply to mention "a beautiful woman"—telling description—if the focus is elsewhere. More often, minor figures and scenes are worth static showing. To give them the attention that action showing requires might make them seem as important as major figures and scenes. The major ones usually demand the attention of action showing, often with touches of static showing.

In some cases, descriptions of major characters do not call for action showing. Static showing is most useful for appearances, action showing for activity. Imagine that the teacher whose dramatic gestures are shown in the paragraph above dresses shabbily. In addition to showing him in action, the writer might have described him in the words a *Newsweek* reporter used in writing that Peter Falk, the actor, has "the wardrobe of a flood victim."

In writing descriptions of appearances or actions, you should use visual words. Avoid telling descriptions such as "He is handsome" and "The game was exciting." To describe the handsome man, use the kind of static showing illustrated by the Capote and Orwell sentences and by the William Faulkner sentence quoted earlier ("Her eyes, lost in the fatty ridges of her face, looked like two small pieces of coal pressed into a lump of dough"). To describe the exciting game, show what happened by sketching it in some detail, trying always to help your readers *see*.

PROBLEMS IN DESCRIPTION

The chief problem in using static showing or action showing is that you are likely to overwrite, as a student did in writing these paragraphs:

> Mari Kajiwawa glides across the stage with super-human fluidity. The performer's presence penetrates the auditorium like a sharp wind as her liquid, bluish form flows through the languid movements of a dance with the consistency of molten wax. The physical reality of a human body becomes as intangible as a breeze.
>
> Mari's solo provided one highlight of the City Center Dance Theater's opening performance yesterday. As the dancers personified the tragi-comic daydreams of convicts on a chain gang or radiated the unfettered joy of a Southern religious revival, the audience was ensnared in a web of choreographed eloquence and infected by the attitude and commitment with which it was woven.

This description is so self-consciously creative that readers are more aware of the writer than of the dancer. Although it is true that active verbs such as glides, penetrates, radiated, ensnared, and infected make the writing vigorous, they combine with strong adjectives to produce an explosion. Perhaps most readers begin to notice the adjectives when they see *superhuman* in the first sentence, an extravagant word that has been used so often so badly that it now has little power. The second sentence is heavy with adjectives: sharp, liquid, bluish, languid, and molten. The alliteration at the beginning of the second sentence (*p*erformer's *p*resence *p*enetrates) is another bit of word-play. Then image collides with image: The dancer's grace is fluid, her presence like a sharp wind, her movements like molten wax, her body a breeze. Considered singly, all the words and images are apt; considered together, they are chaotic.

The writer of the following piece describes much more effectively. But as the comments indicate, other problems come up near the end:

COMMENTS

The writer uses a few adjectives, but consider especially her choice of verbs: hissed, peeked, stretched, fanned, and merged. Because they are visual, such verbs enable readers to see. She shuns verbs such as is, are, was, and were, which express only existence, and wooden phrases such as there is and there are.

Consider the wise use of two kinds of variation. In the first paragraph, only one sentence, the first, begins subject-verb ("The hickory, ash, and oak still hissed. . . ."). The other sentences are constructed differently. In the second paragraph, the first two sentences and the fourth begin subject-verb, the third provides pleasing variation. The sentences are relatively short in both paragraphs, but note that they are also varied in length as well as structure.

Here action showing is mixed with static showing. Describing a place might seem to call for the latter, but the writer is describing the park in terms of how it is affected by people. Actions are essential; showing them is valuable.

Throughout, the writer lets strong verbs do most of the work of describing, makes certain that the nouns have weight, and wisely limits her use of adjectives and adverbs.

DESCRIPTION

The hickory, ash, and oak still hissed in the fire as the two campers peeked with blinking eyes through the small holes of their mummy bags. Directly above, the redwood trees stretched their limbs upwards and fanned away the clouds with their leafy hands. On all sides the blueness merged with the granite peaks.

Nature can provide the simplest example to follow. The campers contemplated emerging from their warm cocoons, unfolding themselves to the new day, standing as purely and solidly as the peaks silhouetted against the sky. But the dawn had grown too old. The campground had already transformed itself into the setting for the daily rape of Yosemite's majestic calm.

The two campers loosened their sleeping bags and peered disbelievingly beyond their campsite property lines. Overnight a neighborhood of prefab canvas monsters had mushroomed around them. Each plot came complete with a one-car driveway. Underwear hung from clotheslines in the backyards. Next door, Martha's voice bulleted through the tent walls, piercing the serenity of the valley floor. "Harry I'm not going to get up. You make breakfast." The canvas window flap was jerked up by a draw string inside. Harry crawled feet first under the canvas door flap dragging along his butane stove. He fumbled with it for awhile and finally set a match to the burner. Harry was surprisingly quick-witted as he sprayed the can of white foam fire extinguisher over the stove and geyser of flames. When the extinguisher's frothy snout somehow caught fire Harry calmly threw it in the pile of foam and crawled back

COMMENTS

DESCRIPTION

into his tent. The canvas flap dropped over the window screen. Not another sound was heard from Martha and Harry.

Like an earlier description, "the daily rape of Yosemite's majestic calm," this one, "the foul breath of suburbia's early-morning yawn," is imaginative personalization of a park. It is especially good because she writes of the impact of people on a place.

The foul breath of suburbia's early morning yawn invaded nature. The man on another side of the two campers filled his lungs with a satisfied beat on his chest and doubled over in guttural coughing. After recovering he pulled out a lighter and stuck a cigarette in his mouth. Cars turned over and chugged out of their stalls. Families eagerly huddled in the front of the cars to view the beauty of the park. In their trail was a wake of grey pollution and dirty kleenex.

This paragraph and the next would be more effective in a more varied structure. First, consider sentence length. In the first paragraph, the sentence lengths in words are 11–16–13–5. In the second, 12–9–9–12–26. Although the sentence at the end of each paragraph provides variation, most sentences are approximately the same length. In the second paragraph, the sentences are in one kind of structure. The combination makes the reading a bit monotonous. True, the writer continues to use visual verbs well, but in such a structure, even they become somewhat monotonous. Worse, the sameness of sentence length and structure places an extraordinary burden on the verbs and makes them stand out so that the writer seems to be straining for effects rather than using them naturally. And although the writer has not used too many adjectives, they also stand out (especially "sizzling embers" and "soothing rustles") in a way that makes it seem that the writer is trying too hard to produce effects.

The two campers could not recapture the time of nature's dawn. Even as they looked up from their sweltering bags, jets crisscrossed white streaks across the blue. They kicked themselves free of their bags and doused the sizzling embers. Packs strapped to their backs, they made their escape through the redwood pillars. Thin shadows stabbed the sunlight.

The sun rose higher as the two campers climbed the valley's wall. Each pitch took them farther away from the babble. The trees below applauded their progress with soothing rustles. The granite allowed them sure moves as they scaled the lichen-filled face. The afternoon passed for the two campers in the happy serenity of breathing the uncolored air, feeling the hard rock, and hearing the noises of nature.

This last paragraph is an argument that has no place. It is not that a writer can never argue in description. The point is that this writer has already made the argument more subtly—and effectively—in the descriptive passages. Every reader who is capable of being

National parks must meet the threat presented by the invasion of nature "lovers." In some areas only a limited number of campers are allowed entrance. Automobile traffic is restricted. Many roads are narrowed or ripped

COMMENTS	DESCRIPTION

persuaded has already been persuaded before reading this paragraph. In effect, the writer is saying here: This should be your attitude—as though readers could not grasp that for themselves. In short, the paragraph is offensive rather than persuasive.

up. Butane buses provide free transportation. There will always be campers who can escape to the granite peaks. For the preservation of the crowded parks, campers must respect the new restrictions and follow the rules of camping etiquette.

FOCUSING ON A PERSON

The writer of the piece above wisely limited her descriptions of Martha and Harry to their actions that affected the national park. But a sketch of a person (which is called a *profile*) uses quotations to help describe. Most of us describe ourselves, at least in part, by what we say and how we say it. A student whose hobby was collecting beer cans decided to write about the World's Greatest Beer Can Collector, a 59-year-old printer of synagogue bulletins who lived in Hicksville, New York. The student began his theme:

"YA GOTTA COME RIGHT OVAH. YA GOTTA SEE MY COLLECTION."

"Well, you see, Mr. Veselsky. . . ."

"CALL ME JOE. CALL ME JOE."

". . . we're in New York City now, near Triboro Bridge . . ."

". . .and well, sir. . . uh . . . Joe, we've come all the way from California just to see your collection."

"FABALOUS, FABALOUS." The voice had a Bronx accent with a Jimmy Durante delivery. "YA GOTTA SEE IT. I'M NUMBAH ONE. YA CAN'T TALK BEER CANS WITHOUT SEEING JOE VESELSKY'S COLLECTION."

Phoning from a creaking old booth and shouting over the roar from the nearby Triboro Bridge, we had nonetheless heard the introductory exhortations of Joe Veselsky. When we had convinced him that we would indeed be on our way there if he would silence his rushing monologue and give us directions, he chortled happily.

"O.K. BOYS YA SAY YOU'LL BE RIGHT OVAH AND YA SAY YOU'RE NEAR THE TRIBORO BRIDGE SURE I KNOW THAT CORNER EXACKLY AND NOW I LIVE IN HICKSVILLE YA SEE AND IF YOU'LL LISTEN TO ME GOOD I'LL GET YA HERE IN ABOUT 44 NO 48 MINUTES."

Tom took copious notes with a laugh-shaken hand as Joe rattled off a complex set of directions involving: five freeways, including one not to be taken under any circumstances, and one not to be taken "but it wouldn't hurt ya much if ya did"; seven streets to turn onto, whose names Joe spelled out twice each; two streets *not* to turn onto, whose names he spelled out twice each; six red lights, "but they might be green so just keep on goin' "; four landmarks, including the Mid-Island Shopping Center and a Walgreen's; two traffic signals to serve as reference points for turns, including one "No-U-Turn sign; and one key place to make a U turn. Yes, *there.*

Finally, with dramatic pause, the address "Numbah Eight Marie Court, Joe and Florence Veselsky."

The writer went on to describe the trip to Number Eight Marie Court, the house, and Florence Veselsky. Each was given only a few sentences to keep the focus on Joe Veselsky and his collection. There was much more to the description of Veselsky, of course, including his appearance, but the quotations above and the way Veselsky uttered them were an important part of the picture of the man.

In the following piece, a complete profile, the student writer mixed static showing and action showing to sketch the man's appearance and actions and described him further by quoting him. Because this piece is twice as long as the description of the national park, the writer had to solve more and greater problems of organization and transition. Because profiles are brief biographies, which make special demands, the writer had to solve many problems that do not come up in other kinds of writing. The comments indicate how often she solved many of the problems:

COMMENTS

The writer shows almost instantly, beginning to describe the professor's actions in the second sentence. Readers are confronted by the man, they are not just told about him. An even more compelling confrontation would have pictured him at his primary work, lecturing (which the writer presents later), but this picture does have the value of showing him in his office, a place that is central to his life and work. The description of the litter on his desk is almost as important as the description of his actions. Both help to describe the kind of man he is.

This blend of static showing and action showing—a sketch of appearance and action—helps to flesh out the figure and attract readers. He is not

PROFILE

Is history his life? "My wife thinks so," confessed Professor Gordon Wright, raising his pale but shaggy brows above the thin black frames of his glasses and grinning sheepishly as he avoided my eyes.

Swivelling his brown leather chair to the right, parallel to his desk, Professor Wright stretched his long legs, and, bending his left knee, eased into a comfortable position. He resembled Ichabod Crane.

Deliberately entrenched behind his desk, which is littered with clippings of James Reston columns and multicolored Bic pens, he prepared for a barrage of questions which would leave him feeling "psychoanalyzed."

His overgrown hands searched for occupation: smoothing his free-hanging paisley necktie against his concave chest, scratching the raised tuft of

COMMENTS	PROFILE
just a man with a title and a name; readers begin to think they can actually see him.	graying hair receding from a wrinkled brow, quietly twirling a pink gum eraser between thumb and forefinger.
	His office, den of creativity and knowledge, is his domain. Yet he was **nervous.**
Perhaps the writer should have devoted more space to the points made in this paragraph. Because he is a historian, his views on history are central to understanding him.	The man is a paradox: "History cannot be free of personal opinion," declares the modern France scholar. "History must be created by each person who reads and studies it."
This is a valuable paragraph. If readers have not already become aware that he is a modest man, those two sentences make that clear in a few words.	The soft-spoken espouser of this philosophy is neither a preacher nor an ivory-tower intellectual. He prefaces all personal judgment with "Well, I *guess* I would say," adding a quick shrug of the shoulders and a cock of the head to emphasize his fallibility.
Now it becomes clear that this modest man is not one who gives in easily. Like most of us, he is complex. This paragraph shows one of his other qualities.	Gordon Wright, whose most emphatic gesture is a sharp chalk thrust as he dots his "i's," asserts himself in quiet ways. At a faculty meeting, for example, he might sit silently, offering no opinions. But back in his office, ten strategic telephone calls assure that his "will" be done.
Here the writer has attributed a direct quotation to many students and teachers. It is highly unlikely that all use exactly the same words. Instead, one student or teacher the writer interviewed used these words; the others agreed in somewhat different words. In such cases, a writer should quote the one person who used the words, then say that others agree.	An excellent academic administrator as well as teacher, scholar, and lecturer, Professor Wright is renowned for his diversity. "He is responsible for the strength of Stanford's history department," claim students and colleagues alike. Secure in his own field and intent on maintaining high standards, the former history department chairman refused to settle for second-best in recruiting faculty.
Note that the writer uses a sentence adroitly to tie his work as an administrator to his work as a teacher—a smooth transition.	As a teacher, Gordon Wright is equally demanding of himself. Although admittedly uncomfortable before large groups, Wright draws many students to his classes. He estimates that he has taught over 12,000 since 1939, when he started teaching at the University of Oregon.

COMMENTS

This, too, is smoothly transitional. The preceding paragraph ends on a historical note. This paragraph begins with a quotation that refers to that time. Then the next paragraph continues to evaluate his teaching ability while moving smoothly back to the present.

Because the quotation by Professor Nelson is about Professor Wright's ability, it does not show Wright but tells about him. Like other quotations, it is valuable because it supports the writer's judgment that Wright is an excellent teacher.

Here the writer enables readers to see the subject at his principal work. Like the other showing descriptions, this one makes Wright a figure of flesh and blood.

Note that the others who appear in this article are not shown. They are minor figures whose comments enable the writer to keep the focus on Wright. Had the others been shown in passages of similar length—or even if they had been the subjects of short descriptions —the focus would have been removed from Wright; the piece would not have been thematic.

The transition here is a bit weak even though the first sentence in this paragraph ends with a reference to history, which seems to be the focus at the end of the preceding paragraph. But the preceding paragraph was actually the end of a long passage showing him at work as a teacher. To make a smooth transition, the writer should have begun this paragraph with a reference to his interests outside of class, perhaps like this: "When he is not lecturing, he may be watching sports, attending the theater. . . ."

PROFILE

A former student of that era, Professor Lyle Nelson, explains why Gordon Wright was his favorite professor: "He was so well-organized, so logical. I could go back to my dorm and repeat his lectures word-for-word. The other fellows didn't need to go to class at all."

His painful sense of duty, his shyness, are the marks of a good teacher, and an intense one. In class, he stands well behind the lectern, leaning against the blackboard, legs casually crossed. His big hands periodically emerge from his pants pockets to make staccato gestures, or to grip a piece of chalk like a cigarette between his first two fingers, or to situate the next yellow legal-sized sheet of lecture notes.

Occasionally his smooth sermonizing voice wavers. His tongue sweeps his thin lips during a momentary pause. His performance is nonstop: when his dry sense of humor evokes laughter, he rushes on to the next point, as if embarrassed by his success.

Wright is a modest man. Ending an informative and searching probe into the origins of the Cold War, he offers: "Maybe this gives us some insight, I don't know."

He characterizes himself as a dilettante in regard to interests outside of history. "I have too many superficial interests: sports, music, theater, looking at art. I'm a decadent Renaissance man."

But he is far from decadent in pursuing his professional responsibilities. During the academic year, teaching is Professor Wright's first priority. He divides discussion group and grading duties with only one teaching assistant.

In a university, he contends, devel-

COMMENTS

The succeeding paragraphs (beginning with "But he is far from decadent") are tied to each other with smooth transitions.

No description of a professor who writes as well as teaches classes is complete without references to his writing. This passage would be better if one or two of Professor Wright's books or articles—those most widely read—had been cited by name. It is also in order in writing a long description of a teacher-writer to quote from his works. If the subject is famous as a stylist or as one whose written arguments are known for their intellectual brilliance, quotations are essential.

Contrast the beginning of this paragraph with the beginning of the preceding paragraph. The preceding one, which begins "His first love, however. . . ," is beautifully transitional. This one is tied to it, but less firmly.

Note especially how smoothly the writer takes the reader back into Wright's history. Instead of making readers stop, take a deep breath, and leap backward *in time (a common flaw), the transition leads them there. A write must work out such movements through time if readers are to derive pleasure from reading.*

PROFILE

oping a field of knowledge, researching and writing are necessary. Wright notes that "the best teachers are usually scholars."

His summer months are devoted to the solid research and consistent writing demanded in creating books. Currently, Professor Wright is revising some older texts and composing several short articles, including one on American cultural policy in the Middle East.

His first love, however, is France. He spent several years in Paris after World War II and in 1967 served there as Cultural Attache. Although he admits to a sense of futility as an outsider trying to synthesize a complicated period, Professor Wright selects as his most enjoyed writing experience his general history of Nineteenth and Twentieth Century France. As an American, however, he sees his greatest advantages in comparing European cultures.

Upon his return to Stanford in 1969, Wright assumed an assistantship under the Dean of Humanities and Sciences, in addition to his teaching responsibilities. He thus reaffirmed his deep commitment to the university, which dates back to his graduate study days. After completing his B.A. at Whitman College in Washington, Wright earned his M.A. and Ph.D. at Stanford.

Professor Wright remembers Stanford in the 1930's as a "stuffy, smug, self-satisfied imitation of the University of Virginia." He returned to the California campus in 1957 as a faculty member, attracted by the Hoover library collection of documents relevant to Twentieth Century history, hoping that Stanford was on the verge of change.

COMMENTS

Written at a time when activism on the campus was most apparent, this theme properly quotes Wright's thought about student actions. His attitudes toward students are obviously important because so much of his work centers on their actions.

This is attractive writing, but except for the information about his poor sight, it adds little or nothing to the picture the writer has already painted of Wright sitting in his office being interviewed.

This is a neat transition from his views to his actions.

Placing this sentence here was bad judgment. It fits better with the earlier references to his work in France. Note that the preceding paragraph and the following paragraph fit together neatly.

He is not "Anticipating his retirement" (at least nothing in this paragraph indicates that he is taking action

PROFILE

Fortunately, his hopes were fulfilled. "There has been a considerable change between students now and 10 years ago," explains Professor Wright. "Today activism is much greater. There is a feeling that the university is not adequate, a groping for something that is, and yet a failure to find it.

"Ten years ago, the mission of most students was to fit into the system. Today, there is a prejudice against that system, and increasing evidence that the system has not been nearly so successful as we thought it was."

Cupping his hands behind his head, elbows spread like wings for support, he stared at the ceiling, lost in quiet thought. His eyes (defined as "blind" by U.S. Army standards) were puzzled.

"Sometimes I don't understand students," he confessed. Youthful impatience, cynicism, lack of enthusiasm bewilder him. He deplores the easy philosophy of "if you can't correct big evils completely, don't try at all."

In his own way, Gordon Wright has tried to embody a philosophy of gradualism and reason. Having devoted himself to the life of the mind, he exists as an example to emulate, which has greater impact than any words of advice he might offer.

His early ambitions have been fulfilled: two cracks at the Foreign Service satisfied his desire for glamour plus his native wanderlust; and his two university posts have satisfied his longing to teach.

Constantly exposed to youth, Professor Wright is painfully aware of his own mortality. A miniature skull reigns ominously over the left-hand corner of his desk. Anticipating his retirement, Professor Wright ex-

regarding it); he is expecting *retirement.*

"Conquer the concertina" indicates that the writer has worked, and successfully, to use words that create pictures.

pressed mixed feelings about the future. He looks forward to travelling, reading, writing—to doing the postponed. He will be able to conquer the concertina, a gift from his wife "in case he ever broke his leg and was confined to bed."

Yet there is uncertainty in leaving the university. It means a drop in income. It means severing oneself from students, from an organization, from a way of life. "When you are on your own, isolated, it is chilling somehow," mused the history scholar.

This is a strikingly apt and readable concluding paragraph. It does not summarize heavily—the writer does not wind up to present a conclusion—it aptly uses the symbol of time passing to refer to the passing of Wright's own time, then ends with just the right symbol for the last working day of a teacher.

He is aware of time passing. But his consciousness of the ticking minutes is as casual as his characteristic glances at his wrist watch, tucked beneath a too-long shirt sleeve, near the end of a class period. When the bell rings, Gordon Wright is never startled.

Like the other students whose work has been quoted in this chapter, this writer had to concentrate to gather the small, vivid details that make description come alive. Learning to observe is essential. John Burroughs points to the value of using all the senses by describing the habits of the naturalist:

> His senses are so delicate that in his evening walk he feels the warm and cool streaks in the air, his nose detects the most fugitive odors, his ears the most furtive sounds. As he stands musing in the April twilight, he hears that fine, elusive stir and rustle made by the angleworms reaching out from their holes for leaves and grasses; he hears the whistling wings of the woodcock as it goes swiftly by him in the dusk; he hears the call of the killdeer come down out of the March sky; he hears far above him in the early morning the squeaking cackle of the arriving blackbirds pushing north; he hears the soft, prolonged, lulling call of the little owl in the cedars in the early spring twilight; he hears at night the roar of the distant waterfall, and the rumble of the train miles across country when the air is "hollow"; before a storm he notes how distant objects stand out and are brought near on those brilliant days that we call "weather-breeders." When the mercury is at zero or lower, he notes how the passing trains hiss and simmer as if the rails or wheels were red-hot.

PROJECTS

1   Study the piece on the national park, looking for examples of telling description, static showing, and action showing. List them down one column on a page, leaving room for another column. Then study the piece on the professor in the same way and make a similar list in another column. Which of the pieces uses more of each type of description?

2   Write a long descriptive paragraph about a member of the class or someone whose appearance is familiar to all members of the class. Do not include in your description the name of the subject or such details as height, weight, and hair color. Instead, focus on gestures, mannerisms, tone of voice, and ways of walking, talking, sitting, and standing. Read your description to the class to determine what percentage of the class can identify your subject.

3   After attending an event on the campus that attracts a large crowd, write an essay of about 400 words on the color, flavor, and excitement provided by the crowd itself. For example, if you attend a football or baseball game, describe the action on the field only to the extent necessary to describe other actions. Focus on the reactions of the crowd, yell leaders, band—those who make a game exciting because of their reactions to it.

4   Write an essay of an least 700 words about one of your teachers. Like the student who wrote the profile of Professor Wright that appears in this chapter, you should take notes on the teacher's actions and mannerisms and interview him and those who know him.

5   Using a dictionary and a thesaurus, substitute in the following passage, which is taken from Vladimir Nabokov's *Speak, Memory*, at least five synonyms for adjectives. Also substitute your own phrases for "a brief crack of light between two eternities of darkness" and "the smug, encroaching air of a coffin." Then compare the two versions in writing a few paragraphs about word choice and phrase-making in descriptive writing.

The cradle rocks above an abyss, and common sense tells us that our existence is but a brief crack of light between two eternities of darkness. Although the two are identical twins, man, as a rule, views the prenatal abyss with more calm than the one he is heading for (at some forty-five hundred heartbeats an hour). I know, however, of a sensitive youth who experienced something like panic when looking for the first time at some old homemade movies that had been taken a few weeks before his birth. He saw a world that was practically unchanged—the same house, the same people—and then realized that he did not exist there at all and that nobody mourned his absence. What particularly frightened him was the sight of a brand-new baby carriage standing there on the porch, with the smug, encroaching air of a coffin; even that was empty, as if, in the reverse course of events, his very bones had disintegrated.

Writing about Actions: Narration

To make the narrative flow along as it ought, every part naturally springing from that which precedes; to carry the reader backward and forward without distracting his attention, is not easy. Yet it may be done.—THOMAS BABINGTON MACAULAY

7 When Theodore White finished writing the manuscript for his book *The Making of the President 1960,* the publisher excitedly advertised that "It reads like a novel." When Carl Bernstein and Robert Woodward of the *Washington Post* published a book on their history-making investigation of the Watergate scandal in 1974, an editor of *Playboy* who had been assigned to select 25,000 words of it for publication in the magazine said, "It reads just like a story!" Most of us react that way to nonfiction books and articles that are skillfully written narratives. Because our love of stories was deeply instilled by fiction in early childhood, we are likely to be pleased by nonfiction that uses the same basic techniques.

In fact, the narrative form is so attractive that many young writers try to use it for nearly every piece. Lured partly by a natural love of stories, they are also attracted to the seemingly simple structure of narratives. First this happened, then that. What could be easier to write?

Unfortunately, few ideas actually fit the narrative form. And although those that do fit *are* easier to organize than most others, imaginative touches are essential to make narration effective. In short, the narrative form may be as deceiving as it is appealing.

FUNDAMENTALS OF EFFECTIVE NARRATION

You should think of a narrative as more than writing organized so that one thing occurs after another chronologically. Printed instructions for driving a car are so organized: the first action a learner must take comes before the second, and so on. Like the theme on Black English in Chapter 5, that is narrative exposition, not true narration.

What makes a narrative? First, narration does depend on a sequence of time, but only in part. One action follows another, grows out of another, is usually *caused* by another. But the actions need not be presented chronologically. You can start with a recent action (preferably a tense or exciting one that will catch the interest of readers), then dip into the distant past to sketch a causal action, then work your way back to the recent time and on to the conclusion. The chronological occurrence of actions is their natural order; their occurrence in your theme is their narrative order. The natural order and the narrative order may be the same —*should* be, in fact, unless you have a reason for changing the natural order. Whatever the organization, sequence of time is not just a convenient way of organizing the theme, as it usually is in narrative exposition and narrative description. Time is pivotal in narration.

But there is more to narration. It also presents life in motion in a story that moves from a beginning to an end. The major purpose is to tell a story, real or fictional. You may occasionally use exposition, description, and argument in a narrative—you may even consider one or all of these important—but story-telling is the larger purpose. This is obviously true of White's book about the presidential election of 1960 and of the book by Bernstein and Woodward about their investigation of Watergate. In contrast, the printed instructions for drivers and the analysis of Black English clearly have an expository purpose.

Finally, when you use sequence of time to present life in motion in a story that moves from a beginning to an end, the narrative should unfold in a way that creates suspense. What will happen next? That question should pull readers along to the conclusion. You should not try to write nonfiction with the edge-of-the-seat suspense that we associate with some fiction, especially mysteries. Such efforts make narratives seem artificial. But an adroit writer can create a degree of suspense in nonfiction, even if the actions that make up the narrative are neither adventurous nor dangerous.

The following is a quiet but effective account of a quiet event. Although the comments beside it indicate that the student could have written it more effectively, it satisfies all the requirements of the narrative form.

COMMENTS

A good writer often uses a few scene-setting sentences or paragraphs at the beginning to establish the theme, especially in writing a narrative that is largely chronological. This writer is using the first three paragraphs to set the scene. He could have started the first sentence with one of the actions that occur in the middle of the narrative, then flashed back to the beginning, then moved forward again. Such a structure is ordinarily used, however, only when the writer can begin with a tense moment that will capture readers. Because this event has no extraordinary tension, the writer wisely chose to use the simplest structure. To begin this with an action from the middle might have been dangerous. It might have tempted the writer to make the action seem more exciting than it actually was so that it would justify its place at the beginning.

This is generalized action, not the sharply focused action that is central to true narration, but it is effective because it makes the scene-setting paragraphs active, not just explanatory.

Now that the scene has been established, the true narrative begins.

This paragraph is deftly written. A less talented writer might have stopped the narrative at this point and devoted a separate paragraph to explaining Zener cards. Here the explanation is part of the story. The writer begins with the action of the young man—who is described only briefly because his part in the story is brief—then de-

NARRATION

Ray Cormier is a mentalist and authority on Extra Sensory Perception, but he is not a public speaker. Demonstrating "Psychic Phenomena" recently, he spoke in a halting, self-conscious voice. He even had to read his patter.

This didn't necessarily mar his show. In fact, the audience, skeptical about this man who claimed to be a mind reader, appeared reassured by his stage-fright. This obviously wasn't any slick professional out to fool the locals.

The program was a benefit for Pets in Need and Pet Birth Control, two animal welfare groups. Most of those in the audience were members or friends of the organizations, there to support the cause. Those who had come strictly to learn about ESP were far outnumbered and easy to spot: They tended to gather in cliques, discussing Edgar Cayce, reincarnation, and how they once knew what a friend was thinking even though he was on the other side of town. Both animal lovers and psychic enthusiasts shared one topic, however: The number of phony mentalists they had heard of. They entered the theater politely, but looking for proof.

"Extra Sensory Perception," Cormier began reading, "is knowledge gained from beyond the five senses. Everyone is psychic to some degree. We'll start tonight with an experiment using Zener cards. Any volunteetrs?"

A long-haired young man in a patched shirt threw up his hand. He was out of the third row and heading for the stage almost before Cormier nodded to welcome him. As the man approached, Cormier explained that Zener cards are a set of five cards with a symbol on each. Five sets form a deck. An experimenter goes through

COMMENTS

NARRATION

scribes Cormier's welcome of the young man and explanation of the cards. The explanation thus becomes part of the narrative.

the deck holding up one card at a time. If, without looking, a subject can guess five symbols out of 25, he's about average. One who guesses nine or more consistently may have psychic powers.

This is also exemplary writing. Because the young man is a minor actor in this little drama, the writer does not devote sentence after sentence to his right and wrong guesses.

As Cormier held up each card, the young man, now seated on the stage, tried to guess them. He got eight out of 25 and was a bit disappointed. "I was tested once before and did much better," he said. Cormier smiled and said it was all right.

The writer's use of "then" ties this action to the preceding action. He makes his description of Jody, like his description of the young man, part of a sentence. To devote an entire sentence to describing her would interrupt the action.

Cormier then called an assistant, Jody Murdock, out of the audience. He explained that Jody, an attractive brunette in a long black dress, had recognized psychic abilities and would now take the same test. Seated where the young man had been, Jody shut her eyes and frowned in concentration as Cormier held up the cards. One by one she correctly named them all.

Impressed, the audience gave her a round of applause that was more than polite.

Because Jody is a major figure, the writer should have described her a bit more in this paragraph or the next because readers should know more about a major figure than that she is an attractive brunette named Jody. Reader interest in Jody is assured because of her actions, but interest would be heightened if the writer had done a bit more to make her a flesh-and-blood figure.

"She could do this all night," Cormier said, facing away from the audience. "We'll try something more difficult. Jody'll stand behind the curtain where she can't see, and a member of the audience will shuffle the cards and show them to the rest of us. I'll try to project the symbol to Jody."

The writer described the audience in the third paragraph and only now returns to it. Should he have described audience reactions earlier? If the audience reacted noticeably, yes. If, for example, the audience was skeptical during the first few demonstrations, the

They took their places and each card was held up by a teenage girl in the front row. Cormier strained in concentration, then clapped his hands to signal Jody. When she named the first card correctly, the audience began to murmur: "How does she do it?" "What's the trick?" When she named the first three out of four correctly, heads started craning, looking for a hole in the curtain, a mirror on the

COMMENTS	NARRATION

writer could have pointed up the skepticism to heighten the suspense.

The passage that begins here and extends through the next two paragraphs is excellent. Instead of spelling out in detail everything that happened, the writer is pulling readers along by giving them just enough information to establish what happened without boring them.

The writer is also using sentence fragments properly in this passage: "Nineteen out of twenty times." "Eight out of ten times." "Eleven out of twelve times." Such fragments focus the attention of readers in a way that complete sentences do not. And, of course, the writer wants readers to focus on these significant numbers.

Here the writer is using audience reaction well. In effect, the audience reflects the thoughts of the readers. Both are waiting for an explanation because both are uncertain and doubtful. Both would be much more uncertain and doubtful, and thus the suspense would be stronger, had the writer described Cormier's manner in giving his answers. Did he pause dramatically before answering? Did he seem to concentrate in a way that contorted his features? Even if such actions were misleading on his part—a showman's flourishes—describing them would heighten the suspense.

Here the writer's description of Cormier's manner contributes to making this a story rather than a mere recitation of one action after another.

stage, or a confederate signalling from the rear. There were none. After Jody correctly guessed the fifth card, Cormier brought her back out. The audience, though puzzled, applauded loudly.

The other experiments went much the same way. People called out names of objects and Jody wrote them next to a number on a blackboard. After 20 objects were named, people called out the numbers at random. Cormier, blindfolded and facing away, correctly named the objects. Nineteen out of twenty times.

A woman pointed to individual playing cards from a pack fanned face down on a table. Cormier told her what the cards were. Eight out of ten times.

People put objects in envelopes which were then mixed up. Cormier correctly gave the objects back to the people. Eleven out of twelve times.

The audience was stumped. There was no doubt in their minds that this shy, hard-to-hear man was a genuine psychic, if not a sorcerer. Some looked perplexed, some giggled nervously, some stared in awe, some wouldn't even look. But all listened carefully.

For his finale, Cormier took the serial numbers from two dollar bills, multiplied them by eight, and wrote the product on the blackboard. A volunteer then called a phone number in San Francisco of a "psychic friend who has put herself in a trance" who would clairvoyantly tell what the number was. The answer was almost anticlimactic: correct to the last digit.

The applause proved that not a skeptic was left in the theater. Cormier, however, motioned for quiet and began his closing remarks. With a touch of a

COMMENTS	**NARRATION**

grin, he began: "I hope this has increased your understanding of psychic phenomena. Many respected researchers are now beginning to explore this field. It is only fair to tell you, however, that none of the demonstrations here tonight were done by psychic means. They were all illusions."

Cormier's explanation turns out to be a bit anti-climactic, a bit of a letdown. That is what happened, though, and the writer of a realistic narrative must report it. Moreover, it turns out to be valuable despite the anti-climax. Cormier taught his audience a lesson worth remembering; the writer taught his readers the same important lesson. Instead of lingering over it and trying to point the moral, the writer wisely lets the narrative itself—the speaker's words and actions—tell the readers what they should know. When a writer selects quotations artfully, they speak more memorably than a writer's own moralizing.

What! Tricks? No one actually fell out of a chair, but the surprise pushed a few to the edge. A woman, frantically waving her hand, called out, "Well, what's the point. If it's just a trick, why'd you do it?"

Cormier quietly answered: "Because some people use psychic powers unscrupulously. I believe in these powers, but not in the trickery people use to make money." The point, he added, carefully and clearly, "is that when people do things 100 percent correct— watch out."

PROBLEMS IN NARRATION

The piece above points up some of the primary problems in writing effective narratives. Note especially the comments on beginnings that appear beside the first three paragraphs. If possible, start a narrative with action rather than scene-setting; you may be able to go on from there to create a pure narrative from beginning to end—all action. But if you try to devise a beginning that will force into pure narrative form a piece that does not lend itself to it, you may create an atmosphere of *contrived* excitement. Instead of attracting readers, you may repel them because the beginning sounds artificial.

The comments on the writer's descriptions of Cormier, Jody Murdock, and the young man indicate the importance of using description in narration. Although Cormier's manner is sketched revealingly in the first two paragraphs, the writer could have heightened the suspense toward the end by describing how Cormier gave answers. Because the young man is a minor figure—little more than a prop in this quiet drama—the writer need not have named him or described him more fully. But Jody Murdock's actions are central in paragraph after paragraph. Readers should be able to see her as a person; she is much more than a prop. The writer could have sketched her without interrupting the narrative flow by describing her in terms of her actions. For example, when she took her place behind the curtain (tenth paragraph), the writer could have told in a few words *how* she took her place, exactly how she walked. The chapter on visual writing and the deft description of movement in the profile of Professor Wright in the preceding chapter suggest how you should write such descriptions.

The chief problem in narration often grows out of an attempt to fit into the narrative form a piece that does not have a narrative purpose. Consider the beginning paragraphs of this one:

> "We're going," said Kim, who meant it as a command.
> I peered over the top of a book I was reading and asked what time it was. "Five minutes to twelve. C'mon, we're late."
> Five minutes to twelve may seem a bit early to be late to a 1:30 football game, but on this campus, anything past eleven is late. Besides, I thought, the pre-game show is the best part. The three of us, Kim, Tim, and myself, climbed in my car and started for the stadium.
> The opposing team was Washington State, which though better than it had been in preceding years, is still mediocre and definitely not the team to pull in large crowds.
> Fortunately, this made for easy parking, and there was no problem finding a place. Once out of the car, we started down Galvez Street, three abreast.
> Off to our left, the band was getting organized—or at least the leaders were trying to make some sort of order out of the mass of intoxicated bodies, all of them carrying some kind of instrument. . . .

The writer went on to describe the instruments (some of them painted in wild colors), the band formations, the agility of the pompon girls, the color of the pre-game show, and the varied actions of the spectators. Although the structure was chronological, the writer's purpose was to describe. As the quoted paragraphs indicate, the writer's attempt to narrate defeated his purpose. Because the passage merely notes (in detail) that three students made a short and uneventful trip to a football game, the action is not compelling. Nor does that passage promise that any actions that grow out of it will be. The effect is entirely negative: The beginning prevents the writer from serving his real purpose, to describe, until he has exhausted the details of the trip—and probably his readers.

In short, the first problem in narration is deciding whether to use the narrative form. Do you have a narrative purpose? If telling a story *is* central, you must decide whether the natural order is the most appropriate narrative order. In writing, you must use description to flesh out each action without allowing it to interrupt the flow of the narrative.

METHODS OF THE NEW JOURNALISM

You can learn much about writing narration by analyzing the writing of those who use fiction techniques in writing nonfiction, among them Tom Wolfe, Gay Talese, Truman Capote, Joe Eszterhas, and Norman Mailer. The basic technique of those Wolfe calls "the new journalists" is scene-by-scene construction of a complete narrative. Here is the first scene of an article by Talese, "Joe Louis—The King as a Middle-Aged Man," which appeared in *Esquire:*

> "Hi, sweetheart!" Joe Louis called to his wife, spotting her waiting for him at the Los Angeles airport.
> She smiled, walked toward him, and was about to stretch up on her toes and kiss him—but suddenly stopped.
> "Joe," she snapped, "where's your tie?"
> "Aw, sweetie," Joe Louis said, shrugging. "I stayed out all night in New York and didn't have time."
> "All night!" she cut in. "When you're out here with me all you do is sleep, sleep, sleep."
> "Sweetie," Joe Louis said with a tired grin. "I'm an ole man."
> "Yes," she agreed, "but when you go to New York you try to be young again."

This scene, the first in the article, pictures Louis with his fourth wife. The concluding scene focuses on Louis's second wife, Rose, in a roomful of people watching a film of Louis fighting Billy Conn. "Rose seemed excited at seeing Joe at the top of his form," Talese wrote, "and every time a Louis punch would jolt Conn, she'd go, 'Mummmm' (sock). 'Mummmm' (sock). 'Mmmmm' (sock)." The article is made up almost entirely of such scenes.

Wolfe, who in recent years has become a strong promoter of this kind of writing as well as one of its leading practitioners, has written of the journalists who began to fashion such narratives:

> They developed the habit of staying with the people they were writing about for days at a time, weeks in some cases. They had to gather all the material the conventional journalist was after—and then keep going. It seemed all-important to *be there* when dramatic scenes took place, to get the dialogue, the gestures, the facial expressions, the details of the environment. The idea was to give the full objective description, plus

something that readers had always had to go to novels and short stories for: namely, the subjective and emotional life of the characters.

Lillian Ross, who writes primarily for the *New Yorker,* was one of the earliest practitioners of what Wolfe calls "saturation reporting." In fact, her book *Picture,* a behind-the-scenes narrative of the making of the film *The Red Badge of Courage,* was probably the first "nonfiction novel." Some of the topics she chooses to develop make it clear that one need not be able to spend days with a celebrity such as Joe Louis or weeks with a motion picture film crew to develop effective scene-by-scene narration. One of her most readable articles for the *New Yorker* reported on the visit to New York of a group of rural Indiana high school students. One scene was written:

> The next morning, a meeting of the class was held in the hotel lobby to take a vote on when to leave New York. . . . The class voted for the extra day in New York and Niagara Falls.
>
> "I'm glad," Becky Kiser said, with a large, friendly smile, to Dennis Smith. Several of her classmates overheard her and regarded her with a uniformly deadpan look. "I like it here," she went on. "I'd like to live here. There's so much to see. There's so much to do."
>
> Her classmates continued to study her impassively until Dennis took their eyes away from her by saying, "You get a feelin' here of goin' wherever you want to. Seems the city never closes. I'd like to live here, I believe. People from everyplace are here."
>
> "Limousines all over the joint," Albert Warthan said.
>
> "Seems like you can walk and walk and walk," Dennis went on dreamily. "I like the way the big buildin's crowd you in. You want to walk and walk and never go to sleep."
>
> "I hate it," Connie Williams said, with passion. . . .
>
> "There's no place like home," Mike said. "Home's good enough for me."
>
> "I believe the reason of this is we've lived all our lives around Stinesville," Dennis said. "If you took Stinesville out of the country, you wouldn't be hurt. But if you took New York out of the country, you'd be hurt. The way the guide said, all our clothes and everything comes from New York."

This scene is worth studying. Although you will need time and practice in writing to undertake a complete narrative made up entirely of scenes, you should try to write a scene of this kind. Writing one effectively is not as easy as it may appear to be. Being in a position to overhear such a conversation, choosing exactly the right quotations and writing them so that they are natural rather than artificial, making certain that not even a hint of your viewpoint affects the scene, letting the dialogue tell the story—all these are difficult. But all are worth practicing to develop narrative skill.

Students of Professor Edward Nickerson at the University of Delaware have successfully written similar scenes in the form of the "dramatic dialogue." He describes it as a passage of conversation that discloses a significant relationship between people without describing their inner thoughts. Using the third person as Lillian Ross does in the quotation above, the writer tries to show inner thoughts through a combination of seemingly detached description of the actions of the people talking, and of an equally detached recording of their words. Mastering the dramatic dialogue is valuable practice for the more demanding work of linking scene to scene in a way that tells a complete story. Here is a good dramatic dialogue:

> A car pulled up to the college.
> "Here we are."
> "Is that where you're going to live?" she asked, pointing to a tall tower.
> "Yes," her daughter answered.
> The girl and her parents got out of the car.
> "I hope you didn't forget anything."
> "I probably did."
> "You know little Jimmy said he'd miss you."
> "Tell him I'll miss him too."
> They took three suitcases and a portable stereo out of the car and walked to the tower. Upon entering, her mother said, "Well this looks nice," trying to be cheerful. "I'm sure you'll like it." They took the elevator to her floor. As they walked into a room a girl and two boys walked out laughing.
> "Hi," said the girl, "I'm Jean White. I guess I'm your roommate." The two boys grabbed her arms and pulled her away, just as she finished her sentence. She yelled "See ya later," and laughed.
> "They don't allow boys in here. Do they?" her father gasped.
> "Of course, Daddy. I'm in college."
> "But Ellen, you never told me that."
> "I didn't think I had to."
> "Your mother and I are going to worry ourselves sick now."
> "Why?"
> "Because we're concerned."
> "You think I'll get pregnant or something?"
> "Don't use gutter talk like that in front of your mother, Ellen! Things like that are not discussed. We love you and are concerned, so naturally we'll worry. But don't think about it. We want you to have a good time, and meet nice boys."
> "Yes, father."

"Don't forget if you want to talk about anything bothering you, you can call anytime. Even at night, just call."
They exchanged goodbyes and parted.

The writer does not need to provide inner thoughts or in some other way tell us that there is tension between this girl and her parents; their words reveal the tension. We would have to read other scenes involving these people to know whether tension is characteristic of their relationship. We may suspect that it is, if only because tension between those of college age and their parents is so common. A dramatic dialogue can be successful, however, showing only tension of the moment.

Note especially how deftly the writer moves the roommate, Jean White, and the two boys in and out of the scene. They are necessary, but only to point up the parents' fear in a way that will create tense dialogue. Instead of placing Jean and the boys in the room when the girl and her parents arrive, where their presence over a longer period would probably make it impossible for the father to speak frankly, the writer has Jean and the boys appear, strike the spark, then move on, leaving the girl and her parents free to speak revealingly.

Further analysis of the scene outlines the method of dramatic dialogue. The thoughts of the characters are not provided, and in no other way does the writer intrude. The writer is camera and recorder, but primarily recorder; this is drama in dialogue. It is as though a documentary film were made without a narrator, a film in which actions are so secondary as to be mere movements while words carry the weight, the meaning, and the drama.

Of course, no successful dramatic dialogue grows out of a mere scene between two or more people, not even if the words they exchange are angry. The writer must have a reason for sketching the scene. What am I trying to show? That is the writer's central question. He does not answer it merely by sketching an interesting scene in which people used memorable words. The closer a scene comes to presenting common but revealing experiences that help to show us what we are like in essence—the closer, that is, it comes to being universally meaningful—the closer it approaches art.

THE FULL SCOPE OF NARRATION

Although much of this chapter emphasizes the structure of narratives and the use of description in them, nearly all of the basic values and devices of writing that were analyzed in the early chapters apply to narration. If it seems that story-telling should allow you to write more loosely, to let your sentences grow and flower, you should be aware that conciseness and simplicity are usually central. If it seems that the need for suspense indicates that you should write vigorously and colorfully throughout—that you should inject suspense to make pale actions seem colorful—be aware that wordy overwriting prevents you from developing the most effective kind of narration: a story simply told. Using strong words to try to make actions seem more exciting than they actually were weakens your narrative.

Robert Wallace wrote these paragraphs, which appeared in *Life* in 1953, as the beginning of an article about a heart attack:

> The pain had begun just before he got on the train. Like most men in middle age he had vaguely considered the possibility that he might someday have a heart attack. His father had died of one. But there was nothing the matter with his own heart, so far as he knew. He was no more of a hypochondriac than any man whose breath comes shorter than it did and whose belt seems tighter than it once was. He had merely considered the possibility and dismissed it.
>
> A specialist might have told him that he was a good candidate for a heart attack. He was 41, 5 feet 8 inches tall, of stocky build and inclined to put on weight; stripped, he weighed 165. He had a nervous stomach. Sometimes, but only sometimes, he worked under pressure and did not readily shake it off when he went home at night. His medical history was undramatic. He had had few illnesses in his life and supposed that he took good care of himself. He rarely drank more than one cocktail a day, smoked about one pack of filter-tipped cigarettes daily and rarely engaged in sudden, violent exercise. He liked to fish, occasionally played golf and puttered gently around the house and garden on weekends.
>
> At 7:55 P.M. on Nov. 10, having worked a long day, he left his office on 45th Street in Manhattan and started to walk East toward Grand Central Station. He lived in Connecticut and traveled to and from his work in New York on the New Haven Railroad, 58 minutes each way. (He was not a native New Yorker and had not always lived in the atmosphere, sometimes thought to be tense, of a big city.) On this particular evening he was more tired than usual, having worked three 11-hour days in a row. His company produces commercial films; between Monday morning and Wednesday night he had torn apart and rebuilt a 30-minute movie for a steel company. He was not worried about the film. He knew it was good. His job had been well done and the pressure was off him.
>
> His train left at 8:09 P.M. He had nearly 15 minutes to walk five blocks to catch it. He moved rapidly through the huge vaulted lobby of the station, through the train gate and down a flight of 28 steps to the platform where the 8:09 was waiting, already largely filled with passengers. He began to walk up the platform, heading for one of the front cars where he habitually sat. The pain commenced just then.
>
> It arrived full-grown. It was as though a small hot bulb had suddenly

started to glow in his chest. It remained constant. The area of pain seemed about the size of a quarter, in the center of his chest, four inches below the knot of his necktie. Never having had a heart pain before, he thought it was indigestion; he often had gas pains and carried a small box of antacid tablets in his pocket.

He had walked halfway up the platform but suddenly did not feel like walking farther toward the head of the train. He stepped into the nearest car and was pleased to find a seat on the aisle near the door. If he were going to be sick, he thought, he could get to the washroom quickly without attracting attention.

The pain was severe but he had felt many worse pains at various times in his life. He leaned back in his seat, took an antacid tablet from his pocket and began to chew it. Presently he felt a second ball of pain beside the first one, to the right of it, and then a third, to the left. Soon all three merged into a bar, hot and high up across his chest. He began to wonder whether his heart might not be involved, but he had the conventional notion that the pain of a heart attack would be lower and on the left side of his chest. He thought briefly of leaving the train and trying to find a doctor, even of taking a taxicab to a hospital, but then considered how ridiculous he would feel if he were told that he had indigstion.

For two or three minutes he sat quietly trying not to think, his body simply a container for the little rod of pain. Then he noticed that his left arm was numb. It felt as though he had been carrying a heavy weight for a long distance and had just set it down. He began to knead the arm with his right hand and felt pain running from his left shoulder down to his elbow. He knew then, beyond doubt, what was happening to him.

These paragraphs, which are a third of the article, create such suspense that surely you are anxious to know this: The man survived. How did the writer build such extraordinary tension into a simple narrative about a common occurrence?

The first sentence is important: "The pain had begun just before he got on the train." The writer fills in the man's background in the rest of that paragraph and throughout the next, but the narrative begins with the first words. The writer sustains it; he does not stop the story. Note that the first sentence in the second paragraph is also keyed to the heart attack. Some of the information in this passage is simple description—"41, 5 feet 8 inches tall"—but all of it is written in relation to the man as a potential victim of a heart attack.

The writer uses simple words and sentences, nearly all of them short. By varying sentence length and structure, he avoids the choppy writing that may result from extreme simplicity. The number of words in each of the sentences in the first paragraph is: 11–20–6–15–26–9. Only four of the six sentences begin in the conventional subject-verb structure.

Next, consider the visual wording of the climactic sentences: "It was as though a small hot bulb had suddenly started to glow in his chest. . . . Presently he felt a second ball of pain beside the first one, to the right of it, and then a third, to the left. Soon all three merged into a bar, hot and high up across his chest." Such word pictures enable readers to see—even to feel.

Moreover, the writer has focused unrelentingly on the man. Appearing in this narrative in a section not quoted above are a woman with a British accent, other passengers, the conductor, a brakeman, two policemen, doctors, nurses, and patients. *All* are presented in relationship to the man who suffers the heart attack.

Throughout, the writer uses specific details to produce extraordinary effects. The man does not just travel to and from work on the train; it is "58 minutes each way." He work "three eleven-hour days." The train left at 8:01. He walked down a flight of 28 steps. In a later passage, he descended four steps to get off the train, and to get to the street from the platform he went up a "dark flight of 28 concrete steps." These details are, of course, spread through the narrative, not piled on one another. So arranged, they create an atmosphere of realism that almost places readers on the scene. Like the numbers that show the museum party in the preceding chapter, these numbers help to make the scene come alive.

Perhaps the most important point to remember about narration is that no story tells itself. When a narrative reads both simply and appealingly, when you are pulled onward by what seems to be the *need* to know what comes next, a writer has had to work hard to affect you that way.

PROJECTS

1 Read again the short dramatic dialogue and the analysis of it that appears in this chapter, then write one. Be sure to decide what you are trying to show. Then read your dialogue to the class or to several members of the class and ask them to tell you what your dialogue shows. If they are unable to do so, ask them whether the dialogue reveals anything about the characters: the kind of people they are—or the kind they were at the moment of the scene. Use the responses in rewriting the dialogue.

2 Choose from your experiences the one that is most likely to interest many readers. Something dramatic or humorous may be the best choice. Write about it in a chronological narrative of at least 1,000 words.

   a Take an incident out of your chronological arrangement and place it at the beginning. Rewrite where necessary, especially to fill the gap left by the rearrangement.

b Write several paragraphs to analyze the difference between the two arrangements of the experience. Was your experience such that it did not lend itself to anything but chronological order? Does the beginning of the chronological piece start slowly? Does the beginning of the revision seem contrived, a too-obvious attempt to lure readers?

Writing to Convince: Persuasion

Thinking is like loving and dying. Each of us must do it for himself.
—JOSIAH ROYCE

8 A group of social scientists once tried to determine whether prejudice could be reduced by making fun of it. Thinking that strongly prejudiced people might be led to laugh their way out of their narrowness, the research team showed some of them a series of satirical cartoons. To the dismay of the researchers, many of the prejudiced people interpreted the meaning of the cartoons in reverse. Instead of laughing at the cartoons, and thus at themselves, these people took the cartoon messages seriously. For example, looking at a cartoon that showed a woman in a hospital refusing to accept a transfusion unless it was "blue blood," one viewer said, "That's a very good idea. I must warn my doctor to be careful if I ever need a transfusion."

A point worth remembering from this example is that persuasion through satire often fails; some people just don't get the joke. A more important point is that it is difficult to persuade anyone to change his mind about anything he believes strongly. This chapter focuses on problems in persuasion and suggests how to solve them.

PRINCIPLES OF PERSUASION

Some authorities on language make a distinction between persuasion and argumentation. The primary purpose of persuasion is to win assent, the primary purpose of argument to establish the truth, and the differ-

ence is sometimes vast. Instead of trying to establish truth, you may try
to persuade someone of a falsehood (or persuade someone to act against
his own best interests or the best interests of others). But it is better for
us to simplify by considering persuasion and argument as one. Both use
the same methods and have the same goal: to convince.

To understand how difficult it is to convince, consider the obstacles
you face in writing exposition, description, and narration. First, people
must be attracted to read what you write. Second, they must accept what
you have written. Then they must interpret it correctly. Finally, if it is
to be effective, they must store it for later use (or for a pleasant memory).
Because all of us are surrounded by so many more messages than our
senses can handle or our nervous systems adjust to, these are high
obstacles. Persuasion faces all of them and others.

One of the central problems in persuasion is that readers have
defenses. They already have beliefs and attitudes, some relatively flexible
but many that they are prepared to defend stubbornly and even irration-
ally (like the prejudiced people who misinterpreted the satirical cartoons). They have personal relationships and loyalties that they may not
change however strong the evidence you offer. They have been lured by
persuasion before, sometimes to their sorrow.

Moreover, readers' beliefs, attitudes, relationships, and loyalties are
so entwined that they can seldom change one without changing another.
If you try to persuade a conservative to become a liberal or a Democrat
to become a Republican, for example, you may have to persuade him to
change some of his friendships and family relationships as well as his
politics. Some friendships are built largely on similar political leanings.
Political beliefs are sometimes so strong that when one member of a
family begins to differ politically with the others, he becomes an outcast.
In trying to persuade someone to change his beliefs, you may actually
be arguing that he should change his life.

It is not impossible, of course, to change strongly held beliefs. Dan
Wakefield, a writer who was a founding member of the Young Republi-
cans Club when he was a high school student in Indianapolis, wrote in
his book *Between the Lines:*

> In looking back for political influences, I have to acknowledge the
> important factor of my peers. For the first time in my life, at Columbia
> College, I was in daily contact with more people who were Democrats than
> were Republicans. I had only one friend in high school who was a
> Democrat, and he was considered a "wild" fellow with weird ideas. I
> thought there was one other, but I recently saw him in Washington and
> he assured me I was mistaken—he'd been a Republican all along.
> I suppose I had made the mistake in my memory because he was rather
> an eccentric guy; but not so eccentric, it turned out, as to be a

Democrat. For a person who is as concerned with other people's approval as I am—and especially as I was in college—I am sure this influenced my thinking simply through the social instinct of wanting to take on the coloring of those around me. To be one of the crowd. Perhaps if I'd gone to a Zulu college I'd have taken to cannibalism. But this may be unfair even to myself, at least in overemphasis. I do believe that one of the factors in moving from right to left was not the herd instinct alone, but the fact that for the first time I was hearing people I knew and liked express views different from any I had ever heard expounded. I had never seen this "other side" before, and the more I saw of it the more it seemed to me to be the one I wished to support.

The things one reads that show the other side can also be influential, but just as the solitary Democrat in the Indianapolis high school did not affect Wakefield's beliefs, a single piece of writing may have no effect. Like Wakefield's friends, who influenced his beliefs over a long period, not all at once, writing is more likely to be persuasive piece by piece, bit by bit.

You are most likely to persuade those with strong beliefs if you take advantage of the fact that human beings try to be consistent; all of us try to keep in balance the things we know and believe and do. When we become aware of inconsistencies, we may change. If we admire and respect the president of the United States, for example, we may find it difficult to continue to admire and respect him if we learn or come to believe that his major policies are evil. To keep our attitudes in balance—to strain toward consistency—we must change at least to some degree.

This suggests a strategy for persuasive writing. Suppose that those who admire and respect the president are not aware of the effect of his policies. If you write a direct attack on the president himself, his admirers will defend him. But if you present evidence and closely reasoned arguments that his policies are bad, you have a better chance of influencing their attitudes toward him.

You can also create persuasive cross pressures. If you can persuade readers who admire and respect both of the U.S. senators who represent your state that the senators disagree with each other on an important issue, the readers will then be more open to arguments against one of the senators.

(As several experiments have shown, the strain toward consistency can also change *you,* the writer. If you write to convince readers of something that you do not believe, you may be led to change your own belief at least slightly to bring it closer to the belief you express in writing.)

But all this focuses primarily on the problems of changing strongly held beliefs and attitudes. What of those that readers are less likely to defend so stubbornly? Confronted by an argument that challenges a belief they defend lightly, or an argument about an issue that they had not considered, readers will more readily be attracted to a reasoned argument, accept it, interpret it correctly, and store it for use.

Reasoning

Whether you are trying to persuade those who hold beliefs strongly, those who hold them lightly, or those who have not considered the issue you are writing about, your argument will be more persuasive if it is based on reason. Persuasion must be rational—or seem to be. Many advertising campaigns, many political campaigns, and many mass movements play on fears and are based on emotion, not reason. Significantly, however, those who devise and lead the campaigns and movements must make it seem that their arguments are rational. Hitler persuaded the Germans that they must kill the Jews and conquer Europe to survive, to prosper, and to fulfill their destiny. Such arguments are deceitful, of course. But the fact that demagogues try to make it appear that they are appealing to reason makes it all the more obvious that reason is central to persuasion. Many large volumes have been written about reasoning and how it works. The basic methods of reasoning are induction and deduction.

Induction. A leading psychologist heard someone say in a cocktail-party conversation that modern adolescents have more trouble with identity crises than did adolescents of earlier times. The psychologist responded quickly: "Oh, no! *I* went through the worst identity crisis you ever saw!" She may have been right in suggesting that identity crises were more troublesome in her time, but her own experience was not proof of it. (Had she been writing rather than chatting, she would never have attempted to prove the point by citing a single case. Like most of us, she is more careful in writing.)

By citing her own experience, the psychologist made an inductive leap. She said, in effect, *I went through the most terrible identity crisis; therefore, my generation experienced worse identity crises.* That conclusion *may* be true, but because her experience does not prove the point, her inductive leap was faulty.

Nevertheless, the psychologist's statement is a good example of the kind of reasoning called *induction,* which means using particular facts to establish a general truth. It is the most common kind of reasoning, used so often that we are usually unaware that we *are* reasoning. One who has been cut by glass reasons that glass cuts. One who has been hit reasons that fists are hard. This is learning by experience, of course, but experience alone is not really a great teacher. Experience teaches nothing without reasoning.

Inductive reasoning is so often accurate that most of us try too often to establish general truths by using particular cases. Consider these examples:

1   All seven freshmen in the college class who were graduated from Lincoln High School write well. Lincoln High graduates write well.
2   Three of the women in the class are members of Pi Phi and have high grade-point averages. Pi Phi's have high grade-point averages.

The particular facts do not support the general conclusion in either case. The Lincoln High graduates may have become friends because they write well—perhaps they had worked together on the school literary magazine or newspaper—and decided to take the same college course. The other Lincoln High graduates may be poor writers. Friendship may also have led the Pi Phi's to enroll in the same course. Their grades prove nothing about the grades of the other Pi Phi's.

These are errors, but they help to point up an essential quality of inductive reasoning: probability. If there is only *one* Lincoln High School graduate in the class, and he writes well, it would be ridiculous to reason that all Lincoln High graduates write well. When you find that all of the seven Lincoln High graduates in the class write well, that increases the probability—but not conclusively. Similarly, if there is only one Pi Phi in the class, and she has a high grade-point average, to assume that all Pi Phi's have high averages would be ridiculous. Three increases the probability.

Inductive reasoning is *always* based on probabilities, not certainties. To use it, you must set aside ridiculous conclusions and test possibilities to determine which are probable. To test the possibilities in the examples cited, you might examine the writing of several Lincoln High graduates who were not in the class and several members of Pi Phi who were not in the class. If the results were positive in each case, the probability would be increased. You could strengthen the tests of probability by examining the writing of every tenth Lincoln High graduate and every tenth Pi Phi. This method (called *sampling*) would give you greater confidence in your conclusions.

Deduction. Deductive reasoning is based on truths already established. In Latin, *de* means "from" and *ducere* means "to lead." In deducing, you lead—or reason—from a premise to a conclusion. The premise must be a statement accepted as true without any demand for proof, such as the axiom in geometry that states, "Things that are equal to the same thing are equal to each other," or, "All oceans contain water." Your premise must be accurate or your conclusion can be accurate only by weird accident. For example, you can reason from premise to conclusion like this:

All soldiers are brave.
John Jamerson is a soldier.
Therefore John Jamerson is brave.

If it were true that all soldiers are brave, you could reason truly from the fact that John Jamerson is a soldier that he is brave. He may be brave, but all soldiers are not brave. The syllogism, as this pattern of argument is called, is valid because the reasoning process is logical. But because the major premise is false, you cannot trust a conclusion that is based on it.

When deduction is based on a premise that actually is a self-evident statement of truth, the conclusion must follow:

All princes are men.
Charles is a prince.
Therefore Charles is a man.

The formality of this kind of reasoning may cause you to doubt that it has much value. It is true that few of us ever argue in precise syllogisms. But *everyone* argues from premises, and deductive reasoning is valuable in testing most arguments that are based on premises. When one English major said to another, "You wouldn't like talking to him; he's in engineering," he said, in effect:

All engineering students talk only about engineering.
He is an engineering student.
He talks only about engineering.

Although the conclusion *may* be true, it does not follow from the premise because the premise is not true.

Mistakes in reasoning by induction or deduction are examples of fallacy, or faulty logic. Although most fallacies result from faults in inductive or deductive reasoning, several occur so often you should consider them separately.

Post Hoc, Propter Hoc   ("This came first so it caused that"). If you tend to think that because one event occurred after another the first caused the second, you are likely to make this common error. Alvin Moscow gives an example in his book *Collision Course* that suggests how absurd cause-and-effect thinking can become. On the night in 1956 when the liner *Andrea Doria* collided with another ship, a woman passenger on the *Andrea Doria* flicked a light switch in her cabin. A great crash and a grinding of metal followed immediately. The woman ran from her cabin into the passageway, where passengers and crew members were running and screaming, and explained to the first person she met that she must have set the ship's emergency brake.

The Fallacy of Equivocation ("Words mean what I say they mean"). This is using a term more than once with different meanings, usually to make it seem that a conclusion follows when it does not. One widely quoted example is:

> Even scientists recognize a power beyond nature, for they speak of "natural law"; and if there is a law, there must be a power to make the law; such a power beyond nature is called God; therefore scientists believe in God.

The writer is equivocating by making the natural law with which scientists describe the regularity of natural processes the same as law in the sense of authority. A respected historian indicated how easy it is to make this mistake when he wrote, "Power, of course, corrupts, and luxury when available is a powerful temptation." By this faulty logic, luxury corrupts. Perhaps it does, but trying to make luxury seem to be the same as power does not prove it.

Argumentum Ad Verecundiam ("He's famous; he must be right about everything"). This fallacy is an argument that attempts to prove a point by appealing to fame or authority. In its crudest form, it appears in advertisements in which entertainment or sports celebrities endorse products. Joe Namath uses Right Guard. So should you.

These arguments are made so often (so strongly) that they do not appear to be arguments but statements of unchallengeable fact. "The president (or the professor or the dean) says . . ."—and the authority who is cited is offered as proof. Sometimes no specific authority is cited. "They say . . ." has become a familiar (and surprisingly persuasive) appeal to authority. It is even more suspect, of course, than the specific appeals.

Argumentum Ad Hominem ("If you don't have the facts, argue personalities"). This fallacy, which is so common that many writers refer to it as "the familiar *ad hominem*," is an argument against the man. You are making that argument when instead of dealing with an issue you attack your opponent. An example is related in Herndon's *Life of Lincoln*. Lincoln's law partner, William F. Herndon, remembered:

> In a case where Judge [Stephen T.] Logan—always earnest and grave—
> opposed him, Lincoln created no little merriment by his reference to
> Logan's style of dress. He carried the surprise in store for the latter, till he
> reached his turn before the jury. Addressing them, he said: "Gentlemen,
> you must be careful and not permit yourselves to be overcome by the
> eloquence of counsel for the defense. Judge Logan, I know, is an effective
> lawyer. I have met him too often to doubt that; but shrewd and careful

though he be, still he is sometimes wrong. Since this trial has begun I have discovered that with all his caution and fastidiousness, he hasn't knowledge enough to put his shirt on right." Logan turned red as crimson, but sure enough, Lincoln was correct, for the former had donned a new shirt, and by mistake had drawn it over his head with the pleated bosom behind. The general laugh which followed destroyed the effect of Logan's eloquence over the jury—the very point at which Lincoln aimed.

Much like the *ad hominem* argument is *argumentum ad populum,* which appeals to passions and prejudices. When a demagogue attacks someone by trying to appeal to our prejudices, *ad hominem* and *ad populum* are the same.

Other Fallacies. There are many other fallacies, the most common of which have self-explanatory names: irrational evidence, begging the question, and irrelevant conclusion.

Do these fallacies and the process of reasoning itself seem too abstract to be useful in learning to write well? They may seem less remote from the writing process if we look at them as devices of propaganda. The Institute for Propaganda Analysis listed seven devices: Name Calling, Glittering Generalities, Transfer, Testimonial, Card Stacking, Plain Folks, and Band Wagon.

Name calling is like *argumentum ad populum* or *argumentum ad hominem,* an appeal to passion and prejudice or an attack on a person. One of the most famous editorials in American journalism, "What's the Matter With Kansas?" by William Allen White, editor of the *Emporia Gazette,* is pure name calling:

> We have an old mossback Jacksonian who snorts and howls because there is a bathtub in the statehouse; we are running that old jay for governor. We have another shabby, wild-eyed, rattle-brained fanatic who has said openly in a dozen speeches that "the rights of the user are paramount to the rights of the owner"; we are running him for chief justice so that capital will come tumbling over itself to get into the state. We have raked the old ash heap of failure in the state and found an old human hoop skirt who has failed as a business man, who has failed as an editor, who has failed as a preacher, and we are going to run him for congressman-at-large. He will help the looks of the Kansas delegation in Washington. Then we have discovered a kid without a law practice and have decided to run him for attorney general.

Glittering generalities are glowing words that may beg the question, present irrational evidence, lead to an irrelevant conclusion, or indeed, make readers blind to almost anything the writer tries to obscure, including absence of all reason. At their worst, glittering generalities ask us to equate the writer's opinions with Home, Mother, Democracy, the Stars and Stripes, and Green, Leafy Vegetables.

Transfer and *testimonial* are much alike; both are usually examples of *ad verecundiam* arguments. In transfer, the prestige of an institution is ordinarily used to give weight to the argument. In testimonial, it is the prestige of a person. Appeals to the memory of Abraham Lincoln— what Lincoln would have thought, said, or done if he were alive—is one of the most common uses of the testimonial device. The *Kansas City Star* commented on concentrated outpouring of appeals to the memory of Lincoln:

> Reading excerpts from some of the fifty Republicans who made Lincoln Day speeches Saturday, we are somewhat confused as to what Lincoln really stood for. The speakers put forth differing views, but each could quote Lincoln in his support.
>
> Governor Aiken of Vermont was sure Lincoln wouldn't have stood for the present Republican leadership. John Hamilton, chairman of the Republican National Committee, brought Lincoln to its rescue. Senator Vandenberg of Michigan proved that Lincoln believes in coalition.
>
> Ministers have found Bible texts in support of many different doctrines, so we should not be surprised at the different interpretations of Lincoln. Perhaps after all, the country will have to admit that Lincoln lived in a different age and faced problems that are different from those of today.

Card stacking is usually the presentation of irrational evidence that leads to an irrelevant conclusion. The card stacker often presents only the evidence that supports his conclusion, as *Time* magazine once did in attacking a famous scientist, J. Robert Oppenheimer. The *Washington Post* carried an editorial that said, in part:

> . . . *Time* carefully selects testimony unfavorable to Dr. Oppenheimer, and winds up its article with quotations from John J. McCloy. . . . Perhaps the editors of *Time* themselves should have taken a closer look at the transcript. For, at the end of his testimony, Mr. McCloy added: "I can't divorce myself from my own impression of Dr. Oppenheimer, and what appeals to me is his frankness, integrity, and his scientific background. I would accept a considerable amount of political immaturity, let me put it that way, in return for this rather esoteric, this rather indefinite theoretical thinking that I believe we are going to be dependent on for the next generation.

Plain folks is usually a subtle *ad populum* argument, with the writer taking pains to assure readers that he is exactly like they are, and thus they should share his views, which are usually presented as good old common sense instead of empty theorizing. That is the stance of publisher William Randolph Hearst, Jr., in this argument:

> Never before, to the best of my recollection, has this column been devoted to a discussion of economics and the mysterious but enormous role it plays in our national welfare.
>
> There are two excellent reasons for this:
>
> A—Economics was a subject I never studied in college.
>
> B—From what I have observed since then there are so many conflicting theories that only experts can pretend to understand them fully, and even then there is no general agreement, much less any semblance of unity of opinion.
>
> Just the same, inflation and the problem of controlling it have become so important that today I thought I'd put in my two bits' worth. And even though I am a non-expert in this non-science, most everybody else is in the same canoe.
>
> So here goes—a collection of thoughts, offered for what they may be worth, by one who was brought up to believe the essence of a sound fiscal policy is to be neither a borrower nor a lender.

Hearst went on and on with homilies, presenting an argument that said, in effect: You and I know more than the egghead experts; we're sensible.

Band wagon, which is also an *ad populum* argument, usually appeals to us to join the majority to be with the winner or to serve with everyone else in an excellent cause. Like *plain folks,* it is used more often by politicians than by writers. An article in *Harper's* magazine by Robert E. Coulson entitled "Let's Not Get Out the Vote" indicates, however, that all of us, especially editorial writers, sometimes argue that everyone should go along with high-minded people in a good cause, not realizing that getting on the band wagon may have a bad result. This short passage from Coulson's article makes his point:

> Let's look at the voting behavior of Mr. and Mrs. Whipcord and Mrs. Whipcord's brother Harold on the day of the local school-board election. Mrs. Whipcord says, "I have studied the candidates and have made up my mind. I will vote for Jones." Mr. Whipcord says, "I know nothing about the candidates or the issues. I will stay home, and allow the election to be decided by the votes of those who have made a study and formed an opinion." Harold says, "I don't know anything about the candidates or the problems, but by golly, I'm going to vote. It's my duty. I'll pick the fellows with the shortest names."
>
> If there is a bad citizen among these three, which one is it? Whose decision is least likely to bring good government to the school district?

The seven devices sketched above are often used to mislead (sometimes unconsciously). By giving them catchy and loaded names, however, the Institute for Propaganda Analysis has probably obscured the fact that most of the devices may also be used for good reasons. For example, we need not avoid all name calling merely because it is most often a device used to mislead. To call a liar a liar and a thief a thief is sometimes in order. Moreover, some causes and opinions should be couched in glowing words—and to call every strongly positive statement a glittering generality is itself name calling of a pernicious kind. Nor is it always wrong to use the prestige of a person or an institution to support a cause or an opinion. In fact, card stacking is probably the only one of the seven devices that should always be condemned. Although the other devices are probably most often evidence of fallacious reasoning or an attempt to mislead, we must analyze each instance to judge truly.

Analyzing the writing of others is essential. We have trouble finding the fallacies in our own reasoning and are always in danger of using propaganda devices in a way that misleads. When we analyze other writing, however, we gradually become so conscious of fallacies and devices that we are more likely to avoid them while we are writing and better able to detect them when our words are on paper.

THREE ESSENTIALS
IN PERSUASIVE WRITING

Even when you think logically and argue honestly, you may not be able to persuade readers unless you present counterarguments and avoid overstatements and insincerity.

Counterarguments

In 1972, the NBC television network broadcast an hour-long documentary titled "Pensions: The Broken Promise." Sharply critical of several pension plans, it concluded that "it is almost inconceivable that this enormous thing [a system of pensions] has been allowed to grow up with so little understanding of it and with so little protection and such uneven results for those involved." Many individual viewers, groups, and corporations protested that the program was distorted; it had failed to emphasize that most pension plans worked well. An NBC executive responded that the program was accurate in making the point that "not all pensions meet the expectations of employees or serve all persons with equity."

This did not satisfy the protesters, of course. An organization called

Accuracy in Media complained to the Federal Communications Commission (FCC) that NBC should be required to show more positive aspects of the pension system as well. The FCC agreed. NBC took the case to court.

This case is important because it may help determine whether the courts will uphold the FCC "Fairness Doctrine," which requires that broadcasters who present one side of a controversial issue afford reasonable opportunity for response by those who represent the other. The case is important to us for another reason: It emphasizes the danger of failing to present counterarguments.

Early in the program, the narrator stated that "the pension system is essentially a consumer fraud, a shell game, a hoax." These were keynote words; most of the rest of the narrator's statements and all of the scenes were in tune with them. But surely this harsh judgment surprised—and perhaps outraged—millions of Americans: those who benefit from good pension plans and their families, not to mention those who administer good pension plans. Worse, the harsh judgment misled many viewers who had not known whether pension plans in general are good or bad. Perhaps some viewers who were counting on pensions to support them in later years began to fear that they were being defrauded.

The narrator, Edwin Newman, did say near the end:

> This has been a depressing program to work on. But we don't want to give the impression that there are no good pension plans. And there are many people for whom the promise has become a reality.

But by the time the narrator made *that* statement, it was too late. It was also too little. Everything else that had been stated and shown argued strongly that the synonyms for "pension system" are "fraud," "shell game," and "hoax." No doubt this emphasis alerted some viewers to analyze their own pension plans. If they found flaws that led to changes for the better, the program served a good purpose. But the cost in misinformation, and perhaps outrage and fright as well, was too high for this small return. It was especially high because it was unnecessary. Had the positive information at the end of the program been presented earlier and more fully, the broadcast might have served the same good purpose without the cost.

In writing persuasion, you must foresee the arguments that will counter your own. If you know that your opponents have a strong case, you must present it yourself, you must present it clearly, and usually you must present it near the beginning. Doing so is both fair and disarming. The ignorant will be informed. Your opponents and those who know their point of view will read your argument more receptively. If you fail to present the counterargument, you will mislead the ignorant and anger members of the opposition and their sympathizers. Angry readers are in no mood to be persuaded.

Overstatement

This is the most common fault in writing persuasion. In trying to argue convincingly, you are likely to state your case too strongly—as did the writer of the script for the broadcast "Pensions: The Broken Promise." Obviously, "fraud," "shell game," and "hoax" are too strong to describe the pension system, even though those words accurately describe some pension plans.

Fortunately, presenting counterargument properly sometimes helps you avoid overstatement. If you present the counterargument near the beginning and state it clearly, you are less likely to overstate; the counterargument will restrain you. How could the scriptwriter for the broadcast have described the pension system as a fraud, a shell game, and a hoax if he had already written that "there are many people for whom the promise has become a reality"?

That script teaches another important lesson in avoiding overstatement. Note the italicized word: "is *essentially* a consumer fraud . . ." The writer did not write that it *is*; he wrote that it is *essentially*, which means in essence but not entirely. He tried (perhaps unconsciously) to reduce the strength of his statement, to qualify it. The effort was worthwhile, but the word is too weak. In a sentence with words such as "fraud," "shell game," and "hoax," "essentially" has no force. Did anyone who watched that program even hear "essentially" as a qualification of the strong words that follow?

Using qualifying words that are forceful enough to reduce the power of strong words is an important technique in avoiding overstatement. A more important one is aiming the strong words at the right target. Is the pension *system* a fraud? No. Are some pension *plans* (parts of the system) frauds? Yes.

Like the television script, the essay on the National Newspaper Board that is criticized in the introduction is heavy with overstatement. The writer was blind to the sensitivity of his readers and to the flaws in his argument because he believes so strongly in the plan he outlined. That suggests a danger. As you read about insincerity, remember that persuasion is also weak when a writer is so sincere that he allows his belief to cloud his vision.

Insincerity

In private moments, entertainers sometimes say half-jokingly, "The most important thing is sincerity. Once you can fake *that,* you've got it made." Unfortunately, some writers also fake it. Or try to. Although readers cannot always detect insincerity, they are usually affected by it. If a writer does not really believe what he has written, or if he tries to make it appear that he is interested in a subject that actually bores him, readers are not likely to be caught up in his argument. This is one of the reasons so few editorials that appear in newspapers and magazines and on radio and television attract us. The writers do not often care about what they are writing. It shows.

Politicians share this failing, which is the main reason so many of their speeches are windy. When a politician has nothing to say that means much to him, he is likely to fill the air with mere words. If he is clever, he may be able to substitute technique for sincerity and to manipulate millions, but technique alone wears thin.

Insincerity is both the greatest danger in writing persuasion and the easiest to avoid. It is the greatest danger because it is usually obvious; the writing is not convincing because the writer is not convinced. It is the easiest to avoid because you need only focus persuasive writing on your beliefs and interests. Never try to write persuasively on a subject that means little or nothing to you. To choose such a subject is to fail from beginning to end. You will probably do research mechanically because no spark of interest is there to make you work imaginatively. In trying to persuade readers, you will probably write with false force.

THINKING AND WRITING

There remains the problem of fitting the principles of thought and the principles of writing together in a coherent and persuasive piece. In the following critical review of the novel *Advise and Consent* by Allen Drury, a student is trying to persuade readers that her judgment of the value of the book is accurate. Her own criticisms of the book provide a counterargument for her praise of it. She does not overstate. It is obvious that she is sincere. And yet the piece is not persuasive—or not as persuasive as it could be—largely because few of the sentences are crisp with concise and precise expression, because the writer tries to make points without illustrating them, and because the last section is poorly organized. The editing of the piece and the comments beside it are to show that persuasion in writing does not depend solely on sound reasoning.

COMMENTS

The writer should not have used such a statement at the beginning. It is too familiar to make compelling reading. Also, limiting the paragraph to those words calls attention to them and thus wrongly suggests that they are worth strong emphasis. It would be better to make one paragraph of the first two and to begin the first sentence with words that signal that the familiar quotation will be presented in a new perspective.

". . . the man and his vote are inseparable" is so obvious that readers wonder why those words are used. The writer must go on to make clear the significance of the statement (if it has any significance).

". . . hangs in the balance" is trite and "much ensues during the battle period" can be deleted.

Like "the man and his vote are inseparable," "the lives of these men cannot be separated from their careers" is puzzling. Do those words mean anything?

REVIEW

"The Senate of the United States shall be composed of two Senators from each State . . . and each Senator shall have one vote."

These words in the Constitution of the United States set up the upper house in our government. But this is not the full story of its place in the American democratic system. This story is left for *Advise and Consent* to tell.

Allen Drury in *Advise and Consent* provides a study of the meaning of the Senate and the integrity of our system of checks and balances. He realizes that the two senators from each state are individual personalities, and that the man and his vote are inseparable.

Advise and Consent is built around the Constitutional power of the Senate to advise and consent to the President's appointment of Robert A. Leffingwell as Secretary of State.

The liberal forces of the country, the President, and the press are pitted against an old Southern senator (Seab Cooley) in a bitter battle over the nomination. Leffingwell's appointment hangs in the balance for two weeks, and much ensues during the battle period; reputations are made and lost, courage is severely tested, and men face what for some is the major crisis of their lives. For the lives of these men cannot be separated from their careers.

The conflict illustrates the real meaning of the Senate, described in so few words in the Constitution. It shows that power politics plays a larger part in our governmental process than sugar-coated government texts indicate. Yet, at the same time, it illustrates that the real strength of our government is not spiritual but me-

COMMENTS

The piece is well-organized up to the paragraph marked (A). (That and the remaining paragraphs are marked with letters that will be referred to in the discussion at the end.)

What is meant by "written journalistically"? Persuasive writing is ineffective when such meanings are in doubt. The writer should illustrate by quoting a few of the clichés so that readers will be convinced that she is right.

The writer is mixing metaphors with "parade" and "dirty laundry." Because "parade" is a symbol for "book," using both in one sentence is graceless.

The writer should quote a bit of the good dialogue and that described as "teen-age." Merely saying that some of the dialogue is good and some immature is not persuasive.

"The characters are good" can be misleading. Are they good people? Or did Drury's words etch clear portraits of them? To be persuasive, the writer must show how they are "overdone" and spell out Munson's appeal.

"One criticism" seems odd because

REVIEW

chanical, and that somehow out of the complex and cumbersome workings of the Senate, a decision emerges.

One is left with the thought that power is a dirty and vital element in government.

(A) In a literary sense, Drury's book is not a great novel. Deadwood could have been eliminated easily. It is written journalistically, and clichés are sprinkled throughout.

(B) In spite of this, Drury has created a behind-the-scenes atmosphere in a skillfully developed plot. One finds this great parade of Washington's dirty laundry impossible to put down until the book is completed.

(C) Part of its appeal undoubtedly stems from the fact that everyone yearns to know what *really* happens among the higher-ups in the smoke-filled rooms of politics. This book gives you the feeling that you are there.

(D) The dialogue is good in spots, although some of it sounds a little teen-age for dignified Senators. However, this may reflect the image of Senators as men, which is the great lesson gleaned from *Advise and Consent*.

(E) The characters are good, although overdone occasionally. But Munson, the Senate Majority Leader, is particularly appealing. The most powerful character is Seab Cooley, who in the eyes of many is a sly and evil old man. His opposition to Leffingwell's appointment provides the spirit of the book.

(F) Attempts to identify the characters with actual governmental figures add interest.

(G) One criticism of the book is that

COMMENTS

the writer has already made several other criticisms.

Because readers of this piece may not have read the book, the writer should make it clear why she thinks Van Ackerman commands too much respect. What is it about him that suggests that Drury made a mistake in making Van Ackerman a respected figure? The writer cannot persuade readers that her judgments are accurate when she offers readers no more than a bare indication of what she thinks.

REVIEW

it is unrealistic in several areas. One bothersome character is Fred Van Ackerman, a self-appointed liberal leader, who commands too much respect.

(H) The most disturbing aspect is that the book ends with the death of the President. An ending with a roll-call vote would have been more realistic.

(I) Still, *Advise and Consent* has a point to make, and it makes it well. It is an outstanding novel about Washington, in spite of its flaws.

Like the other forms of writing, persuasion is most effective when readers are led smoothly from point to point. Consider the badly organized passage that runs from the paragraph marked *A* to a paragraph near the end of the theme.

In the first seven paragraphs, the writer provides an overview of the novel. In paragraph *A*, she begins to criticize Drury's style, drifts back to the overview in paragraph *B*, devotes *C* to overview, then, unaccountably, reverts to criticism of Drury's style in *D*. Paragraph *E* seems to be much like *B*: part overview, part criticism of Drury's style. Paragraph *F* is different: an example of the writer's insight, it seems to belong with *C* because both allude to the same kind of public interest in political reality. *G*, *H*, and *I* are satisfactory concluding paragraphs: a salient criticism, then *the* most disturbing aspect, then a transitional word ("Still") that leads into the central judgment.

Obviously, the passage from paragraph *A* to paragraph *F* should be reorganized so that like elements can be read together. This does not mean that all criticisms of an author's style must appear in one place. Here, though, they should be brought together because there is no reason for scattering them and a good reason for integrating them: Readers can better understand the writer's argument.

The effect of some arguments depends almost entirely on deft writing and on arguing imaginatively. Because the following piece is satire, the student who wrote it could safely overstate and ignore counterarguments—provided he succeeded in making it clear, subtly, that he was writing satire. A satirical argument that seems to readers to be conventional argument is the worst kind of failure. This student succeeded, and in doing so illustrated how much more persuasive an argument is when the writing is attractive.

COMMENTS

The first two paragraphs may be dangerously subtle. If readers do not catch the writer's tone, they may think that he means what he seems to be saying: that futurology is so wonderful that everyone should get in on it. Note that he says "Even more astounding," which may suggest that he is wide-eyed about the money-making possibilities. In fact, of course, the writer is beginning to ridicule futurology. Most readers will catch the writer's tone in the first two paragraphs. Those who do not may stop reading because they think futurology is nonsense. Although this is the principal danger of subtle writing, overstating too strongly at the beginning to make certain that every reader understands may change satire to slapstick.

This explanatory passage is necessary both to define futurology and to make the point that its practitioners are serious about it.

ARGUMENT

The word "futurology" is so new that it doesn't appear in most dictionaries. Yet people all over the country —consultants, authors, academics—are earning big money out of the science of futurology right now.

Even more astounding is the fact that futurology is simple to learn. Almost anyone can be a futurologist in only a few hours of study in the comfort of his own home!

What is futurology? Basically, it is predicting the future by identifying and projecting current trends. These predictions need not be believable, just as long as they are derived from numbers, or what the scientists call data. In a recent book, *The Limits to Growth,* a group of futurologists took data on existing trends—birth rates, resource use, pollution, etc.—and projected or "extrapolated" them into the future. They showed clearly that we will soon run out of precious resources such as aluminum, copper, mercury, molybdenum, food and water. The end will come quickly:

The behaviour mode of the system . . . is clearly that of overshoot and collapse . . . (T)he collapse occurs because of nonrenewable resource depletion . . . (T)he industrial base collapses, taking with it the service and agricultural systems . . . For a short time the situation is especially serious because population . . . keeps rising. Population finally decreases when the death rate is driven upward by lack of food and health services.

COMMENTS

Here the writer ridicules strongly, making clear to readers who may not have been certain *of his purpose that he is satirizing futurology.*

Readers who have gotten in the spirit of the writing will probably chortle at the use of the method of futurologists to poke fun at them. If futurologists and their supporters are humorless, they *are likely to be irritated.*

Note that this paragraph quoting Twain and the following paragraph quoting Ruckelshaus indicate that the writer has done research. Instead of hitting upon a bright little idea for ridiculing futurologists, then writing whatever came into his mind, the writer prepared carefully. Subtle and light though the theme may be, it is built on a solid foundation. The danger is that the writer may allow the research to dominate the writing. This writer wisely uses research briefly, then returns to his own engaging commentary.

What if in research he had found many others he could quote? To quote them would have been to alter the character of the piece.

ARGUMENT

In other words, within a lifetime we will probably all be dead. This book has sold thousands of copies.

Yet the astonishing fact is that with very little practice you too can make predictions every bit as alarming as these.

The easiest tool of the futurologist is extrapolation of *linear growth*. A quantity grows in a linear fashion if it increases by a constant amount in a constant time period. If you knew for example that a certain child grew at the rate of one inch a year, or that a man saved $10 a week, this would be linear growth. With very little mathematical ability you could, say, extrapolate these growth trends to figure out when the child will be 42 feet tall, or when the man will be able to purchase France.

Mark Train, a futurologist who was well ahead of his time, showed deft use of this technique in a passage from his *Life on the Mississippi:*

In the space of one hundred and seventy-six years the Lower Mississippi has shortened itself two hundred and forty-two miles. That is an average of a trifle over one mile and a third per year. Therefore, any calm person, who is not blind or idiotic, can see that . . . seven hundred and forty-two years from now the Lower Mississippi will be only a mile and three-quarters long, and Cairo and New Orleans will have joined their streets together, and be plodding comfortably along under a single mayor and a mutual board of aldermen.

There is little doubt that Twain could have earned a healthy consulting fee

COMMENTS

ARGUMENT

if he had taken these findings to the Corps of Engineers.

Keep in mind that this technique can easily be adapted for use with quantities that are decreasing by a constant amount. William D. Ruckelshaus, Administrator of the Environmental Protection Agency, showed this clearly in a speech he made last year in Detroit:

> Statistics now show that the rate of occupancy of cars during peak load periods is down to 1.2 persons per vehicle, and at the present rate of passenger decline by 1980 one out of every three cars will be tooling along without a driver.

This paragraph marks an important change. Instead of continuing with examples like those used earlier, and thus running the risk of spinning out a single thread that readers would eventually tire of following, the writer introduces a new element. The theme is the same, but the new element promises a different kind of development of it that pulls readers along.

The problem with linear growth is that it's too slow. The man saving $10 a week may not be able to afford France until he's too old to enjoy it. Luckily, science has recently come up with something a lot faster called "exponential" growth. A quantity grows exponentially when it increases by a constant *percentage of the whole* in a constant time period.

For example, let's say you know a man who has a 256-square-foot garden. One day a patch of crab grass appears that is one square foot in area. The man asks you to consult him on the future of his garden, and you show up the next day to find that there are now two square feet of crab grass. The crab grass could be growing linearly (at one square foot per day) or exponentially (100% increase per day). In the former case the man will have a full 8½ months before the crab grass completely overruns his garden, while in the latter he has only a week. You immediately inform the man that his

COMMENTS

By this point, you may wonder whether the writer is actually trying to persuade his readers that futurology is nonsense or whether he is just having fun. The fact is that the writer respects some studies of the future but thinks that such projections have become a ridiculous craze.

The more important question is whether readers think the writer is just having fun. If all think so, this persuades no one of anything—and probably should not be defined as persuasion. Sixty students who read this were asked whether it should be considered persuasion; more than half thought so. Several said that it persuaded them that projections have become ridiculous. One said that he had noticed in reading news items and textbooks that projections seemed to have become "the thing to do" in many fields but that he might not have considered the practice ridiculous had he not read this. Others agreed.

Because "linear growth," "exponential growth," and "systems extrapolation" are real terms that symbolize real practices, using them is sure to enhance the belief of some readers that

ARGUMENT

garden is suffering from a bad case of exponential growth, which shakes him up so much that he fails to notice the exorbitance of your fee.

With this simple tool you can produce in the comfort of your livingroom predictions that will rival those from the computers of M.I.T. Let's say that you are a rabbit fancier and know among other things that rabbits can reproduce at eight months of age, that they can have one litter per month, and that the average litter is six bunnies. You wish to determine whether there will ever be a problem of excess rabbits.

Like all good scientists, you make some conservative assumptions—that the life expectancy of a rabbit is one year, that there are only two rabbits presently in existence—and then begin to calculate. You quickly determine that at the end of one year there would be only 24 rabbits taking up a measly 12 square feet, and after two years only 288 rabbits taking up a manageable 144 square feet. But then the little bunnies begin to proliferate at an alarming rate until by the 15th year there are 15 quadrillion of the damn things and the entire land area of the world is hip-deep in hoppers. Immediately you call Civil Defense officials to say you have some information that might interest them.

The main tools of futurology are linear and exponential extrapolation, but if you really want to make the big time there is one more skill you must master: systems extrapolation. This involves gathering all identifiable trends and quantifying them into one huge system of interdependent equations forming a dynamic simulation of the future of the entire world. It is this

COMMENTS	ARGUMENT
the writer intends his argument to be taken seriously. Because the examples are ridiculous—see especially in the next-to-last paragraph the "most advanced model"—no reader is likely to think that the writer is citing actual examples. It is important to use overstated examples in such cases to avoid misleading readers who may be ignorant. This is valuable overstatement.	"systems" approach that sells books, that brings speaking engagements, that wins academic chairs at large universities, that guarantees lucrative consulting contracts.
	Unfortunately, the complex techniques of systems design are beyond the scope of this article. Suffice it to say that M.I.T.-type dynamic computer systems have produced predictions far more incredible than any we have touched on so far. Indeed, the most advanced model we have seen predicts that the world will end in the year 2035 during a battle between a giant crab grass-eating rabbit and a 42-foot-high child who owns France.
Note that the writer does not end with a savage denunciation of futurology. He wisely ends in the tone in which he began. If readers are not convinced by what has preceded the last paragraph, the writer is not likely to convince them at this point with an editorial statement.	There is money, glamor and fame in this new science. But the time to get involved in futurology is *now,* before everybody tries to get on the bandwagon. Our projections show that at the present rate of growth there will be more futurologists than people in this country before the turn of the next century.

In writing satirically, this student placed himself in the position of the editorial cartoonist. A cartoonist's work would have no force if he were to draw his satirical picture, then draw another beside it to say, in effect, "On the other hand. . . ." Also, to make his point in a single picture, the cartoonist must overstate, usually by caricaturing figures and exaggerating their actions. Finally, we can seldom be certain in looking at a cartoon whether the cartoonist is as sincerely savage as the picture he has drawn makes him appear to be.

Similarly, the student's satire would have had no force had he worked into it a counterargument pointing up the value of some projections of the future. Because satire is overstatement, the writer had to overstate. And, of course, we cannot be certain of the degree to which he was sincere in ridiculing futurology and the degree to which he was having fun.

All this suggests reasons for using satire infrequently. Most objects of attack deserve to have their arguments presented. Overstating an attack on them is usually unfair. Finally, some readers of satirical writing are almost certain to think that the writer is presenting truth (or his version of it), not satire, unless the satire is written so heavily that it becomes slapstick. The writer runs the risk of seeming more ridiculous than the subject he satirizes. But when a writer can carry it off, as few can, satire makes most reasonable arguments seem pale and weak, most fiery arguments seem shrill.

Although persuasion is only one of the four forms of writing, the examples in this chapter show how much you can learn from it about all writing. The review of *Advise and Consent* shows that one who thinks clearly must also learn the principles of the craftsman. The piece on futurology shows how one who thinks clearly and is a craftsman can use his imagination to write artfully. It may be that a thoughtful writer is not ready to become an artist until he has mastered the principles of the craftsman. Perhaps only then is his mind free to let his imagination work.

However that may be, this much is certain: Writing well requires that you combine craftsmanship and clear thought.

PROJECTS

1   A famous eighteenth-century preacher noted for overstatement, Jonathan Edwards, delivered a sermon that included the following. Look back at the seven propaganda devices described in this chapter and determine whether this passage reflects the use of any of them. What modern audience —what kind of people—might be persuaded by such sermonizing?

> The God that holds you over the pit of hell much as one holds a spider or some loathsome insect over the fire, abhors you, and is dreadfully provoked; his wrath towards you burns like fire; he looks upon you as worthy of nothing else but to be cast into the fire; he is of purer eyes than to bear to have you in his sight; you are ten thousand times so abominable in his eyes as the most hateful and venomous serpent is in ours. You have offended him infinitely more than ever a stubborn rebel did his prince: and yet it is nothing but his hand that holds you from falling into the fire every moment. Tis ascribed to nothing else, that you did not go to hell the last night; that you was [sic] suffered to awake again in this world after you closed your eyes to sleep; and there is no other reason to be given why you have not dropped into hell since you arose in the morning, but that God's hand has held you up. There is no other reason to be given why you have not gone to hell since you have sat here in the house of God, provoking his pure eyes by your sinful wicked manner of attending his solemn worship. Yea, there is nothing else that is to be given as a reason why you do not this very moment drop down into hell.

2   Look in newspaper or magazine advertisements or editorials for examples

of propaganda devices. As pointed out in this chapter, the devices can be used for good purposes and have good results. Using five of the examples you find, write several paragraphs about each to give your opinion. Consider in each case whether you approve the use of the device because the writer's argument squares with your beliefs or disapprove because it does not.

3   Gore Vidal wrote the following description of Ronald Reagan. Write a short paper commenting on his use of description for argument. Consider whether Vidal's argument is more persuasive in a paragraph that seems to be descriptive than it would be in a paragraph obviously devoted to presenting the writer's opinion.

Ronald Reagan is a well-preserved not young man. Close to, the painted face is webbed with delicate lines while the dyed hair, eyebrows, and eyelashes contrast oddly with the sagging muscle beneath the as yet unlifted chin, soft earnest of wattle soon-to-be. The effect, in repose, suggests the work of a skillful embalmer. Animated, the face is quite attractive and at a distance youthful; particularly engaging is the crooked smile full of large porcelain-capped teeth. The eyes are the only interesting feature: small, narrow, apparently dark, they glitter in the hot light, alert to every move, for this is enemy country—the liberal Eastern press who are so notoriously immune to that warm and folksy performance which Reagan quite deliberately projects over their heads to some legendary constituency at the far end of the tube, some shining Carverville where good Lewis Stone forever lectures Andy Hardy on the virtues of thrift and the wisdom of the contract system at Metro-Goldwyn-Mayer.

4   Write a critical review in about 700 words of any book, film, play, concert, or dance performance.

5   Study the piece on futurology in this chapter, then try to write a short satire on another subject. You may find that you can develop ideas about satire by reading the work of three satirical columnists, Art Buchwald, Art Hoppe, and Russell Baker. Their columns appear in hundreds of newspapers. If you find that you are not comfortable with satire—many writers are not—write a quietly worded argument in a wry or skeptical tone.

A Handbook for Writers: Conventions and Principles

This alphabetical list is made up of conventions of punctuation and spelling and principles of usage and grammar. No one could ever compose a true list of the precepts of good writing, and few of the entries in this list are rigid rules. Instead, the practices of good writers establish conventions and principles; and their practices change, often to reflect changes in speech patterns. A few of the conventions and principles are always in the process of change. Usage experts try to keep pace with the practices of those who write well, but Roy Copperud's *American Usage: The Consensus* shows that the leading usage experts sometimes disagree.

The usage entries in the following list try to avoid the bookish, the stilted, and the stuffy on one side and colloquialisms, slang, and clichés on the other. The purpose is to promote conventions and principles that make writing similar to speech but to avoid the looseness of the spoken language.

A, an. See *Articles.*

Abbreviations.   Most publications have a style book or a style guide that tells writers which words should be abbreviated. Newspapers, which try to present a great deal of information, tend to abbreviate more words than do most other publications. These abbreviations are used by nearly all publications:

1   B.A., B.S., M.A., M.S., Ph.D., M.D., Ed.D., D.D.S., and other academic degrees.
2   Mr., Mrs., Ms., Dr., Jr., and Sr.

3 Political and military titles when they precede the full name, as in Gov. John Jones, Sen. Margaret Atkin, Col. Reuben Johnson, and Lt. Henry Douglas. When such a title is used only with the last name, it is not abbreviated: Senator Atkin, Colonel Johnson.

4 Mph, rpm, P.M., A.M., A.D., B.C., and No. when they are used with figures: 90 mph, 1,500 rpms, 8 P.M., 4 A.M., 104 A.D., 450 B.C., and No. 1 choice.

5 U.N., U.S., C.O.D., TV, hi-fi, and stereo.

Above. Avoid using "the figures above" where possible, and always avoid using *above* as a noun (the above will make clear). "These" or "these figures" is preferable. When it is necessary to use *above*, make it "the figures above" rather than "the above figures."

Acronyms. An *acronym* is an abbreviation, pronounced as a word, which is made up of the first letters of the major words in the title: CREEP for Committee for the Re-Election of the President, SAC for Strategic Air Command. When a writer is not certain that all his readers know what an acronym stands for, he usually writes the full name and puts the acronym in parentheses—South East Asia Treaty Organization (SEATO)—then uses only the acronym in later references and removes the parentheses: "The SEATO nations decided. . . ." This is a common practice in writing all initials, but many readers consider it odd to see widely known organizations so identified, as in Federal Bureau of Investigation (FBI).

Active voice. See *Verbs.*

Actual, actually. See *Modifiers.*

Adjectives. See *Modifiers.*

Advance planning, future planning. Planning is laying out a future course, "advance" and "future" are superfluous.

Adverbs. See *Modifiers.*

Affect, effect. These words are often confused. The verb *affect* means to influence, concern, or assume, as in these examples:

> Hemingway's writing *affected* (influenced) the writing of John O'Hara
>
> Brando *affected* (assumed) the manner of Hamlet.

The verb *effect* means to cause or to bring about, as in this example:

> The manager *effected* (caused) a change by substituting Pete Rose.

Affect is used as a noun only as a technical term in the social sciences. The noun *effect* means the result, as in this example:

> The *effect* (result) was that Oakland won the game.

Aggravate.   This word is not a synonym for irritate or exasperate. *Aggravate* means to increase or make worse.

Agreement.   This term means the formal correspondence of one word with another. Most of the common errors in agreement result from carelessness, as in:

> If a writer has any ability, the teacher will help *them* develop it

Verbs and pronouns must agree in number with a preceding noun or pronoun, a verb with its subject, a pronoun with its antecedent. Most problems of agreement can be solved easily by keeping pronouns close to their antecedents and verbs close to their subjects. But even professional writers are sometimes troubled by a few problems that are covered in the following:

1   Collective nouns take either singulars or plurals, depending on the writer's intent. If the writer is thinking of a group as a unit, he must use singular verbs and pronouns:

> The group *has* been ready to act on *its* major assignment since November.
> The team *prays* before every game.
> The committee *is* to meet at 8 P.M.

If the writer thinks of members of a group as individuals taking individual actions, he should use plural verbs and pronouns;

> By the time the committee had been in session for an hour, *they* were shouting.
> When the team took the field, *they* ran from the dugout.

2   A compound joined by *and* takes a plural verb and pronoun:

> John Kennedy and Lyndon Johnson *were* at *their* best in political debate.

3   After a compound joined by *or* or *nor,* the number of the verb and pronouns is determined by the nearer subject or antecedent:

> We don't know whether the quarterback or the linebackers *are* to appear on the television program.
> The senators *or* the president is certain to be here soon.

4   Most good writers seem to decide that indefinite expressions such as *an-*

other, anybody, each, either, everybody, everyone, neither, nobody, no one, and *none* take singular verbs and pronouns:

No one *is* likely to want to go if *he* must buy a ticket.

But some writers and grammarians hold that *no one* and *none* can be singular or plural depending on the sense. In this example, "none are" seems preferable: "The children's home has received no contributions, and none are expected."

All ready, already. *All ready* means that everything is ready, *already* means "by this time" or beforehand in time. (She was already at the bus stop.)

All right, alright. *Alright* is all wrong.

Allude, allusion, refer, reference. To *allude,* or to make an *allusion,* is to mention indirectly, leaving it to the reader to use the allusion to make the identification. A *reference* is direct, as in, "I refer to the first sentence, not to the entire paragraph."

Although, though. *Although* is preferable.

Ambiguous, ambivalent. Writing that is *ambiguous* has more than one meaning or interpretation and is thus uncertain or obscure. *Ambivalent* refers to simultaneous attraction and repulsion.

Among, between. Use *between* for two elements (between you and me), *among* for more than two (among the three of us).

Amount, number. *Amount* is used to refer to many things of the same kind or to many similar things considered as a whole, as in, "The amount he paid was not enough." *Number* is used to refer to separate units, as in, "The number of coins was different when she counted."

Anachronism. This error involves misplacement of words or actions in time. For example, "George Washington was a bit stern even when he was a teen-ager" uses *teen-ager* in referring to a time when the word was unknown.

And/or. This legalism is seldom useful in nonlegal writing and always sounds legalistic. *Or* will usually do the work of *and/or.* When it will not, use "_____ or _____, or both."

Angry, mad. Use *angry* to refer to the emotion. Use *mad* to refer to the mental condition. Using *mad* for *angry* sometimes leaves readers wondering, at least for a moment, whether the writer is referring to the emotion or to the mental condition.

Another.   See *Agreement.*

Antecedents.   See *Agreement.*

Anybody, anyone.   *Anybody* should not be written *any body* unless the meaning intended is "any corpse" or other inanimate object such as a body of water. *Anyone* should not be written *any one* unless the intended meaning is "any one thing." See also *Agreement.*

Any more, any way.   *Any more* is always written as two words. *Any way* should be written as two words unless the intended meaning is "in any case" (He didn't care anyway).

Anyplace, someplace.   Use *anywhere* and *somewhere.*

Apostrophes.   Among the many uses of the apostrophe are to:

1   Mark the possessive of nouns:

> John's book
> the boys' books

(Except for *one*—one's best book—the apostrophe is not used to mark the possessive of pronouns: *hers, yours, his, its, ours, theirs.*)

2   Mark the omission of one or more letters in contractions:

> doesn't
> it's (Note that *it's* means "it is"; *its* is the possessive.)
> I'll
> we've
> she'll
> who's (Note that *who's* means "who is": *whose* is the possessive.)

3   Mark the omission of one or more numbers:

> a '75 Cadillac

4   Form the plurals of symbols:

> He rolled three 7's.
> She earned two A's.
> I use too many the's in writing.

Article.   *A* should be used before *h* when the first syllable is accented:

a *hus*band, a *half*back. *An* should be used before a silent *h*: *h*umble, *h*erb. Using *an* before *historian* and *historical* is an affectation.

A and *an* are indefinite articles. They refer to members of a class: a book, a football, a man, an ostrich. *The* is the definite article. It refers to individual persons or objects: the woman, the table. A fairly common fault is for a writer to forget that his readers know nothing about his topic and to write, say, "Henry was pushing *the* wheelbarrow when he stumbled." In most instances, an object should be introduced indefinitely —"Henry was pushing *a* wheelbarrow when he stumbled" so readers will not wonder: *The* wheelbarrow? What wheelbarrow? When it is mentioned again, the writer should shift to the definite article: "A dozen bottles of gin spilled from *the* wheelbarrow and broke on the sidewalk."

As, like.   Use *as,* not *like,* as a conjunction: The cigarette tastes good, as a cigarette should."

Avoid using *as* for *because.* If a writer uses *as* and *because* interchangeably, readers have no way of knowing what is meant by expressions such as this: "As I was swimming, I began to think." Did he begin to think *because* he was swimming or merely *while* he was swimming?

At.   Avoid using *at* after *where.* "Where is it at?" says no more than "Where is it?"

At present, at the present time, presently.   Instead of using *at present* and *at the present time,* use *now,* which says the same thing crisply. Some writers misuse *presently,* thinking that it means now. It means soon, and when that is the intended meaning, use *soon.*

Because.   Avoid using ambiguous substitutes such as *since* and *as.*

Behalf.   "In his behalf" means in his interest. "On his behalf" means representing him.

Between.   See *Among.*

Bimonthly, biweekly.   *Bimonthly* means every two months, *biweekly* every two weeks. These are so often confused with *semimonthly* and *semiweekly,* which mean twice a month and twice a week, that it is better to write every two months, every two weeks, twice a month, and twice a week.

Blond, blonde.   *Blond* refers to a man, *blonde* to a woman.

Boat, ship.   A boat is usually a small open craft. Larger vessels are ships.

Brackets.   A writer uses [brackets] to insert his own words in a direct quotation. Parentheses should not be used for this purpose because one who is quoted may say something parenthetical that will require parentheses. Most newspapers use parentheses for brackets because their type fonts have no brackets.

Burglary, robbery.   These words are not the same. *Burglary* is breaking and entering with intent to commit a felony. To *rob* is simply to steal from.

Can, may, could, might.   *Can* and *could* usually express ability or physical possibility: "He *can* play on Saturday." "He *could* win if he tried." *May* and *might* usually express permission or possibility: "You *may* attend the game." "She *might* want to go."

Cannot, can not.   Either word may be used. *Cannot* is used more often, perhaps because *can not* seems more emphatic.

Can't hardly, couldn't hardly.   Both expressions have the force of double negatives and should be avoided.

Capital Letters.   The style books (or style guides) adopted by publications spell out rules for capitalizing that differ somewhat from one publication to another, but all are based on one principle: The name of anything unique begins with a capital letter. The term *proper noun* is derived from names that are the property of something unique: Susan Sanders, Sears and Roebuck, Continental Can Company, November, Texas, New Year's Day, Germany, William Shakespeare, Tuesday, the Mississippi River. Adjectives that grow out of such nouns are also capitalized: Texan, Shakespearean. In addition, titles that are used in place of names are capitalized: "I'm writing, Mother, to ask whether you can send me an advance on my allowance." "Please, Mayor, listen to the voice of the people."

The principle of uniqueness in capitalizing is a fair guide, but there are several exceptions. A writer should refer to "John's mother," not to "John's Mother," and to "a call from the mayor," not to "a call from the Mayor." In these instances, the writer is not using a title in place of a name but is using descriptive words.

Seasons (spring, fall) are not capitalized in constructions such as "next spring" or "last fall." Sections of the country are capitalized when referring to a region or culture—"the West," "the South"—but not in referring to them as directions: "I expect to go north in September."

Titles of books, plays, films, and the like are capitalized, but not conjunctions, articles (a, an, the) and prepositions of fewer than four letters unless one of these is the first or last word: *The Man Who Was Not With It, One Flew Over the Cuckoo's Nest, The World We Live In, Once Upon a Mattress, Pride and Prejudice.*

Capitalize the initial letter in an independent clause after a colon (It was a wild collection: She had everything from campaign buttons to camp tents), but do not capitalize the initial letter of a dependent clause after a colon (It was a wild collection: everything from campaign buttons to camp tents).

Centers around.   This is often used. It is wrong. *Center* refers to a point. Use *centers on* or *revolves around.*

Chord.   Do not use with *vocal,* as in "vocal chord." It is *vocal cord.*

Cite, site.   To *cite* is to refer to or to quote. A *site* is a location.

Classic, classical.   *Classic* connotes importance, as in "The Battle of Gettysburg was a classic." *Classical* refers to Greek and Roman culture, serious music that has lasted, and basic bodies of knowledge (*classical Hebrew, classical philosophy*).

Cohort.   A *cohort* cannot be one person, or even several. The word refers to a large group.

Colon.   The colon usually tells readers that a pointed explanation of the preceding part of the sentence comes next, as in:

> He had only three choices: flight, surrender, or suicide.

The colon is also used to introduce a quotation:

> Hemingway wrote of Gertrude Stein: "It seemed to me at first that she was always right."

Commas.   An old printer said he used this rule for punctuating: "I set type as long as I can hold my breath, and then I put in a comma. When I yawn I put in a semi-colon. And when I want to chew of tobacco I make a paragraph." Some beginning writers are likely to sympathize. The conventions of punctuation, especially those governing the use of the comma —the most common and the most commonly misused mark—may seem unbearably complicated. The many conventions will not seem complicated to one who remembers that punctuation is an attempt to reflect the pauses, intonations, and pitch of the spoken language. Thus, the writer who reads his work aloud can often guide himself to the appropriate marks.

Commas are used to impart meaning and prevent confusion. Their primary functions are to separate clauses (usually with the help of conjunctions), to separate items in a series, to set off introductory words and phrases, to set off parenthetical groups of words, and to avoid ambiguity. Following are the main conventions of comma use:

1 Commas should be used to separate clauses, but not to splice groups of words that should be independent sentences. Here the comma is used appropriately:

> The team won, but every player was exhausted.

Here the comma splices two sentences:

> The president spoke at length, later he said that he regretted speaking so long.

Reading the first sentence aloud shows the slight pause and makes it clear that the words before the comma and those after it are naturally connected. Reading the second sentence aloud shows the much stronger pause at the comma, which suggests that the comma should be a period.

When an independent clause is short, no comma is needed:

> If I win I'll be happy.

But a pair of commas is always needed to set off a nonrestrictive clause— the kind that does not define or limit as restrictive clauses do but could be made a separate sentence, as in:

> The player, who was injured throughout the 1974 season, decided that his baseball career was over.

That sentence could have been written:

> The player decided that his baseball career was over. He was injured throughout the 1974 season.

2 Commas separate items in a series like this:

> The tree was alive with lizards, bugs, and birds.
> She went to the kitchen, to the bedroom, and to the porch.

Some publications prescribe that no comma should be used before the *and* that signals the last item in a series: "The tree was alive with lizards, bugs and birds." That system works in most instances, but in some it causes ambiguity: "The relationship of industrial recruitment, airport expansion and public transit and the problems of pollution and land use will soon be known." Readers cannot be certain whether "airport expansion and public transit" together represent one item or whether "public transit" is the last item in the series.

3 Commas set off introductory words and phrases like this:

> Well, you know I wouldn't do anything like that.
>
> When the quarterback tried to pass, he was overwhelmed.

As reading each sentence aloud will show, the comma reflects a break. The words "know I wouldn't" in the first sentence, for example, run smoothly together, not at all like "Well, you." In most instances, failing to use commas to set off such introductory words causes confusion for at least a few readers.

4 Commas are used to avoid ambiguity like this:

> Below, the senator was speaking to his colleagues.

Had the sentence been written, "Below the senator was speaking to his colleagues," many readers might expect the words after the first three to tell what was below the senator.

5 Some conventions of comma usage have become established because commas are needed to show pauses, or to reflect a drop in the voice of a speaker, or both. Commas are used:

> To separate cities from their states: Kansas City, Missouri, is growing.
>
> To separate the parts of dates: It happened on November 12, 1958, in Boston.

(When only the month and year are used, a comma is optional: November 1958 or November, 1958.)

> To indicate direct address: You told me, John, that Harry would go.
>
> To set off mild interjections: Oh, why should I care?
>
> To separate modifiers: She wore a pair of old, tie-dyed jeans.
>
> To set off appositives: Amy, the valedictorian, has the highest scholastic average.
>
> To introduce quotations: He said, "Let the music begin."

Compare to, compare with. In likening one thing to another, use *compare to*. In examining two things to show differences and likenesses, use *compare with*.

Complected. Use *complexioned*.

Complement, compliment. *Complement* refers to making something whole or complete: "The dancers complement each other neatly." *Compliment* refers to praise: "Applause is the compliment actors seek."

Compose, comprise.   To *compose* is to constitute or make up. Thus, the parts compose the whole. To *comprise* is to consist of, or to be made up of. Thus, the whole comprises the parts.

Consensus.   Because a *consensus* is a general opinion or belief, both "general consensus" and "consensus of opinion" are redundant.

Consider, consider as.   When *consider* is used to mean "believe to be," *as* should not be used:

> Jim Plunkett is considered the greatest quarterback.

In a sentence meaning "speak about" or "think about," *as* should be used:

> In judging him fit for the job, they considered him as a worker as well as a leader.

Contact.   Avoid *contact* as a verb by stating the action specifically:

> The workers should call [write, visit] the precinct leader.

Contemporary.   Use *contemporary* to mean "at the same time," but make certain that the time meant is clear to readers. "Babe Ruth's contemporaries" is clear, but perhaps not "The contemporary view of Babe Ruth's batting records. . . ." The "contemporary view" could mean that of Ruth's time or that of the present. In such cases, it is usually better to use "Babe Ruth's contemporaries" or "In his time, the view of Ruth's batting records. . . ."

Continual, continuous.   One can practice the piano continually—in frequently repeated practice sessions—but not continuously; *continuous* means without interruption. (One could, of course, practice continuously for several hours.) *Continual* and *continually* are meant much more often than *continuous* and *continuously*. It is wise to mark the difference by thinking of the o-u-s at the end of *continuous* as standing for *one* uninterrupted *sequence.

Contractions.   See *Apostrophe*.

Could have, could of.   Use *could have*, never *could of*.

Council, counsel.   A *council* is a group with legislative or administrative functions. *Counsel* is advice, and *a counsel* is one who gives advice, such as a lawyer.

Couple, couple of. A *couple,* like a *pair,* is singular. Using either term sometimes leads to awkward expressions. The phrase "a couple of" is too breezy for any writing except the most relaxed.

Criteria. See *Greek and Latin words.*

Curriculum. See *Greek and Latin words.*

Dash. The dash is one of the most useful—and one of the most over-used—marks of punctuation. Dashes are used to set off a strongly paren-thetical expression within a sentence, as in the preceding sentence. The dash is also used in informal writing to indicate a break in a sentence:

> It was horrible, terrifying—oh, I can't tell you how bad it was.

The dash is often misused near the end of a sentence:

> The club should also be a place where all members of the commu-nity can relax and be comfortable—adults as well as children.

The dash is misused in that example (a comma would have been better) because the dash is strong punctuation that demands strength of the words it isolates. A dash used near the end of a sentence asks readers to pause, then rush into the remaining words. Readers should not be made to rush into weak words.

In typing, the dash is made with two hyphen marks to distinguish it from the hyphen.

Data. See *Greek and Latin words.*

Different from, different than. *Different from* is preferable because things differ from each other. In a few instances, *different than* is accept-able, as in:

> The constitutions of all the nations are different, but those of the democracies are more different than the others.

Dilemma. A *dilemma* is a choice between two distasteful alternatives. The word is often mistakenly used to refer to a choice that one wants to make and a choice that one should make.

Discreet, discrete. *Discreet* means prudent. *Discrete* means distinct or separate.

Disinterested, uninterested. To be disinterested is to be impartial, to have no selfish, private, or emotional interest. The word suggests neutral-ity. *Uninterested* suggests lack of concern or enthusiasm, even boredom.

Double negative, more than one negative.   The need to avoid double negatives is widely known. "He did not do nothing" means that he did do something. Not so widely known is the need to avoid using more than one negative in a sentence even though the negatives may not cancel each other. When readers come upon "The City Council decided not to consider the failure of the city manager to void the contract," they must stop and puzzle out the meaning of three negatives: "not to," "failure," and "void."

Due to.   The broadcast networks often apologize with "Due to circumstances beyond our control," thus further popularizing the use of "due to," which has long been wrongly used. *Due* is an adjective. In nearly all cases, "because of" is preferable.

Each, every.   *Each* is singular. So is *every.* "Each and every" is merely an emphatic way of saying *each* and should take a singular verb: "Each and every man was ready to join the posse."

Each other, one another.   Use *each other* for two, *one another* for more than two.

Effect.   See *Affect.*

E.g., i.e.   *E.g. (exempli gratia)* means "for example." *I.e. (id est)* means "that is." Thus, in giving one or more examples, *e.g.* is appropriate. In naming all the members of a class, *i.e.,* is appropriate. But both expressions are better used in footnotes or in scholarly texts than they are in other writing.

Either, neither.   *Or* is used with *either, nor* with *neither.* When *either* means one or the other, it takes a singular verb: "Either John or Bill is to play third base." When the meaning of *either* is "both," it takes a plural verb: "Either John or Bill are capable of playing."

Ellipsis.   The ellipsis (plural, *ellipses*) is made up of three periods and indicates that part of a quotation has been omitted. A fourth period is used if the omitted material occurs at the end of the sentence. Here is an example of both kinds of omission:

> The man who would be greater than he has been . . . will make a greater effort. . . .

That sentence reads in its entirety:

> The man who would be greater than he has been, greater than his

friends think he can be, will make a greater effort than he has made.

Some who have discovered ellipses use them too often. Journalists seldom find ellipses necessary because in most instances readers understand that quotations are not complete.

Emigrant, immigrant. An *emigrant* leaves a country. An *immigrant* enters a country.

Enormity, enormousness. *Enormity* means atrociousness, wickedness. An *enormity* is an outrage. The word for great size is *enormousness*.

Enthuse. A back formation from *enthusiasm, enthuse* is a gushing word that should be avoided.

Equally as. *Equally* does not need *as:* "The books were equally readable."

Etc. Using *etc.* seems lazy and makes a sentence trail off. It is better to name specific items, but when naming them would become tedious for readers, or unnecessary, substitute "such as" or "including" at the beginning of a list to indicate that there are others. When *etc.* or a substitute for it seems unavoidable, use "and so on" or "and the like."

Euphemism. Some *euphemisms*—substitutes for plain words—are useful in avoiding vulgarity or grossness. Some are damaging because they substitute fanciness or abstractions for words that are weighty. To write "pass away" for "die" and "casket" for "coffin" is too fastidious. The task of the writer is to decide when he is avoiding vulgarity and when he is using words as veils to hide something better displayed in its plain form.

Everybody, everyone. See *Agreement.*

Exclamation point. Like the dash, the exclamation point is strong and calls so much attention to itself that it should be used infrequently. It should be used, of course, with all exclamations:

> Oh!
> Damn!
> How sweet it was!
> Then I understood. It was Dave wearing the mask!

A writer should not merely be wary of using many exclamation points; he should guard against their frequent use. The tendency to use many exclamatory sentences is usually a sign of general overstatement.

The fact that.   It is not possible to purge writing of this phrase, but it should be used sparingly.

Farther, further.   The first is used to express physical distance, as in, "It is farther from Los Angeles to Chicago than it is from New York to Chicago." *Further* is used to express figurative distance: "I have much further to go on this term paper than I thought I had." Many good writers sometimes use the terms interchangeably, but *further* is indispensable in expressing "more," as in, "The committee will consider the matter no further."

Fewer, less.   *Fewer* refers to how many and is used with countable units: "San Francisco has fewer people now than it had in 1970." *Less* refers to how much and is used with abstract and inseparable quantities: "There is less bourbon in the bottle today." In general, *fewer* is used for numbers, *less* for amounts, but some units that could be counted, such as money, are often considered single quantities, as in, "I have less than a hundred dollars in the bank."

Figuratively, literally.   These words are responsible for two bad writing habits. One is using *literally* for *figuratively,* probably because it seems stronger. The other is using *literally* with an old metaphor to intensify it or to try to make it seem fresh, as in, "He literally ate them out of house and home." Neither *figuratively* nor *literally* is often useful. If a writer who uses *figuratively* correctly will examine his use of it, he is likely to find that the expression "The banker was figuratively at the edge of disaster" is obviously figurative; the meaning is the same without the word. *Literally* is of no use as an intensifier. It should be used to make a point, as in, "Justices Black and Douglas believed that the Constitution means literally what it says: that there should be no restriction on free expression. They held that anyone may call another a liar, or a murderer, whatever the truth of the charge, without fear of successful court action." Here *literally* is useful to make it clear that the other justices did not interpret literally.

Firstly.   This word and its companions, such as *secondly* and *thirdly,* are old-fashioned. Cut *ly.*

Flaunt, flout.   To *flaunt* is to wave, to make a boastful display, to parade, as in, "The candidate flaunted his military record." To *flout* is to ignore, to reject, to treat with contempt, as in, "The candidate flouted the law of slander."

Folks.   Except in letters home, use the specific terms: parents, mother, father. To write of people as *folk* or *folks* is usually both arch and archaic.

Foreign words and phrases.   Some foreign words and phrases, such as *matinee* and *negligee,* are now part of the American version of English and should be used. The task of the writer is to decide whether he is using a foreign word or phrase because it best expresses his meaning and will be understood by readers or whether he is using such a word or phrase merely to show off his knowledge. See also *Greek and Latin words.*

Former, latter.   Avoid using these when they make readers look back. Repetition is usually better. In using *former* and *latter,* make certain that there are only two antecedents. It is wrong to write, "Senators Long, Church, and Mansfield spoke yesterday, but only the latter spoke at length."

Formula.   See *Greek and Latin words.*

Fortuitous, fortunate.   *Fortuitous* means "accidental" or "happening by chance." *Fortunate* means "lucky."

Fulsome.   This does not mean full. It means "overfull, offensive, insincere."

Future planning.   See *Advanced planning.*

Gender.   This refers to the sex of words, not people. Unlike many other languages, English has many neuters, with the gender usually indicated by the sense of sentences.

Gerund.   See *Verbal.*

Greek and Latin words.   The plural forms of some Greek and Latin words that are commonly used in English are widely known and used: *criterion* is the singular, *criteria* the plural; *appendix* is the singular, *appendices* the plural; *curriculum* is the singular, *curricula* the plural; *phenomenon* is the singular, *phenomena* the plural. But the plural forms are not entirely consistent, and we have further complicated the use of some Greek and Latin singulars and plurals: *formula* becomes either *formulae* or *formulas; index* becomes either *indexes* or *indices; datum* is the singular, but some good writers use *data* as both singular and plural; the plural of *stigma* is neither *stigmas* nor *stigmae* but *stigmata; agendum,* the singular of *agenda,* has all but disappeared; the plural form of *spectrum, spectra,* is rarely used except in technical exposition. The only way to steer through such confusion, especially with change occurring relatively rapidly, is to consult a recently published dictionary.

Hanged, hung.   *Hanged* is the past tense for the execution of a person. *Hung* is used to refer to the suspension of objects.

Hopefully.   This does not mean "I hope," "We hope," or "It is to be hoped." It means "full of hope." "Hopefully, the motel will have a vacancy," means that the motel is hopeful, which is ridiculous.

However.   Many sentences in which "however" is used as a conjunction meaning "but" are smoother if *however* is tucked into the sentence rather than used at the beginning. If it is used at the beginning ("But" or "Nevertheless" is sometimes preferable there), it must be set off with a comma so readers will not confuse it with *however* as an adverb, as in "However haltingly he speaks, he is certain to win the election."

Hyperbole, litotes.   Hyperbole is heavy exaggeration, as in, "He worked like a demon." Like all strong techniques, hyperbole loses force, and may seem extravagant or even odd if it is used often. *Hyperbole* sometimes misleads readers who do not realize the writer is purposely overstating. The same dangers are apparent in using *litotes,* which is understatement. "Henry is able to restrain his enthusiasm for politics" may be an admirably dry way of saying that he dislikes politics, but some readers may take it to mean that Henry must work to restrain his enthusiasm. The effects of *hyperbole* and *litotes* depend on the context in which they are used and especially on the writer's control of tone.

Hyphen.   The hyphen has many uses:

1   To indicate compound nouns: "father-in-law."
2   To indicate compound adjectives: "jet-black hair." The effect of the hyphen in compound adjectives (and in compound nouns) is to make two or more words read as one. In contrast, "father in law" and "jet black hair" seem halting. Phrases that are customarily read as one word, as when "high school" becomes a compound adjective in "high school student," are not hyphenated because readers are accustomed to the combination. Compound adjectives are hyphenated only when they appear *before* the noun. Write "nine-year-old boy," but "The boy was nine years old." Compound

adjectives should not be confused with combinations of adverbs and adjectives. No hyphen should be used in "overly praised performance" because "overly" is an adverb; readers are accustomed to reading "ly" words into the next word so that they seem to be one, which produces the same effect as the hyphen in the compound adjective.

3 To prevent confusion: "He re-covered the furniture" makes it clear that he put on a new covering. The hyphen marks the difference between that action and the action suggested by "recover." Other words, such as "re-creation" and "re-form" are hyphenated to indicate their difference from "recreation" and "reform." Many publications favor using the hyphen to avoid the awkwardness that results from doubling vowels at syllable breaks: re-elect, pre-eminent, re-entry.

4 To join prefixes and suffixes: anti-Semitic, senator-elect, self-evident, ex-wife, arch-conservative.

The hyphen is also used, of course, to break a word at the end of a line when there is not room to type the entire word. Such breaks should be made between syllables: *drug* at the end of the line, *store* on the next line, not *drugs* at the end and *tore* on the next.

Idiom, idiomatic.   Foreigners can learn the proprieties of the American version of English, but they have trouble learning our idiom (just as we have trouble when we try to learn theirs). They find it difficult, for example, to understand why we "go to *the* stadium to watch a game" but go to town to buy some clothes." Why not "go to stadium"? Why not "go to the town"? There is no reasonable answer. Over centuries, we have come to develop the idiom. In some instances, of course, native Americans use unidiomatic constructions, as when some say, "I graduated high school." To write idiomatically is to write sentences as they are used by most educated Americans: "I graduated from high school," and "I am able to do that work," not "I am capable to do that work."

i.e.   See *E.g.*

If and when.   *When* usually has no value in this tired phrase. If it happens, it will happen at a particular time.

Immigrant.   See *Emigrant.*

Implement.   Use it as a noun, not as a verb.

Imply, infer.   One who speaks or writes *implies;* one who hears or reads *infers.*

Importantly.   Like "hopefully," this word is often misused. "Importantly, he then made the decision" means that he made the decision with a sense of his own or its importance. The writer meant that it was important that the decision was made at that time, but the sentence does not say that.

Include, including.   To write either word immediately before a list indicates that not all items are listed.

Incredible, unbelievable.   Both words are misused often to express amazement at actions that are actually credible or believable. It is far better to reserve their use for occasions when one wants to say that something cannot be considered credible or believable.

Index.   See *Greek and Latin words.*

Individual.   This is often used when "person" would serve better. The *Oxford English Dictionary* says that substituting "individual" for "person" is a "colloquial vulgarism."

Infer.   See *Imply.*

Infinitives.   Like the rule that a writer must not use a preposition at the end of a sentence, the rule that a writer must not split an infinitive is now weak. Good writers point out that in some instances splitting an infinitive produces a more readable sentence, as in, "The news caused the soldiers to simply shout in happiness." Placing "simply" before "to shout" or after would not be as smooth as splitting "to shout" to make room for "simply." But splits should be infrequent, limited to natural sounds. Most readers have been taught that an infinitive should not be split, and many are likely to pause when they see one. Moreover, a writer who feels free to split infinitives may insert adverbs as weak intensifiers: "to really understand," "to better see the picture." In general, do not split infinitives. In particular, judge whether a split is better than a solid infinitive.

Interesting.   In most instances, to refer to something as *interesting* is to say nothing worthwhile. A writer should substitute specifics for this generality. To begin a sentence or a pragraph with "It is interesting to note" or "It is interesting to consider" is usually no more than a lazy way to begin. Is the point that is about to be made important, significant, pivotal? If so, say so. If not, do not salute the point. To say that what follows is interesting does not persuade readers that it is, and if they are not taken with what follows, it is made doubly insignificant by the salute.

Irregardless. This is a non-word that tries to say what *regardless* says.

Italics. Italics are made in typing by underlining and are used:

1 To emphasize words or parts of words: "He said that he would *not* run for office" and "No, I told you I *dis*like apricots." Although such emphasis is occasionally necessary, writers who underline often to emphasize should remember that all strong techniques become weak when they are overused. Emphasis can usually be expressed by words carefully chosen and sentences carefully constructed.

2 To show the titles of periodicals, books, films, theater productions, paintings, and vehicles: *Chaucer's Use of Imagery, Saturday Review/World, The Heart Is a Lonely Hunter, Bonnie and Clyde, Mother with Child, Merrimac.*

3 To mark foreign words and phrases that have not become part of our language (as, for example, "matinee" has): *dossier, Realpolitik.*

Its, it's. See *Apostrophe*.

-ize. Americans are turning nouns and adjectives into verbs by adding *ize* so freely that writers who care for the language are beginning to complain. Perhaps there was no outcry when, long ago, *civilize, familiarize, patronize,* and the like grew out of *civil, familiar,* and *patron.* Good writers are not happy, however, with the pace of change that has brought us words such as *utilize, personalize,* and *familiarize.* The "ize" words that are trying to make their way into the language are better avoided.

Joined together. The first word says it all. Delete *together.*

Kind of, sort of. Although *kind of a* and *sort of a* should never be used, *kind of* and *sort of* are useful to indicate an item in a species: "Winesap is a kind of apple." *Kind of* and *sort of* cannot be properly used to mean "somewhat" or "rather," or "in some way," as in, "He is kind of angry" and "She is sort of pretty." In the first instance, the writer should specify how angry. In the second, the writer should describe the features that make her pretty or say in what way she is pretty.

Latter. See *Former.*

Lay, lie. These words are often confused because of one confusing element: *Lay,* which means "to put" in its own right, is also the past tense of *lie,* which means "to recline." Thus, one should write, "I lay my books on the desk," "I lie down every night at 11:30 to try to go to sleep," and

"I lay down last night at 11:30, but sleep wouldn't come." The best way to distinguish these is to remember that *lay* as an independent verb needs a direct object, *lie* never needs an object, and *lay* is the past tense of *lie* in addition to its independent status.

Leave, let.   The first means "to go away"; the second means "to allow." Either can be used with *alone,* but the meanings are different. To *leave* someone alone is to leave him in solitude. To *let* someone alone is to allow him to be undisturbed.

Lend, loan.   The first is the verb; the second is the noun. To write "The bank loaned him $500" is wrong.

Less.   See *Few.*

Lie.   See *Lay.*

Like.   See *As.*

Literally.   See *Figuratively.*

Litotes.   See *Hyperbole.*

Loan.   See *Lend.*

Mad.   See *Angry.*

Manner, nature.   Both words are often superfluous. "He worked in a skillful manner," "The work was simple in nature." Such sentences say no more than "He worked skillfully," and "The work was simple."

Masterful, masterly.   *Masterful,* which means "domineering" or "imperious," is often misused for *masterly,* which means "expert" or "skillful."

May.   See *Can.*

Media, medium.   *Media* is the plural. *Medium* is the singular.

Militate, mitigate.   *Militate* is nearly always used with "against" (sometimes with "for") and means to have influence or effect, as in, "The evidence gathered by the House Judiciary Committee militated against the President." *Mitigate* means to soften, to make milder or less severe, as in, "The jury's sympathy for the prisoner's wife mitigated his punishment."

Modifiers.   Adverbs, adjectives, and participles (verbal adjectives) are the main modifiers. Nouns also modify, sometimes too much, as in an example the grammarian Bergan Evans found in a newspaper: "the River Street fire house Christmas Eve party funds." And, of course, phrases and clauses modify. Remembering that modifiers are not independent but do their work on other parts of speech—they are qualities, and have neither the substance of things nor the vigor of actions—should help a writer limit their use. But modifiers are strong enough to be dangerous. They sometimes wander around sentences, pillaging and plundering. In these examples, where the writer places *only* determines meaning:

> Only he scored a first-quarter touchdown.
>
> He only scored a first-quarter touchdown.
>
> He scored only a first-quarter touchdown.

Dangling modifiers sometimes seem to modify nothing, but more often they seem to modify the wrong thing, as in these examples:

> Opening the door, the room seemed huge. (Did the room open the door?)
>
> Attractive from a distance but gaudy on closer examination, he decided not to buy the picture. (Was he attractive but gaudy?)
>
> While driving the car, her eye was caught by an odd scene. (Was her eye driving?)

Modifiers such as *actual* and *actually* are useful only when they contrast the truth with error, as in, "He thought the paper would have to be long. Actually, he was assigned to write only three pages." Never use *actual, actually, real, really,* and *true* (as in "true facts") as intensifiers.

Momentary, momentous.   Anything *momentary* lasts only a moment. Anything *momentous* is extremely important.

Myself.   This word is misused by some writers who fear *me* (probably because they are uncertain about *I* and *me*). "The book was written by Bill and myself" should be "Bill and me"; "Bill and myself wrote the book" should be "Bill and I." *Myself* can be used intensively, as in, "He was punished for that? Why, I myself have done the same often." Or *myself* can be used reflexively: "I injured myself."

Nature.   See *Manner.*

Nausea, nauseous.   *Nausea* is a sick feeling in the stomach. But one who is nauseated is not necessarily *nauseous.* To be *nauseous* is to cause others to be nauseated. An object as well as a person can be *nauseous,* can turn the stomach.

Negative. See *Double negative.*

Neither. See *Either.*

No one, none. See *Agreement.*

Not too, not un-. *Not too,* as in, "He is not too handsome," and "The play was not too good," is an increasingly popular form of understatement that may be acceptable in speaking but is much too imprecise in writing. *Not un-,* as in, "The film is not unlike a Hitchcock production," is precise in that it expresses a distinction finer than "The film is like a Hitchcock production." But writers are sometimes so seized with *not un-* that they use it merely for the sake of using it. George Orwell suggested that they memorize this sentence: "A not unblack dog was chasing a not unsmall rabbit across a not ungreen field."

Numbers. In trying to conserve space, most newspapers use Arabic numerals for all numbers above nine. Other publications have established different rules, with many requiring numerals for numbers over ninety-nine, many others requiring numerals for numbers over twenty. Nearly all publications use numerals in these cases:

1 All numbers that have decimal points or involve fractions or other technical figures: 18.5 percent, $9.98, 7½.
2 Dates: March 17, 1925, June 1975.
3 Addresses: 7803 Cayman Road.
4 Numbered items in a series: 7 Catholics, 14 Protestants, 11 Hindus.
5 Page numbers: Page 50, Pages 104–111.

Off of. Delete *of.* Write "The plan was already off the ground" and "He jumped off the ledge." In some cases, *from* is more natural: "She came down from the ladder." *Of* is seldom useful with *outside* and *inside.* Use "outside the classroom" and "inside the building."

One. Using *one* for *you* or for impersonal expressions sometimes sounds stilted, as in, "*One* must do what *one* can to make *one's* own way in this life." In an earlier time, grammarians tried to change idiom by ruling that *one* must be followed by *one, one's,* and *oneself,* never with *he, his,* and *himself.* There are signs of change, with some good writers and some grammarians holding that this construction is now permissible: "One should do it in the traditional way, but he can change if the tradition seems outdated." It is probably safer to observe the old rule, avoiding stilted expressions by using *a person, a man, a woman,* and the like. To speak of *oneself* as *one* to avoid using "I" is pretentious: "One saw *The Sting* and recommends it to all who enjoy comedy."

One another.   See *Each other.*

One of the . . . (those).   A common error is to use the singular verb in these constructions: "One of best actors who was ever on stage" and "One of those women who is smooth on a tennis court." The intention in these examples is to place one person among many. The ability of the many is the pivot and determines the form of the verb: "One of the best actors who *were* ever on a stage" and "One of those women who *are* smooth on a tennis court."

Only.   See *Modifiers.*

Parallelism.   This is a technique writers use to match two or more concepts or two or more grammatical elements, usually placing the same word forms in phrases or clauses. "I came, I saw, I conquered" is a sentence made up of parallels. Caesar would have jarred the ear had he written, "I came, I saw, and victory was the result." In its simplest form, parallelism is contained in sentences that begin, "First . . . , second . . . , third . . . ," or sentences that contain balancing words such as either . . . or," "neither . . . nor," and "both . . . and." The more imaginative parallels satisfy the reader's sense of rhythm and balance, but using many calls attention to the technique. Had Caesar written many sentences on the order of "I came, I saw, I conquered," readers would have begun to pay more attention to the sound than to the sense. Most conventional parallelism, however, merely repeats tense, person, voice, and grammatical structure to make sentences smooth. These are the constructions to avoid:

1 Shifting tense: He visited his home town and *sees* his old friends. *(saw)*
2 Shifting person: First hit the ball, and then *you* run. (*First you* or *and then run*).
3 Shifting voice: The speech was made by the senator, and then he shook hands. (The senator spoke, then shook hands.)
4 Shifting grammatical structures: The president was subdued and his voice was low, and he seemed to be apologizing with every word. (Subdued, the president spoke in a low voice and seemed to apologize with every word.)

To make appropriate parallels, a writer should use articles and prepositions consistently. *A, an,* and *the* can be used once for all items in a series (The sun, sea, and sand are inviting in Hawaii) or they can be used with each item (The sun, the sea, and the sand), but they cannot be used irregularly (The sun, sand, and the sea). Similarly: In speaking, writing, and studying we should do our best. Or: In speaking, in writing, and in studying we should do our best. Not: In speaking, writing, and in studying we should do our best.

Parentheses.   Use parentheses:

1   To show the initials of organizations that will be mentioned later: Committee for the Re-Election of the President (CREEP).

2   To enclose numbers or letters that divide the items in a series: The points are: (1). . . .

3   To direct the reader's attention to similar or more detailed references (See *Who's Who in America*), or in some instances, to indicate a source: (*Harper's*, July 1974).
    (In most instances, sources are shown in footnotes or are written as part of the text: In Larry King's article in the July 1974 *Harper's*. . . .)

4   To enclose material that digresses and is not important enough to be enclosed in commas or in dashes: To make the point clear (or as clear as it is now), we must. . . .

Commas always appear after parentheses, as is demonstrated in items 3 and 4 above.

Periods go inside parentheses if the parenthetical expression is a complete sentence and is not contained in another sentence; outside if the parenthetical expression is not a complete sentence.

Participles.   See *Verbals.*

Passed, past.   *Passed* is a form of the verb *pass.* *Past* is a noun or an adjective. "Time *passed* slowly." "The *past* is prologue." "*Past* time should not dictate present action." *Past* is often used redundantly, as in, "His past experiences taught him much" and "All that is past history." *Past* serves no purpose in either example because "experiences" and "history" are in the past.

Passive voice.   See *Verbs.*

People.   Use *people* for large numbers, as in "Many people enjoyed the game." Use *persons* for small, exact numbers, as in "Ten persons attended the performance." Both *people* and *persons* are used too often. More specific terms are usually better: fans and play-goers. Instead of referring to students as "people," as many student writers do, refer to them as "students." If the context calls for more specificity, write "art students" and the like.

Per. Use *per* in technical writing, *a* and *each* in all other writing: 90 miles an hour, $50,000 a year, $100 payment for each (rather than *per*) person.

Person. See *People*.

Personal, personally. As intensives—"It is my personal opinion," "Personally, I think"—these words have no value. "I think" serves well in both cases, although writing that is dotted with such phrases is usually unconvincing. *Personal friend* has no value because we have no impersonal or nonpersonal friends. *Personal acquaintance* says no more than *acquaintance*. *Personal* and *personally* can be used, of course, to distinguish from the impersonal: "Professionally, he rejects such actions, but personally he enjoys them." Restrict *personal* and *personally* to such uses.

Phase. This refers to a stage in a cycle and should not be confused with *faze*, which means "to daunt."

Phenomenon. See *Greek and Latin words*.

Plagiarism. This means using the work of others without giving credit. Extensive plagiarism is *piracy*.

Possess. This is often misused to mean nothing more than *have*, as in, "I *possess* a strong mind." Writers who know the weakness of *has* and *have* tend to use *possess* hoping that it will add strength. Choose another verb.

Practical, practically. Do not use these as substitutes for *almost, almost always*, and *almost never*. *Practical* is derived from "practice" and refers to the terms of practice and practical purposes, as opposed to the terms of theory or theoretical purposes.

Prepositions. Prepositions, which relate nouns to other words, should ordinarily be used within sentences instead of at the end. But many good writers think it nonsense to torture sentences merely to follow the no-preposition-at-the-end rule, as in, "He doesn't know from where his next meal is coming." In such instances, write, "He doesn't know where his next meal is coming from." Observe the old rule when it makes sense.

Presently. See *At present.*

Principal, principle. The adjective *principal* means leading, chief, fore-most. The noun *principal* is closely related, meaning "chief official," or, used as a financial term, "the sum on which interest is calculated." *Principle* is only a noun and means rule, truth, or assumption. One could speak of the "principal principle of Roman law."

Proof, proved, proven. Be careful in writing of *proof.* Anything *proved* (*proven* is archaic) must be demonstrated beyond doubt. In most instances, instead of "This is proof that . . . ," one should write, "The evidence seems to show that. . . ."

Prophecy, prophesy. *Prophecy* is a noun meaning a prediction, as in, "The *prophecy* was defeat." *Prophesy* is a verb meaning "to predict," as in, "To *prophesy* defeat is to give up before the battle has begun."

Protagonist. The *protagonist* is the leading or main character in a literary work. "The main protagonist" is redundant. It says "The main main character."

Proved. See *Proof.*

Proven. See *Proof.*

Provided, providing. Except when *provided* is used as the past of *provide,* it sets a condition, as in, "He will get the loan provided he has collateral." *Providing* should not be used as a substitute.

Punctuation. See *Brackets, Colons, Commas, Dash, Exclamation Points, Parentheses, Quotations,* and *Semicolons.*

Pupil, student. One who attends an elementary school is a pupil. One who attends an institution of learning higher than an elementary school is a *student.*

Quotations. Indirect quotations are remarks a writer attributes to others without using the exact words. No quotation marks should be used when quoting indirectly: It is not true, the mayor said, that the city will sell bonds for the project. Note that *the mayor said* is set off between commas just as such words of attribution would be set off in attributing a direct quotation. The British base their practices in quoting on single quotation marks. The American practice is to use double quotation marks, except that a quotation within a quotation takes single marks. (Quotations in American newspaper headlines, but not in news stories, are placed within single quotation marks.)

The primary use of quotation marks is to show which words are quoted directly, or verbatim. A secondary use is to mark words that are used in an unusual sense or in an unfamiliar way, as in, A politician can seldom indulge in the "luxury" of integrity. This secondary use should be infrequent. Placing quotation marks around slang or cliches—The candidate has always won with a real "blast" of a campaign because he never hesitates to "tell it like it is"—is like apologizing for using such expressions.

Most of the conventions in using quotation marks are strictly observed:

1 Commas and periods are placed within quotation marks whether the quotation is one word or many:

> "Let us make merry while we can," said the king.
> The king said, "Let us make merry while we can."
> According to Franklin Roosevelt, we have nothing to fear except "fear itself."

2 Colons and semicolons are always placed outside quotation marks.

3 Exclamation points and question marks go inside or outside quotation marks depending on the sense:

> Who was it who said, "Eat, drink and be merry, for tomorrow we die"?
> He asked, "Why won't you vote for me?"
> He had the nerve to say "Vote for Kennedy"!
> Patrick Henry said, "Give me liberty or give me death!"

4 Titles of literary works shorter than books are placed within quotation marks (most newspapers place book titles within quotation marks):

> The article is entitled "The Public Agony of Political Journalists."
> T. S. Eliot wrote the poem "The Waste Land."
> The winning short story is "The Egg Is All."

5 Nicknames are customarily placed within quotation marks the first time they are used, then are used without quotation marks.

0 When one paragraph ends with a quotation that continues without interruption at the beginning of the next paragraph, no closing quotation marks are used at the end of the first paragraph, but quotation marks are used at the beginning of the next paragraph.

In scholarly writing and in many books, quotations longer than fifty words are introduced by a colon, begin on the next line, and are indented at both margins. Because the indentions indicate quotations, no quotation marks are used, but if an indented quotation itself contains a quotation, the writer sets off the interior quotation with double quotation marks.

Quote.   The word *quote* is not a noun. One should not speak of "a quote" but of "a quotation."

Re-.   See *Hyphens*.

Real, really.   See *Modifiers*.

Reason . . . because, reason . . .why.   "The reason is because" and similar constructions weaken sentences by adding needless words. "The reason the Forty-Niners can't win is because they have no quarterback" can be said more crisply: "The Forty-Niners can't win because they have no quarterback." "The reason why" is more acceptable than "The reason is because," but it can usually be eliminated as easily. "The reason why they won is that they followed the game plan for a change" can be revised to say, "They won because they followed the game plan for a change."

Rebut, refute.   To *rebut* is to argue against. To *refute* is to disprove. Be careful in saying that an argument was refuted.

Redundant.   This means excessive or superfluous.

Refer.   See *Allude*.

Reference.   See *Allude*.

Replica.   A *replica* is not a model or a miniature. It is a facsimile or close copy.

Respectively.   This word is often used redundantly. Its purpose is to relate the members of one group to the members of another in order. "John, Bill, and Joe became professional athletes in baseball, football, and basketball respectively" means that John plays baseball, Bill plays football, and Joe plays basketball. In most instances, readers automatically make the appropriate connections without *respectively*.

Robbery.   See *Burglary*.

Semicolons.   The semicolon is sometimes called "the intellectual's punctuation mark" because using it well seems to demand study and because it sometimes connects the parts of long sentences. But no one should fear it, and the mere length of a sentence is not decisive. The semicolon is used:

1   As a substitute for the comma when the comma has already been used: Study is difficult because one must find a quiet place, perhaps a corner of the library; because one's mind wanders, especially in the evening; and because friends are eager to have fun.

2   To separate the independent clauses of a compound sentence that are not joined by a coordinating conjunction: He worked hard; he was paid well; he enjoyed life.

3   To show more separation and a stronger pause between the independent clauses of a compound sentence that has a coordinating conjunction: The senator decided not to run for re-election; and his wife was happy.

As these examples show, the semicolon marks the midway point between the comma and the period. It can be considered a strong comma, or a weak period, or both.

Shall, will; should, would.   Nice distinctions were once made, but they have largely given way to idiom that does not observe the old rules. In an earlier time, *shall* and *should* were to be used with *I* and *we; will* was to be used with *I* to express determination (I *will* go to the concert). *Should* was to be used instead of *would* in conditional statements: I *should* not have won the office without your help. *Will* is now more idiomatic than is *shall* in most instances, and using *should* conditionally sounds stilted. Idiom now dictates that *will* shows determination, as before; *should* shows obligation (You *should* give him a hand); and *shall* is used only interrogatively (Shall I pay him? and Shall we go to the movie?).

Ship.   See *Boat.*

Should.   See *Shall.*

Sic.   This Latin word meaning "so" or "thus," should be placed in brackets immediately after an error in a quotation to show that the error was made by the source, not by the writer:

> *Editor & Publisher* magazine carried an editorial saying that "The media is [sic] certain to be blamed for the government's troubles."

The use of *sic* often seems affected or pedantic. *Sic* should be used only when readers might wonder who made the error.

Sort of. See *Kind of.*

Spelling: These words are frequently misspelled:

absence	deity	initiative
accept	dependent	inoculate
accommodate	describe	irrelevant
achievement	desert/dessert	irritable
acknowledgment	desirable	its/it's
acoustic	diesel	khaki
advice/advise	diphtheria	lacquer
all right/already	disastrous	leisure
allusion	dissension	liaison
amateur	dissipate	library
annual	divide	lieutenant
argument	eccentric	liquor
arraign	ecstasy	lonely/loneliness
auxiliary	eligible	lose/loose
battalion	embarrass	maintenance
beginning	enforceable	maneuver
believe	exaggerate	marshal
benefited	existence	memento
business	exorbitant	necessary
capital/capitol	experience	occur/occurred/
category	explanation	occurrence
cemetery	exuberant	omit/omitted/omission
chose/choose	fiery	pantomime
colossal	fluorescent	perennial
coming	forcible	personnel
committee	forty/fourteen	Philippines/Filipino
commuter	friend	prevalent
comparative	fuchsia	privilege
competition	fulfill	procedure
complement/compliment	gauge	questionnaire
connoisseur	grammar	quiet/quite
conscious/conscience	height	recommendation
consensus	hemmorhage	rhythm
council/counsel	homogeneous	separate
counterfeit	hypocrisy	sergeant
decision	independent	similar
definite	influential	villain

Split infinitives. See *Infinitives.*

Stet. A Latin word for "let it stand" used by an editor to show that an editing mark he made was mistaken. *Stet* means the word or words indicated should stand as they were written, not be changed to conform to the editing.

Stigma.   See *Greek and Latin words.*

Structure.   Use it as a noun, not as a verb. *Structured* can be used as an adjective, especially in the social sciences. A *structured* interview, for example, is different from a free-flowing interview.

Student.   See *Pupil.*

Such as.   Like "including," *such as* used before one or more examples means that not all members of the class are listed. It is pointless and redundant to use "and so on," "and others," or "and the like" after a list preceded by *such as.*

That, which.   *That* defines and restricts:

> The car *that* needs repair is in the garage.

In this example, *that* introduces information to define the car being discussed and to restrict the reader's attention to that car.
Which is nonrestrictive:

> The car, *which* has no fenders, will run well if it has a grease job.

In this example, the information after *which* tells more about the car being discussed, but the clause does not attempt to define the car. The information in the *which* clause could have been placed in another sentence:

> The car will run well if it has a grease job. It has no fenders.

In contrast, making two sentences of the first sentence above would require:

> The car is in the garage. It's the one that needs repair.

In short, making two sentences that carry the same sense forces a definition.
That is appropriately used much more often than *which.*
See also *Commas.*

Total of.   Except when "a total of" is used to begin a sentence to avoid beginning with a numeral, "total of" is usually redundant.

Toward, towards.   Although either may be used, *toward* is preferred.

Try and. Use *Try to*.

Type. Use *type* cautiously and remember these points:

1 Like "kind of" and "sort of," *type of* should not be used to mean "some-what" or "rather." Instead, *type of* refers to a member of a class.
2 Many uses of *type* can be deleted to make crisper sentences. Change "He was a strong type of leader" to "He was a strong leader."
3 Never use *type* without *of* before a noun: It was a different *type* examination. That *type* beauty doesn't attract me. It's hard to describe their *type* operation. *Of* is needed in all these examples.
4 Use "type" as part of a compound adjective only in writing on technical subjects.

> "I have B-type blood" is acceptable.
>
> "He is a Kennedy-type candidate," is colloquial.

Uninterested. See *Disinterested*.

Unique. Use *unique* only to refer to anything that is one of a kind. Nothing is "a bit unique," "fairly unique," or "very unique." It is unique or it is not. In most instances, "unusual" is meant.

Unknown. This is often misused for "undisclosed" and "unidentified," as in:

> The president's destination is unknown.
>
> What she thinks of him is unknown.

The president's destination is known to him. Her thoughts, if she knows her own mind, are known to her. In each example, "undisclosed" is the meaning. In the case of the "Unknown Soldier," "unidentified" would be more precise.

Use, utilize. Utilize and utilization seldom have any value that is not better expressed by *use*.

> He utilized all the garden tools.
>
> He used all the garden tools.
>
> They were unhappy with our utilization of stringed instruments.
>
> They were unhappy with our use of stringed instruments.

Many sentences containing *use of* can be better written without it:
> Gardening is improved with the use of the right tools.
>
> Using the right tools improves gardening.

Verbals. Gerunds, participles, and infinitives are derived from verbs and are known as verbals:

> Gerunds end in *ing* and are used as nouns: *Dancing* is fun.
>
> Participles are used as adjectives: This *driving* manual is dull.

Infinitives, which are made up of *to* and a verb, are used primarily as nouns, occasionally as adjectives or adverbs: We began *to sweat* after an hour.

Like most verbs, most verbals lend vigor.

Verbs, voice. *Verb* comes from the Latin word meaning "word," which suggests the importance of verbs. Their value is pointed up in so many passages in this book that it is necessary here only to mention the property of verbs known as *voice*.

> Active voice: Susan wrote the paper.
>
> Passive voice: The paper was written by Susan.

In nearly all instances, the active is preferred because it *is* active, and thus lends vigor to writing. The passive is better only when the focus is on what was acted upon.

When, where. Resist the temptation to use these to introduce definitions:

> Passing a law is *when* the legislature votes in favor of a bill and the governor signs it.
>
> Making good in this society is *where* you're able to buy many things.

Whether or not. Use *or not* only to give equal emphasis to the alternative. In most instances, *whether* does all the needed work.

Which. See *That.*

While. Use *while* to indicate time, not as a substitute for *although, even though, but* or *and.*

Who, whom. Although *whom* is seemingly disappearing in speech, it is still useful in writing when it is used appropriately, as an object. *Who* is always a subject. *Whom* is always an object.

Will. See *Shall.*

-wise.   Like *-ize, wise* is being married to words it dislikes: gradewise, pricewise, saleswise. It is comfortable with "otherwise" and "clockwise." Let it rest there.

Would.   See *Shall.*

Index

Abbreviations, 173, 174
Accuracy, in persuasive writing. *See* Persuasive writing, accuracy
Accuracy In Media, 160
Acronyms, 174
Action showing description. *See* Descriptive writing, action showing description
Active voice. *See* Verbs
Addison, Joseph, 8, 9
Adjectives, 48, 49. *See also* Descriptive writing; Modifiers; Visual writing, visual words
Adler, Mortimer, 14
Adverbs. *See* Descriptive writing; Modifiers; Visual writing, visual words
Advise and Consent, 162–65, 171
Agreement, of verb and subject, noun and pronoun, pronoun and antecedent, 175, 176
American Journal of Psychology, 51
American Usage: The Consensus, 173
Analogies. *See* Visual writing, analogies
Analysis. *See* Expository writing, topic development
Anderson, Jack, 11
Anecdotes. *See* Visual writing, anecdotes
Antecedents. *See* Agreement
Apostrophes, 177
Argument, in writing. *See* Persuasive writing
Argumentum ad hominem. *See* Persuasive writing, *argumentum ad hominem*
Argumentum ad populum. *See* Persuasive writing, *argumentum ad populum*
Argumentum ad verecundiam. *See* Persuasive writing, *argumentum ad verecundiam*

Aristotle, 98
Article, 177, 178
Associated Press (AP), 11
Attitude Change: A Critical Analysis of Theoretical Approaches, 28
Audience, 8–12, 42, 52–56. *See also* Expository writing; Persuasive writing

Bacall, Lauren, 65, 66
Bacon, Francis, 1
Baker, Russell, 172
Balance. *See* Concise sentences, balance
Balzac, Honoré de, 4, 5
Barnes, Clive, 82, 85
Bay, Robert, 28
Benchley, Robert, 25
Berkeley Barb, 76
Bernstein, Carl, 134, 135
Between the Lines, 150, 151
Brackets, 179
Broadcasting, persuasive writing for, 160, 161
Bromfield, Louis, 4
Buchwald, Art, 172
Burroughs, John, 132

Capital letters, rules for use, 179, 180
Capote, Truman, 32, 120–23, 141
Catcher in the Rye, 32
Cayce, Edgar, 136
Chronological writing. *See* Flow
Churchill, Winston, 4, 5, 78, 86
Ciardi, John, 85
Cicero, 88
City of San Francisco Oracle, The, 4
Classification. *See* Expository writing, topic development